Study Guide

to accompany

Principles of
Macroeconomics

Robert H. Frank
Cornell University

Ben S. Bernanke
Princeton University

Prepared by

Jack Mogab
Bruce McClung
Both of Southwest Texas State University

Boston Burr Ridge, IL Dubuque, IA Madison, WI New York San Francisco St. Louis
Bangkok Bogotá Caracas Kuala Lumpur Lisbon London Madrid Mexico City
Milan Montreal New Delhi Santiago Seoul Singapore Sydney Taipei Toronto

McGraw-Hill Higher Education

A Division of The McGraw-Hill Companies

Study Guide to accompany
PRINCIPLES OF MACROECONOMICS
Robert H. Frank and Ben S. Bernanke

Published by McGraw-Hill/Irwin, an imprint of the McGraw-Hill Companies, Inc., 1221 Avenue of the Americas, New York, NY 10020. Copyright © 2001 by the McGraw-Hill Companies, Inc. All rights reserved. No part of this publication may be reproduced or distributed in any form or by any means, or stored in a database or retrieval system, without the prior written consent of The McGraw-Hill Companies, Inc., including, but not limited to, in any network or other electronic storage or transmission, or broadcast for distance learning.

1 2 3 4 5 6 7 8 9 0 BKM/BKM 0 9 8 7 6 5 4 3 2 1 0

ISBN 0-07-228968-6

www.mhhe.com

To the Student

Welcome to the study of economics. We believe you will find the subject thoroughly intriguing as you gain a clearer understanding of many important issues that may now seem perplexing. For example, what determines the cost of a car, or the salary you will earn when you graduate? Why does the economy experience booms and busts? How does the banking system create money? Why are federal deficits and surpluses so controversial?

These and many other topics are addressed in *Principles of Economics, Principles of Microeconomics,* and *Principles of Macroeconomics,* by Robert H. Frank and Ben S. Bernanke, for which this Study Guide has been written. The Study Guide chapters parallel the chapters in the corresponding textbook, and each contains the following six sections designed to assist your learning and to enhance your understanding of economics:

1. **Key Point Review.** The chapter's main ideas are summarized, and new terms are highlighted and defined.
2. **Knowledge and Skills**. These are the important concepts to master. Each learning objective is keyed to specific questions and problems in sections 3, 4, and 5 of the Study Guide.
3. **Self-Test: Key Terms**. All new terms are listed. Check your understanding by completing the sentences using key terms from the provided list.
4. **Self-Test: Multiple-Choice Questions.** Strengthen your grasp of the chapter material by choosing the correct answer from the alternatives for each question. Your ability to answer multiple-choice questions should serve as a good indicator of success in exams. You may wish to study for exams by reviewing these questions.
5. **Self-Test: Short Answer/Problems.** Here you will discover how the tools of economics can be used to explore and clarify important issues. Problems are developed step by step. You are asked to analyze graphs and tables, to perform basic computations, and to select the best answers to a variety of fill-in statements.
6. **Solutions**. Solutions, with explanations for the more complex and difficult items in the self-tests, are provided for the key-term, and multiple-choice questions, as well as for the short answer/problems.

Here are some suggestions to help make your study of economics successful:

Class Preparation or Must I Turn Off the TV?
It is essential that you prepare assignments BEFORE attending class so that you can understand the lecture and ask questions. The instructor typically will not present all the materials in the text, but will rather concentrate on explaining the more complex ideas and applications.

In preparing for class, first read the "Key Point Review," and the learning objectives listed under "Knowledge and Skills " in the Student Guide. Next, go to the chapter in the text. Read the "Summary," "Core Principles," and the "Key Terms" at the end of the chapter. Then, read the introductory section that will provide an overview of the topics to be covered in the chapter. The number of topics will range from 4 to 7. Read and study one topic at a time, i.e., begin at the bold, upper-case red color heading and read until you get to the "Recap box." Look for the paragraphs in the chapter that define and explain the concepts, principles, and laws of that topic. These concepts, principles, and laws are listed at the end of each chapter as "Key Terms." As you read, mark these "terms" (as many as 3 to 5 per topic). You will notice that each topic can be presented in three modes--verbal, numerical (tables), and visual (graphs). This variety of presentation is important since economics is communicated through all three modes, and the test questions will reflect all three. After you have completed reading a topic, take a few minutes to read the Recap box. Verify that (1) you know (i.e. remember) the topic and important terms; (2) you understand (i.e. comprehend) that material; (3) you can relate the terms to one another when appropriate; and (4) you can relate the topic to the other topics in the chapter. Complete all the assigned topics in the above manner and write down any questions you have for the instructor.

Class Attendance or Why Not Go To the Rec Center?
Frankly, economics is such a demanding course that you will need all the help you can get. A great deal of that help comes from your instructor's lectures. The instructor's style and presentation will show you not only what the instructor considers to be important, but also how s/he approaches this subject. Getting notes from a friend will not give you this information. If you have followed the above suggestions in preparing for class, you will have some knowledge and understanding of the assigned topics. In class, the trick is to carefully combine four classroom skills - listening, taking notes, answering questions, and responding to questions. Listen with your mind. Be selective in what you write down. If you try to write everything that the instructor says, you will not have time to learn anything. For example, do not write a definition that has been given in the text. Listen for examples that differ from those in the text, special emphasis on a relationship between topics, and frequently repeated principles. Asking questions is the responsibility of the student. If you don't know enough to ask questions, you haven't done your job. If you have difficulty formulating questions during class, you should spend some time before class developing a list of questions you need to have answered. On the other side of the coin, you should also respond to the instructor's questions. You should not be shy about answering questions in class. An incorrect answer given in class is a free shot, while the same wrong answer on the test is very costly. The most effective way to use class time is to develop your ability to comprehend and apply economics concepts.

After Class or Do I Have To Do This Again?
Even if you have meticulously prepared for class and performed those four classroom behaviors, you still have a couple of things to do before you will be at the mastery level of the material. First, your class notes should be sketchy. You need to rewrite these notes in a more complete way before they get cold. Next, return to the Study Guide. Select 4-5 questions on the first learning objective listed in the Knowledge and Skills section. Answer those questions without referring to the text, and check your answers with the Solutions at the end of the

Study Guide chapter. If your answers are correct, go onto the next learning objective, continuing in this manner until you have covered the assigned topics. If your answers to the questions on a learning objective are incorrect, go back and study the text and your class notes. Then attempt several more questions (there are additional problems at the end of the text chapters) on the learning objective. If your answers are still incorrect, either ask questions in the next class or go see your instructor for help.

If You Want To Learn It, Teach It.
Before going on to the next chapter in the text and Study Guide, go to the end of the text chapter and read the "Review Questions." If you can answer those questions, you have learned what the authors of the text and Study Guide hoped you would learn. To further test your comprehension of a topic, try explaining it in your own words to a classmate. Illustrate the idea with an example. If you can explain it clearly and give a good example, you have mastered the concept and its time to move on to the next chapter.

A Final Word
If the strategy outlined above seems like a lot of work, it is. You cannot achieve success in economics without hard work. An estimate is that the average student should spend 2-3 hours of quality study time for every hour spent in class.

Acknowledgments
It is a pleasure to acknowledge the assistance and support of Irwin McGraw-Hill in the preparation of this Study Guide. Particular thanks go to our capable and patient editors Tom Thompson and Paul Shensa.

Bruce McClung
Jack Mogab

October 2000

Contents

Chapter 1
Thinking Like an Economist

Key Point Review

Economics is the study how people make choices under conditions of scarcity and how the results of those choices affect society. **Microeconomics** is the study of individual choice under scarcity and its implications for the behavior of prices and quantities in individual markets. **Macroeconomics** is the study of broad groups of markets, including the behavior of the economy as a whole. The subject of this chapter is how rational individuals make choices between alternative courses of action. A **rational person** is someone with well-defined goals who tries to fulfill those goals as best he or she can.

There are two core ideas that relate to making rational choices. The first core idea is the **scarcity principle**, also called the **"No-Free-Lunch principle."** The scarcity principle derives from the fact that although we have boundless needs and wants, the resources available to us are limited. So having more of one thing usually means having less of another. The extra benefit is the **marginal benefit**, or the increase in total benefits, that result from carrying out one additional unit of an activity. The extra cost is the **marginal cost**, or the increase in total cost that result from carrying out one additional unit of an activity. The optimal quantity of an activity exists where the marginal benefit of the activity equals the marginal cost of that activity. The marginal benefit can be estimated by determining a consumer's **reservation price**, or the highest price the consumer would be willing to pay for a good or service. The marginal cost is also called the **opportunity cost**, and is the value of the next-best alternative that must be forgone in order to undertake an activity. Economists use the second core idea, the cost-benefit principle, to analyze such tradeoffs. The **cost-benefit principle** that states an individual, firm, or society should take an action only if the extra benefits from taking the action are at least as great as the extra costs. An **economic surplus** results when the benefit from taking an action is greater than its cost. To facilitate the analysis, the marginal benefits and costs of an activity can be represented either numerically (tabular format) or graphically. The textbook authors applied these principles when choosing which of the many topics in economics to include in the book. The authors have chosen to cover a limited number of core ideas that explain a great deal of the behavior and events of the world. The benefit of learning a small number of core ideas is that you will be able to internalize these ideas as they are applied to a variety of issues. The opportunity cost of this strategy is a host of other ideas that are not presented. The authors believe, however, that this approach will result in an optimal level of learning. This approach will enable you to become an economic naturalist, seeing the details of life in a new light and understanding them in a way others do not, and thus transforming you into a better decision maker.

Knowledge and Skills

The student must master the knowledge and skills listed below each number topic.	Key Terms	Multiple-Choice Questions	Short Answer/ Problems
1. Essential Economic Concepts			
A. Define economics and discus economic naturalism	8		
B. Define the principle of scarcity (aka the No-Free-Lunch Principle) and discuss its applicability		4, 5, 7, 16	
C. Define the cost-benefit principle and discuss it relationship to the Principle of Scarcity	1	8, 17	3
2. Application of the Cost-Benefit Principle			
A. Define a rational person, reservation prices, economic surplus, and opportunity cost	2, 5, 7	6, 15, 18, 22, 24	3
B. Discuss the distinction between economic models and individual behavior			
C. Define marginal benefit and marginal cost	3	13, 14, 19, 20	1
D. Apply the cost-benefit principle and locate the optimal choice		9, 12, 21, 23, 25	1, 2
E. Analyze examples of irrational choice	2	10, 11	3
3. Two Major Fields within Economics			
A. Define microeconomic and identify examples of micro level questions	4	1, 3	
B. Define macroeconomic and identify examples of macro level questions	6	2	

Self Test: Key Terms
Use the terms below to complete the following sentences. (Answers are given at the end of the chapter.)

- economics
- economic surplus
- macroeconomics
- marginal benefit
- marginal cost
- microeconomics
- opportunity cost
- rational person
- reservation price

1. A person who has well-defined goals and tries to fulfill those goals as best he/she can is a
   _____.
2. If the benefit of taking an action equals $15 and the cost is $10, there is a(n)
   _____ of $5.
3. An action should only be taken if the _____ is equal to or greater than
   the _____ .
4. To describe the study of individual choices and group behavior in individual markets,
   economists conventionally use the term _____ .
5. The highest price you are willing to pay for a good is your _____ for that
   good.
6. Concepts such as the national unemployment rate, the overall price level, and the total value
   of national output are explained in _____ .
7. If you choose to attend your economics class tomorrow rather than going to a movie, the
   movie is the _____ of going to class.
8. How people make choices under conditions of scarcity and the results of those choices for
   society is the definition of _____ .

rational person
economic surplus
marginal cost, marginal benefit
microeconomics
opportunity cost
macroeconomics
reservation price
economics

Self-Test: Multiple-Choice Questions
Circle the letter that corresponds to the best answer. (Answers are given at the end of the chapter.)

1. Economics is conventionally divided into two subjects called:
   A. marginal benefit and marginal cost.
   B. reservation price and opportunity cost.
   C. microeconomics and macroeconomics.
   D. rational economics and irrational economics.
   E. economic surplus and economic deficit.

2. Macroeconomics differs from microeconomics in that:
   A. the concept of scarcity applies to the microeconomics but does not apply to the macroeconomics.
   B. the microeconomics studies individual markets while the macroeconomics studies groups of markets, including the whole economy.
   C. rational decisions are relevant to the macroeconomics but not the microeconomics.
   D. the macroeconomics is the study of how people make choices under conditions of scarcity while the microeconomics is concerned with the results of those choices for society.
   E. the macroeconomics explains such concepts as how prices are determined in markets while the microeconomics explains the overall price level.

3. In deciding the number of students to allow to enroll in the economics classes, the Chairperson of the Economics Department is making a(n) _____ decision.
   A. microeconomic
   B. macroeconomic
   C. economic surplus
   D. marginal choice
   E. imperfect

4. When economists say there is no such thing as a free lunch, they mean that
   A. we must pay money for everything we get.
   B. it is against the law to accept goods or services without paying for them.
   C. the more lunch a person eats the more weight the person will gain.
   D. each day we decide to eat lunch is another day we must pay out money.
   E. every choice we make involves a tradeoff.

5. The concept of scarcity applies equally to Bill Gates and a homeless person because
   A. both have the same legal rights protected by the U.S. constitution.
   B. they have the same access to the markets for goods and services.
   C. there are only 24 hours in the day for both of them.
   D. they are both consumers.
   E. both must breathe air in order to live.

6. Maria spends her afternoon at the beach, paying $2 to rent a beach umbrella and $10 for food and drinks rather than spending an equal amount of money to go to a movie. The opportunity cost of going to the beach is
    A. zero, because the money she spent was for food, drinks, and an umbrella rather than to enter the beach.
    B. the $12 she spent on the umbrella, food, and drinks.
    C. only $2 because she would have spent the money on food and drinks whether or not she went to the beach.
    D. the movie she missed seeing.
    E. the movie she missed seeing plus the $12 she spent on the umbrella, food, and drinks.

7. Jose is vacationing on Padre Island during Spring Break. He goes to the beach early on a sunny afternoon because he knows it will become crowded and he wants to have sufficient room to put out a large beach towel to lie on while sunning himself. Later that afternoon the beach fills to capacity and the family next to Jose raises a large beach umbrella to shade themselves from the sun. The shade from the umbrella also covered the area where Jose was laying. In this case, the sunlight was
    A. scarce because Jose would have to forego a place on the beach to receive the sunlight.
    B. not scarce because it is freely available (i.e., Jose did not have to pay money for it).
    C. scarce because the neighboring family absorbed all the sunlight with its umbrella.
    D. not scarce because Jose could move to another location to receive the sunlight.
    E. scarce because the beach was full to capacity.

8. The cost-benefit principle
    A. is not one of the authors' core ideas in economics.
    B. implies that the cost of all alternatives should be included when choosing among alternative.
    C. states that an action should be taken only if the extra benefit is at least as great as the extra cost.
    D. states that an action should be taken only if the extra benefit is greater than the extra cost.
    E. states that an action should be taken only if the extra benefit is less than the extra cost.

9. Samantha has estimated that with a college degree she will be able to earn an additional $40,000 of income annually. The cost of attending a state university is $25,000, while a private university costs $40,000 (all estimates are calculated in current dollars). Samantha would make a rational decision if she chooses to attend
    A. the private university, but not the state university.
    B. the state university, but not the private university.
    C. neither the state nor the private university.
    D. either the state or the private university
    E. any university regardless of the cost and income.

10. Joe has decided to purchase his textbooks for the semester. His options are to purchase the books via the internet with next day delivery to his home at a cost of $250, or to drive to campus tomorrow to buy the books at the university bookstore at a cost of $245. Last week he drove to campus to buy a concert ticket because they offered 20 percent off the regular price of $20.
    A. It would not be rational for Joe to drive to campus to purchase the books because the $5 saving is only 2 percent of the cost of the books, and that is much less than the 20 percent he saved on the concert ticket.
    B. It would be rational for Joe to drive to campus because it costs less to buy the books there than via the internet.
    C. It would be rational for Joe to drive to campus because the $5 saving is more than he saved by driving there to buy the concert ticket.
    D. It would not be rational for Joe to drive to campus to purchase the books because the cost of gas and his time must certainly be more than the $5 he would save.
    E. There is insufficient information to determine whether it would be rational or not for Joe to purchase the books via the internet or on campus.

11. Assume the minimum that Joe would be willing to accept to drive to the university campus is equal to the amount he saved on the concert ticket (see Question 10). What would be the amount of his economic surplus if he bought his textbooks at the university bookstore rather than via the internet?
    A. $5
    B. $1
    C. $50
    D. $20
    E. There would be no economic surplus from purchasing the books at the university bookstore.

12. Steve has estimated that the marginal benefit of studying an additional hour of economics (instead of biology) is an increase of 15 points on the weekly test, and the marginal cost is a decrease of 10 points on his weekly biology test. Applying the optimal quantity rule to maximize his test scores, he should
    A. not study the additional hour of economics, but rather should study an additional hour of biology.
    B. study the additional hour of economics, but no more than one additional hour.
    C. not study the additional hour of economics, but rather should study an additional one-and-one-half hours of biology.
    D. study the additional hour of economics, plus some additional time studying economics.
    E. not study economics or biology.

13. The Third Wave Computer Company employs Sally to assemble personal computers. Sally can assemble 1 computer if she works 1 hour, 4 computers in 2 hours, 7 computers in 3 hours, 9 computers in 4 hours, and 10 computers in 5 hours. Each computer consists of a motherboard that costs $250, a hard drive costs $150, a case that costs $25, a monitor that costs $200, a keyboard that costs $50, and a mouse that costs $25. The cost of employing Sally is $50 per hour. What is the marginal cost of producing the computers Sally assembles during her second hour of work?
    A. $2,150
    B. $2,850
    C. $2,800
    D. $700
    E. $750

14. The Third Wave Computer Company sells each computer for $725. Using the cost data in multiple-choice Question 13, how many hours should the Third Wave Computer Company employ Sally in order to maximize its benefit from her employment?
    A. 1 hour
    B. 2 hours
    C. 3 hours
    D. 4 hours
    E. 5 hours

15. Sophia wants to go to a friend's house this evening, but has promised her mother that she would clean the house during that time. Her brother, James, has offered to clean the house for her if she will pay him $10. Sophia replies, "I'll pay you five dollars (and not a cent more!)." The
    A. $10 represents Sophia's reservation price of going to her friend's house this evening.
    B. $5 represents Sophia's opportunity cost of cleaning the house this evening.
    C. $10 represents James' reservation price and Sophia's opportunity cost of going to her friend's house this evening.
    D. the difference between the $10 James has asked for to clean the house and the $5 Sophia has offered represents the economic surplus of going to her friend's house this evening.
    E. $10 represents the opportunity cost and the $5 is the marginal benefit of going to her friend's house this evening

16. The web site for this textbook can be viewed simultaneously by thousands of students around the world without paying money to view it. Does this suggest that the concept of scarcity does not apply to web sites?
    A. No, because each of the students incurs an opportunity cost measured by the next best alternative to viewing the web site.
    B. Yes, because an additional student viewing the web site does not prevent another student from viewing it.
    C. Yes, because the students do not have to pay money to view the web site, and thus they do not have to forgo something else to view it.
    D. No, because the more students who view it, the slower the transmission of the information to each of the students.
    E. Yes, because the technology of the internet and the world wide web has made the principles of economics outdated.

17. In applying the cost-benefit principle one should calculate the
    A. total cost and total benefit and choose that quantity of an activity where they are equal.
    B. marginal cost and marginal benefit and choose that quantity of an activity where the marginal benefit exceeds the marginal cost by the greatest amount.
    C. total cost and total benefit and choose that quantity of an activity where the total cost exceeds the total benefit by the greatest amount.
    D. marginal cost and marginal benefit and choose that quantity of an activity where the marginal benefit equals the marginal cost.
    E. marginal cost, total cost, marginal benefit, and marginal cost and choose that quantity of an activity where the marginal cost equals the total cost and the marginal benefit equals the total benefit.

18. Salvador bid on a Mark McGuire baseball card that was offered in an auction on an internet web site. Another bidder quickly surpassed his first bid for $10, and he entered a second bid for $20. This was also eventually surpassed, at which time he entered a bid for $50 (the maximum he was willing to bid for the card). When the auction deadline passed, he was notified that his was the highest bid and he would soon be receiving the card. In his excitement, he logged onto a chat board for baseball card collectors and posted a notice that he had just purchased the Mark McGuire card. Soon he received a reply from another collector offering to buy the card for $60, but Salvator politely declined the offered. During the next few days a series of offers were made, all of which he turned down until a collector offered to pay $75 for the card. Salvator decided he could not pass up this offer and accepted it. From this we can conclude that Salvator's economic surplus from purchasing the Mark McGuire card was equal to
    A. $75.
    B. $25.
    C. $50.
    D. $125.
    E. $40.

19. Another name for the marginal benefit of an activity is the
    A. reservation price.
    B. opportunity cost.
    C. economic surplus.
    D. No-Free-Lunch Principle.
    E. scarcity.

20. If Sally works for 10 hours she can sell 15 insurance contracts, and if she works for 11 hours she can sell 18 insurance contracts. The marginal benefit of the 11th hour of Sally's work equals
    A. 18 insurance contracts.
    B. 15 insurance contracts.
    C. 33 insurance contracts.
    D. 1 insurance contract.
    E. 3 insurance contracts.

21. Rajiv has estimated that the additional benefit of writing 100 more lines of computer programming code is $10 and the additional cost is $6. He should
    A. not write the code because it would not be a rational choice.
    B. write the code because it would be a rational choice and an optimal quantity.
    C. write the code because it would be a rational choice but is not an optimal quantity.
    D. not write the code because it would not be a rational choice but would be an optimal quantity.
    E. not write the code because it would not be a rational choice, nor would it be an optimal quantity.

22. Sonya's is employed at a stock brokerage firm where she earns $25 per hour. The office she works at is located downtown. To get to work each day, she must either ride a series of buses that takes one-and-a-half hours at a cost of $2 or take a cab that takes 30 minutes and costs $20. The opportunity cost
    A. of riding the bus is $2, and taking the cab is $20.
    B. of riding the bus is $37.50, and taking the cab is $12.50.
    C. of riding the bus is $35.50, and taking the cab is -$5.
    D. of riding the bus is $39.50, and taking the cab is $32.50.
    E. of riding the bus is $27, and taking the cab is $20.

23. Given the information in Question 22, in order to maximize her income, Sonya should
    A. ride the bus because it costs less money.
    B. take the cab because the opportunity cost is less than that of riding the bus.
    C. ride the bus because the opportunity cost is less than that of taking a cab.
    D. take the cab because the opportunity cost is greater than that of riding the bus.
    E. ride the bus because the opportunity cost is greater than that of taking a cab.

24. If your reservation price for a precooked meal is $15 and the opportunity cost of the pre-
cooked meal is $12, the economic surplus of having a precooked meal equals:
   A. $3.
   B. minus $3.
   C. $27.
   D. $12/$15.
   E. $15/$12.

25. The Smithville Elementary School Teachers Association petitions the Smithville School
Board to provide a computer lab for its school. To support its argument the Association
presents data from a national study that show students earn an average of $5,000 of
additional income during their lives when they have had computer training in elementary
school. In order for the School Board to make a rational choice, it should
   A. determine if other elementary schools have computer labs.
   B. build the computer lab because the children will be able to earn a higher income during
      their lives.
   C. not build the computer lab because the study was not based on a study of the Smithville
      area.
   D. build the computer lab if the additional cost per student is less than or equal to the
      additional income.
   E. build the computer lab if the additional cost per student is greater than or equal to the
      additional income.

Self-Test: Short Answer/Problems
(Answers and solutions are given at the end of the chapter.)

1. An Economic Naturalist's Study Choices
Ben has two tests this week, one in biology and one in mathematics. As an economic naturalist, he has estimated in the table below the expected benefits, measured in terms of his test scores, of studying for each test.

Hours of study	Mathematics test score	Marginal benefit of studying math	Biology test score	Marginal benefit of studying biology
0	37	XXXX	58	XXXX
1	53		70	
2	67		80	
3	79		88	
4	89		94	
5	96		98	
6	100		100	

A. In column 3 of the above table, calculate the marginal benefit of studying mathematics for 1 to 6 hours.
B. In column 5 of the above table, calculate the marginal benefit of studying biology for 1 to 6 hours.
C. If Ben has allocated a total of 6 hours of studying for these two tests, each additional hour of studying for the mathematics test means that he will forego an additional hour of studying for biology. Within this context, an additional hour of studying for mathematics will result in an increase in his _____ test score (the marginal benefit), but there will be a tradeoff that can be measured as a reduction in his _____ test score (the marginal cost).

D. Assuming that Ben has allocated a total of 6 hours of studying for the two tests, complete Table 1-D below by calculating the total score on the two tests combined for the different combinations of studying time.

Hours studying for the math test	Hours studying for the biology test	Combined test scores
6	0	
5	1	
4	2	
3	3	
2	4	
1	5	
0	6	

E. The maximum combined test scores are achieved if Ben studies _____ hours of mathematics and _____ hours of biology.

2. A Graphical Analysis of An Economic Naturalist's Study Choices
A. On the graph below, using the data in Table 1-A, plot Ben's marginal benefit curve for studying additional hours (1-6 hours) of mathematics.

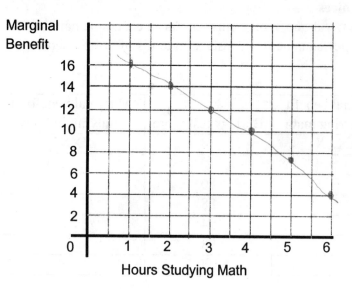

B. Using the data on the graph below, the marginal cost and marginal benefit of studying for the mathematics test are equal when Ben studies _____ hours for the mathematics test.

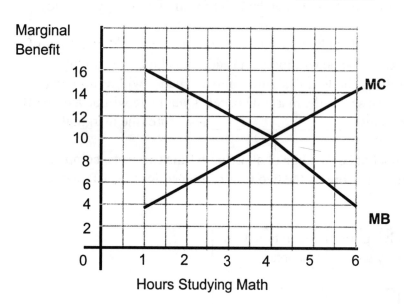

C. Based on the information in the graph above, if Ben wants to maximize his combined test scores, he should study _____ hours for his mathematics test. Assuming that Ben has allocated a total of 6 hours of studying for the two tests, this would imply that Ben should study _____ hours for the biology test.

D. Compare your answer to Question 2C with your answer to Question 1E. Are the answers consistent? _____

3. Reservation Prices and Economic Surplus

The One-Hour Cleaners will clean and press shirts, dresses, pants and suits. To obtain a competitive advantage over other cleaners in town, One-Hour Cleaners picks up and returns the garments to their customers' homes, charging $1.50 per garment. Charles is new in town and his neighbor, Tina, tells him about the One-Hour Cleaners laundry service. The next week, Charles tells Tina that he had his suits cleaned and pressed at the One-Hour Cleaners. He also tells her that he did not have his suits picked up and delivered, because $1 was the most he would be willing to pay for such service. Tina tells him she would pay him $.75 per dress if he would be willing to take her dresses to the cleaners and pick them. Charles agreed to do so (thinking to himself that he would not have agreed to do it for less).

A. Charles' reservation price for having his suits picked up and delivered is $ _____ .

B. Charles' reservation price for picking up and delivering garments is $ _____ .

C. Charles's reservation price for having his suits picked up and delivered represents the (benefit/cost) _____ of the service, while his reservation price for picking up and delivering garments represents the (benefit/cost) _____ of the service.

D. Is Charles is making a rational decision by agreeing to pick up and deliver Tina's dresses for $.75 per dress? _____ Why, or why not? _____

_____

E. The economic surplus that Charles receives from taking and picking up Tina's dresses equals $_____ per garment.

Solutions
Self-Test: Key Terms

1. rational person
2. economic surplus
3. marginal benefit; marginal cost
4. microeconomics
5. reservation price
6. macroeconomics
7. opportunity cost
8. economics

Self-Test: Multiple-Choice Questions

1. C
2. B
3. A It is a microeconomic decision because affects the supply in an individual market.
4. E
5. C Scarcity applies to anyone that has limited resources. Bill Gates and a homeless person both have a finite amount of time in a given day.
6. D Since the movie and the beach require the same amount of money, by going to the beach Marie only foregoes the entertainment value of the movie.
7. A Since Jose must forego his beach location to receive sunlight after the family put up its umbrella, the sunlight is scarce.
8. C
9. D Since the marginal benefit ($40,000 of additional income) is equal to or greater than the marginal cost of both schools, it would be rational to go to either school.
10. C It is rational to purchase the books on campus because his willingness to drive there to save $4 on the concert ticket implies that the minimum he would accept for driving to campus is less than the $5 he would save by buying the books there.
11. B The benefit of driving to campus to buy the books is the $5 saving on the price of the books and the $4 saved on the concert ticket represents his cost of driving to campus. The difference between the benefit and the cost is the economic surplus.
12. D He should study more than the additional hour of economics because at the end of the next hour his marginal benefit would still be greater than the marginal cost of studying economics.
13. A Sally produces an additional 3 computers during the second hour of employment, the components of each costing $700 (3 x $700 = $2,100). In addition you must add the $50 cost of employing Sally for the hour to the $2,100 cost of the 3 computers.
14. D The marginal benefit of the 4th hour of work is 2 computers that can be sold for $1,450, and the marginal cost of producing 2 computers is $1,450.
15. B Since we don't know if Sophie and her brother agreed to the transaction, all we are certain of is that Sophie was willing to pay a maximum of $5 to have her brother clean the house that evening. The maximum someone is willing to pay for something represents the opportunity cost of the activity to that person.

16. A
17. D When marginal benefit equals marginal cost, total benefit exceeds total cost by the greatest amount.
18. B Economic surplus is equal to the benefit of taking an action minus its cost. The benefit of selling the card was $75 and the cost was $50.
19. A
20. E The marginal benefit equals the 18 contracts she could sell in 11 hours minus the 15 contracts she could sell in 10 hours.
21. C It is a rational choice because the additional benefit is greater than the additional cost, but it is not an optimal quantity because the additional benefit is not equal to the additional cost.
22. E Because Sonya has only the two options to get to work before she can begin earning her salary, taking a cab is the quickest means of getting there and requires that she forego the $20 cab fare. Taking the bus she foregoes $2 in bus fare, but, because it takes an hour longer, she foregoes $25 in income as well.
23. B
24. A The reservation price ($15) minus the opportunity cost ($12)
25. D Rational choices require that the additional benefit be greater than or equal to the additional cost of an activity.

Self-Test: Short Answer/Problems

1. A., B.
Table 1-A

Hours of study	Mathematics test score	Marginal benefit of studying math	Biology test score	Marginal benefit of studying biology
0	37	XXXX	58	XXXX
1	53	16	70	12
2	67	14	80	10
3	79	12	88	8
4	89	10	94	6
5	96	7	98	4
6	100	4	100	2

C. mathematics, biology

D. Table 1-D

Hours studying for the math test	Hours studying for the biology test	Combined test scores
6	0	158
5	1	166
4	2	169
3	3	167
2	4	161
1	5	151
0	6	137

E. 4, 2

2. A.

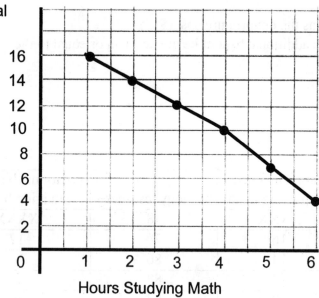

B. 4
C. 4, 2
D. yes

3A. $1
B. $.75
C. benefit, cost
D. Yes, it is a rational decision because the additional benefit is greater than the additional cost of picking up and delivering the dresses.
E. $.25

Chapter 2
Some Common Pitfalls for Decision Makers

Key Point Review

In order to properly apply the cost-benefit principle discussed in Chapter 1, it is important to avoid the errors people often make when implementing it. Three of the most common pitfalls are discussed in this chapter. The first pitfall is ignoring **opportunity costs** (the value of the next best alternative that must be foregone in order to engage in an activity). The cost-benefit criterion states that an activity should be engaged in if its benefits exceed its costs. When considering the costs of an activity it is necessary to take into account not only the outlays required, but also the value of foregone opportunities. The key to using the concept of opportunity cost is in recognizing precisely what a given action prevents one from doing. In addition, the timing of the action that one is prevented from doing must be taken into account. The value of an action in the future is less than the value of that same action today. This is referred to as the time value of money. The **time value of money** refers to the fact that a given dollar amount today is equivalent to a larger dollar amount in the future because the money can be invested in an interest-bearing account in the meantime. Future values should be discounted by an appropriate discount (interest) rate to determine the present value of the future action.

Another common pitfall that people should avoid when implementing cost-benefit analysis is the failure to ignore sunk costs. A **sunk cost** is a cost that is beyond recovery at the moment a decision must be made. Because sunk costs must be borne whether or not an action is taken, they are irrelevant to the decision of whether to take the action. Failure to ignore sunk costs will result in overstating the costs of an action, and may result in a less than optimal decision.

The third pitfall to avoid when implementing cost-benefit analysis is the failure to distinguish between average and marginal costs and benefits. Marginal costs and benefits correspond to the *increment* of activity under consideration. The **average cost** of undertaking *n* units of an activity is the total cost of the activity divided by *n*. The **average benefit** of undertaking n units of an activity is the total benefit divided by n. Sometimes the failure to distinguish between average and marginal costs arises from a failure to distinguish fixed costs and variable costs. A **fixed cost** is a cost that does not vary with the level of an activity, while a **variable cost** is a cost that varies with the level of an activity. Within the context of cost-benefit analysis only marginal costs and benefits are relevant. Nonetheless, many people seem inclined to compare average costs and benefits. The appropriate criterion for allocating a resource that is not perfectly divisible across different activities is to allocate each unit of the resource to the production activity in which its marginal benefit is highest. For a resource that is perfectly divisible, the rule is to allocate the resource so that its marginal benefit is the same in every activity.

The chapter is concluded by introducing the core principle "**Not All Cost Matter Equally.**" This core principle indicates that some costs (e.g., opportunity costs, and marginal costs) matter in making decisions, while other costs (e.g., sunk costs and average costs) do not matter.

Knowledge and Skills

The student must master the knowledge and skills listed below each number topic.	Key Terms	Multiple-Choice Questions	Short Answer/ Problems
1. Pitfall #1. Ignoring Opportunity Costs			
A. Define and identify the opportunity cost of an activity		1, 10	
B. Define the time value of money	3	2, 4	1
C. Illustrate the importance of incorporating opportunity cost and time value of money into cost-benefit analysis		3, 19	1
2. Pitfall #2. Failure to Ignore Sunk Costs			
A. Define and identify sunk costs	1	18	
B. Illustrate the error of including sunk costs into cost-benefit analysis		5, 6, 11, 12, 14	2
3. Pitfall #3. Failure to Understand the Average-Marginal Distinction			
A. Define fixed costs, variable costs, average costs and average benefits	2, 4, 5	8	
B. Calculate average costs and benefits		7, 15	3
C. Analyze the efficient allocation of resource across activities		9, 16, 20	3
D. Illustrate the error of decision making based on average measures			
4. Relative Importance of Different Types of Costs			
A. Explain the Principle of Not All Costs Matter Equally			
B. List and discuss the costs which matter most and least		13, 17	

Self-Test: Key Terms
Use the terms below to complete the following sentences. (Answers are given at the end of the chapter.)

average cost
fixed cost
sunk cost
time value of money
variable cost

1. A cost that is beyond recovery at the moment a decision must be made is a(n)
    _____.

2. Because it varies with the level of activity, a(n) _____ should be taken into
    account when making a decision.

3.- The opportunity cost of resources that are expended in the future will be lower than the
    opportunity cost of resources expended today because of the _____.

4. The total cost of an activity divided by n equals the _____ of undertaking
    n units of the activity.

5. In deciding whether or not to drive your car to the beach during Spring Break, the monthly
    payment on your car loan is considered a(n) _____ and, therefore, would not
    be included in your cost-benefit analysis.

Self-Test: Multiple-Choice Questions
Circle the letter that corresponds to the best answer. (Answers are given at the end of the chapter.)

1. Sonja is the sole owner of Words.com, providing translation services via the internet, where
    she earns an annual salary of $50,000 plus the potential for future profits. She is considering
    an offer for a top management position with another internet firm at a salary of $75,000 per
    year, but without profit sharing.
    A. She should accept the management position because she would earn more income with
        the other firm.
    B. She should refuse the management position because, despite the higher salary, the future
        profits from her current business will be greater.
    C. A cost-benefit analysis of her decision to retain her current position should include an
        opportunity cost of $75,000.
    D. A cost-benefit analysis of her decision to retain her current position should not include an
        opportunity cost of $75,000 because her current salary plus future profits could be greater
        than the salary offered by the other firm.
    E. A cost-benefit analysis of her decision to retain her current position should include an
        average cost of $75,000.

2. The time value of money implies that the value of
    A. a dollar earned today is worth less than a dollar spent tomorrow.
    B. a dollar earned in the future decreases as the interest rate that can be earned on interest bearing money market accounts increases.
    C. a dollar earned in the future decreases as the interest rate that can be earned on interest bearing money market accounts decreases.
    D. a dollar earned in the future increases as the interest rate that can be earned on interest bearing money market accounts decreases.
    E. a dollar earned in the future is unrelated to the interest rate that can be earned on interest bearing money market accounts.

3. Ian paid $475 for an airline ticket to fly to Acapulco, Mexico, for a spring break vacation. Unfortunately, he fell ill and could not go to Acapulco. When he called the airline to cancel the ticket, he was reminded that the ticket was nonrefundable, but that he could exchange it for another ticket within one year if he pays a $75 fee at the time of the exchange. Several months later he is deciding whether to exchange the ticket for a ticket of the same price to Acapulco. The opportunity cost of go to Acapulco would equal the
    A. ticket price of $475 plus the $75 exchange fee, if he has no other trip that he will take within the year.
    B. ticket price of $475 plus the $75 exchange fee, if he has another trip that he will take within the year.
    C. $75 exchange fee, if he has no other trip that he will take within the year.
    D. $75 exchange fee, if he has another trip that he will take within the year.
    E. $0, if he has no other trip that he will take within the year.

4. Darla is a computer specialist who works for Ibid.com. Ibid.com, like most internet companies, is a recent startup that gave her stock options when she joined the firm, but she must wait one more year before she can sell the stock. Darla is now considering a job offer from a firm in the real estate industry that provides a higher salary, but no stock options. If she leaves her current job, she loses her stock options with Ibid.com. Her best estimate is that in one year the stock options would sell for $125,000. The current value of her stock options is
    A. $125,000.
    B. $100,000 at an interest rate of 10 percent.
    C. $100,000 at an interest rate of 15 percent.
    D. $100,000 at an interest rate of 20 percent.
    E. $100,000 at an interest rate of 25 percent.

5. Jim, a student at Southern State University, is enrolled in 15 credit hours this semester. His grade in the Calculus class is a passing grade, but below his expectations. Fearing that his grade may slip into the failing range, he is considering withdrawing from the course. He tells a friend, "I would drop the course but I don't want to waste the $500 I paid in tuition for the course." His friend replies, "The $500 tuition you paid for the course is irrelevant to your decision. Your grade in the course is the only thing that is important, now." The friend is
   A. incorrect, because the tuition will have to be paid again when Jim retakes the course.
   B. correct, because the tuition is a fixed cost and fixed costs should never be considered when making decisions.
   C. incorrect, because the tuition is a variable cost and variable costs should always be considered when making decisions.
   D. correct, because the tuition is a sunk cost and sunk costs should not be considered when making decisions.
   E. incorrect, and obviously so rich that money means nothing to him/her.

6. Monica has purchased a $25 ticket to attend a Back Street Boys concert on Friday evening. Subsequently, she is asked to go to dinner and dancing at no expense to her. If she uses cost-benefit analysis to choose between going to the concert and going on the date, she should
   A. include only the entertainment value of the concert in the opportunity cost of going on the date.
   B. include the cost of the ticket plus the entertainment value of the concert in the opportunity cost of going on the date.
   C. include only the cost of concert ticket in the opportunity cost of going on the date.
   D. include neither the cost of the ticket nor the entertainment value of the concert in the opportunity cost of going on the date.
   E. have a psychiatric evaluation because dates cannot be evaluated using cost-benefit analysis.

7. Jason studied 5 hours for his first History test and his test score was 85; 6 hours for his second History test and scored 90; and 7 hours for his third History test and scored 95. He also studied 5 hours for his first Math test and his test score was 68; 6 hours for his second Math test and scored 78; and 7 hours for his third Math test and scored 88. The average benefit per hour studied for the History tests was _____ and the average benefit per hour studied for the Math tests was _____ .
   A. 15; 13
   B. 5; 10
   C. 90; 78
   D. 13; 15
   E. 10: 5

8. At the University of the Heartland tuition is $50 per credit hour up to a maximum of 12 credit hours, student fees are $150 per student per semester, room and board is $1,500 per student each semester, and books cost an average of $60 per course. For a student taking 12 or fewer credit hours
    A. fixed costs would include tuition, students' fees, and room and board, while variable costs would include only the cost of books.
    B. fixed costs would include students' fees and room and board, while variable costs would include tuition and the cost of books.
    C. fixed costs would include tuition, students' fees, room and board, and the cost of books, but no variable costs.
    D. fixed costs would include tuition and room and board, while variable costs would include students' fees and the cost of books.
    E. fixed costs would include tuition and students fees, while variable costs would include room and board and the cost of books.

9. To efficiently allocate a resource that is perfect divisible across different activities, one should allocate the resource such that the
    A. marginal benefit is greatest for each unit of production.
    B. marginal cost is greatest for each unit of production.
    C. marginal benefit is the same for every activity.
    D. marginal cost is the same for every activity.
    E. marginal cost equals the marginal benefit for every activity.

10. Anticipating a lack of food in stores as a result of the Y2K computer bug, the Adams family took funds from their savings account to purchase the equivalent of 3 months of canned goods to stockpile in their pantry. Fortunately, there were no shortages as a result of the Y2K computer bug, and the Adams family will eventually consume the food. As a result of their pre-Y2K preparations, the Adams family incurred
    A. no opportunity cost because they will eventually consume all the food they bought.
    B. an opportunity cost equal to the cost of the food purchased.
    C. an opportunity cost equal to the benefit of the food.
    D. an opportunity cost equal to the foregone interest income on the funds removed from their saving account.
    E. an opportunity cost equal to the cost of the food purchased plus the foregone interest income on the funds removed from their saving account.

11. Keyshawn Smith, a professional football player, has been offered two different compensation packages by his team from which he must choose one. Package A will pay him a signing bonus of $2 million when he signs his contract at the beginning of the year and a monthly salary during the season of $500,000. Package B will pay him a monthly salary during the season of $500,000 and a $2. 1 million bonus at the end of the year. The minimum interest rate on a one-year certificate of deposit that would make Package A at least as valuable a benefit as Package B is
    A. 10 percent.
    B. one percent.
    C. 5 percent.
    D. 2.5 percent.
    E. 15 percent.

12. Jackson just paid $1,000 cash for a 1979 Corvette and he needs to travel to San Francisco this summer. He can either drive his car or take a bus. In order to make a rational decision, he decides to calculate the costs of driving the car on the trip. He knows the cost of the car was $1,000, he estimates the cost of gas at 10 cents per mile, the car repair shop estimates maintenance at 3 cents per mile, his car insurance premium is $600 for 6 months, and from a web site he determines that depreciation is about $1 per mile. Which of the above costs are sunk cost and, therefore, should not be included in his analysis?
    A. Maintenance, depreciation, insurance premium, and loan payment costs are sunk cost and, therefore, should not be included in his analysis.
    B. Maintenance, depreciation, and insurance premium costs are sunk cost and, therefore, should not be included in his analysis.
    C. Depreciation, insurance premium, and the cost of the car are sunk cost and, therefore, should not be included in his analysis.
    D. The insurance premium and the cost of the car are sunk cost and, therefore, should not be included in his analysis.
    E. Only the cost of the car is a sunk cost and, therefore, should not be included in his analysis.

13. Ms. Trimble dabbles in the stock market, investing a portion of her retirement funds in individual stocks. Among her holdings she has 1,000 shares of XYZ Corp. that she bought at $50 per share. During the last quarter, the company's profits failed to meet the analysts' predictions and, further, the company indicated that the next quarter would also be below expectations. As a result, the stock price has fallen to $40 per share. Ms. Trimble is considering selling the shares in XYZ Corp. in order to purchase shares of ABC, Inc. because she thinks that ABC, Inc.'s prospects are better than those of XYZ Corp. Her stockbroker agrees with her evaluation of the prospects of the two firms, but recommends that she wait until the price of the XYZ Corp. stock gets back to $50 per share so that she won't loose money on the investment and she will be able to buy more shares of ABC Inc. Her stockbroker's advice is
    A. correct because cost-benefit analysis requires that one not only look at the marginal benefit of owning the shares but also the marginal cost.
    B. incorrect because if she sells the shares of XYC Corp. she will loose money that can never be recovered.
    C. incorrect because it does not take into account the cost of buying the shares of ABC, Inc.
    D. correct because if she buys more shares of ABC, Inc. she will have a larger fund to live on during her retirement.
    E. incorrect because the $50 per share price she paid for the XYZ Corp. shares is a sunk cost and should not be consider when making a decision.

14. Shelia is a volleyball player who wears out 10 pairs of shoes each volleyball season. Before the season she purchases all ten pairs because she can get a volume discount from the manufacturer's representatives. She gets a price quote from two representatives from whom she has previously purchased shoes. Representative A will sell her 10 pairs for $495 plus a shipping fee of $11. Representative B will sell her the same 10 pairs for $509. The average cost of buying the shoes from Representative A is _____ and from Representative B is _____.
    A. $50.60; $50.90
    B. $506; $509
    C. $56; $59
    D. $49.50; $50.90
    E. $495; $509

15. Using the information in multiple-choice Question 12 and assuming Jackson decides to drive his car to San Francisco and back on a two-month trip, which of the listed costs would be fixed costs and which would be variable costs?
    A. The cost of the car would be a fixed cost, and the cost of gas, insurance, maintenance, and depreciation would variable costs.
    B. The costs of the car and insurance would be a fixed cost, and the cost of gas, maintenance, and depreciation would variable costs.
    C. The costs of the car, depreciation, and insurance would be fixed costs, and the cost of gas and maintenance would variable costs.
    D. All of the costs would be variable costs.
    E. All of the costs would be fixed costs.

16. Susan studied 2 hours for her first English quiz and scored 90 and 3 hours for her second English quiz and scored 95. During the same week she also studied 1 hour for her first History quiz and her test score was 68, and 2 hours for her second History quiz and scored 78. She would have more efficiently allocated her study time if she had
    A. studied more time for her second History quiz and less time for her second English quiz.
    B. studied more time for her second English quiz and less time for her second History quiz.
    C. studied the same amount of time for both the second English and second History quizzes.
    D. studied more time for both the second English and second History quizzes.
    E. not studied for the second History quiz and allocated all of her study time to prepare for the second English quiz.

17. Which of the following costs should be included when analyzing choices within a cost-benefit framework?
    A. Fixed costs
    B. Sunk costs
    C. Marginal costs and opportunity costs
    D. Sunk costs and marginal costs
    E. Fixed costs and opportunity costs

18. Mark recently switched his long distance telephone service from MTI to AC&C and had to pay his local telephone company a $10 fee to make the change. As an incentive to try their long distance services, AC&C promised to reimburse him for the switching fee if he choose to switch to another carrier after trying their service. From Marks perspective, the switching fee is a.
    A. fixed cost and a sunk cost
    B. fixed cost, but not a sunk cost.
    C. variable cost and a sunk cost.
    D. variable cost, but not a sunk cost.
    E. neither a fixed cost nor a sunk cost.

19. While eating dinner one evening, you receive a phone call from a telemarketing firm. The firm's representative informs you that your name is one of only five names drawn in a recent lottery. Each of the five people will receive a prize. In order to claim your prize, however, you must visit Summer Resorts, Inc. the following Friday (with no commitment to purchase anything), take a 90-minute tour of their facilities, and, at that time, your prize will be awarded. In order to visit Summer Resorts, Inc. the next Friday, you would have to miss 8 hours of work ($15 per hour), pay for the gas to drive there and back home ($20). Because you won't go to work that day you won't have to pay the $3 for gas to drive to and from work, nor pay to park for which you have a monthly pass that costs $50. Using cost-benefit analysis, you determine that it is rational for you to visit Summer Resorts, Inc. if the prize has a minimum value to you of
   A. $35
   B. $140
   C. $187
   D. $137
   E. $87

20. Samantha is the owner of a small bus company that has permits to run two routes daily in the city. The company has six buses and, currently, Samantha has three buses on each route. On Route 1, the daily revenue per bus is $75 and the third bus on the route takes in $50 in fares a day. On Route 2, the daily revenue per bus is $60 and the third bus to run this route takes in $60 in fares each day. To efficiently allocate the buses between the two routes, Samantha should
   A. shift the third bus from Route 2 to Route 1.
   B. shift all three buses from Route 2 to Route 1.
   C. shift the third bus from Route 1 to Route 2.
   D. shift all three buses from Route 1 to Route 2.
   E. leave the bus allocation as it is currently.

Self-Test: Short Answer/Problems
(Answers and solutions are given at the end of the chapter.)

1. Time Value of Money and Cost-Benefit Analysis
Tom put $10,000 in a two-year certificate of deposit (CD) at his bank. One year later, Tom finds out that his CD is currently valued at $11,000. During the same time period, his friend Shirley invested the same amount of money in a stock market mutual fund and it increased in value to $12,500. She suggests to Tom that he should withdraw his money from the CD and invest it in the mutual fund. Tom is hesitant to do so because he knows that there is an early withdrawal penalty of $500 if he takes the money out of the CD before the two-year period expires.

A. Calculate the interest rate that Tom is earning on his CD. _____

B. Assume the interest rate on the CD in the second year is 8%. What would be the value of the CD at the end of the second year? $ _____

C. What would be the opportunity cost if Tom removes the money from the CD at the end of the first year? $ _____

D. Assuming the same rate of return on the mutual fund in the second year as Shirley earned during the first year, what would be the marginal benefit to Tom of investing in the mutual fund? _____

E. Based on the assumptions in the questions above, would it be rational for Tom to shift his money from the CD to the mutual fund? _____ Why?

_____

_____.

2. March Madness Analysis
One week before the championship game of the NCAA Basketball tournament, Manuel and Scott were shopping at the mall where they each enter a free nationwide contest for tickets to courtside seats for the championship game. On the way home, they talked about the likelihood that someone would offer to purchase their tickets outside the arena on the day of the game if the two top-ranked teams were playing for the national championship. If that were the case, Manuel said that he would not sell his ticket for less than $75, to which Scott replied that he would only sell his if he could get at least $100. Recognizing the very small probability of winning the tickets to the basketball game, two days later Manuel pays $50 for a reservation to attend a March Madness Party on the day of the championship game. The next day they are notified that they have each won a free ticket to the game.

A. The minimum Manuel should be willing to accept for his ticket to the championship basketball game is $75. Therefore, Manuel's reservation price for attending the championship basketball game is $_____

B. The minimum Scott should be willing to accept for his ticket to the championship basketball game is $ _____. Therefore, Scott's reservation price for attending the championship basketball game is $ _____ .

C. If Manuel's reservation price for attending the March Madness Party is $110 and it is too late to sell his ticket to the March Madness Party, should he attend the game or the party? _____ Explain your answer. _____

    _____

D. If Manuel's reservation price for attending the March Madness Party is $110, and he can get a full refund for his ticket to the March Madness Party, should he attend the game or the party? _____ Explain your answer.

    _____

    _____

3. Resource Allocation

Seth owns a company that employs homeless people to sell flowers each Saturday evening between 10pm and midnight on the downtown street corners of Centerville and Outerville. The following table shows their total revenues earn in each town when Seth employs 1-4 sellers. Answer the questions below based on the information in the table.

Number of sellers	Total Revenue in Centerville	Average Revenue	Marginal Revenue	Total Revenue in Outerville	Average Revenue	Marginal Revenue
0	$0	XXXX	XXXX	$0	XXXX	XXXX
1	30			$50		
2	55			65		
3	75			75		
4	90			80		
5	100			80		

A. In columns 3 and 6, calculate the average revenue for sellers 1-5 in Centerville, and in Outerville, respectively.

B. In columns 4 and 7, calculate the marginal revenue for sellers 1-5 in Centerville, and in Outerville, respectively.

C. If Seth has three sellers working in Centerville and three sellers working in Outerville, are his resources efficiently allocated? _____ If not, what combination of the six sellers would give him the most efficient allocation of sellers? _____ sellers in Centerville, and _____ sellers in Outerville.

D. If Seth efficiently allocates a total of 4 sellers, he should deploy _____ in Centerville, and _____ in Outerville.

Solutions
Self-Test: Key Terms

1. sunk cost
2. variable cost
3. time value of money
4. average cost
5. fixed cost

Self-Test: Multiple-Choice Questions

1. C There is insufficient information to determine which choice she should make, but an optimal choice should include the opportunity cost of the $75,000 salary offer if the management position is the best alternative to her current position.

2. B As interest rates rise, it takes fewer dollars today to reach a given value at some specified time in the future.

3. C If he has no other trip to take within the year the unused ticket will be unredeemable (and thus represents a sunk cost) and should not be consider an opportunity cost. Thus, the opportunity cost is only the cost of the exchange fee. If he has another trip to take within the year, the opportunity cost of going to Acapulco would depend, in part, upon the price of the ticket to the new location.

4. E To calculate the present value of future earnings, divide the future value by one plus the interest rate to the nth power, where n equals the number of years. Thus, $125,000 divided by 1 + .25 = $100,0000

5. D

6. A The entertainment value of the concert will be foregone is she goes to dinner and dancing and, thus, is an opportunity cost. The cost of the concert ticket, however, is a sunk cost and should not be considered an opportunity cost of going to dinner and dancing.

7. A The average benefit of studying for the History test would equal the total points received on the tests (85 + 90 + 95) divided by the total number of hours studied (5 + 6 + 7).

8. B The student fees and the room and board costs do not change with the number of credit hours and are, therefore, fixed costs. All other costs change with the number of credit hours and are variable costs.

9. C

10. D Because the Adams family is foregoing interest on the savings used to buy the canned goods, it incurs an opportunity cost equal to the interest on the money expended.

11. C

12. D Because the cost of the car and the insurance and are not redeemable they should not be included in the opportunity cost of the trip.

13. E The $50 she paid for the XYC Corp. stock is a sunk cost (i.e., nonredeemable) and should not be considered in her analysis.

14. A

15. B The cost of the car and the insurance do not change with mileage and, thus, are fixed costs. All other costs vary with mileage and, therefore, are variable costs.

16. A The marginal benefit of the last hour of studying for the second History quiz was greater (10 points) than the last hour of studying for the second English quiz. She, therefore, would have more efficiently allocated her study time if she had studied more for the second History quiz and less for the second English quiz.

17. C

18. B The fee does not change with the number of long distance phone calls Mark makes and is, therefore, a fixed costs. If he decides to change his long distance carrier he will be reimbursed the amount of the switching fee. The switching is redeemable and, thus, is not a sunk cost.

19. D The opportunity cost of visiting Summer Resorts, Inc. is equal to the loss of wages ($120), plus the net cost of gasoline ($20 - $3). The cost of the parking pass is a sunk cost and, therefore, not included in the opportunity cost.

20. C The marginal benefit of the third bus on Route 2 is greater than the marginal benefit of the third bus on Route 1, and, therefore, a more efficient allocation would be achieved by shifting the third bus from Route 1 to Route 2.

Self-Test: Short Answer/Problems

1.
A. 10% ($11,000 minus $10,000 divided by $10,000)
B. $11,880 ($11,000 times 1.08)
C. $1,380 ($11,000 times .08 = $880 in foregone interest income plus the $500 early withdrawal penalty.)
D. $2,625 (The value of the CD minus the early withdrawal fee would give Tom $10,500 to invest. The mutual fund would earn 25% a year. Thus, $10,500 times .25).
E. Yes, because the marginal benefit ($2,625) is greater than the marginal cost ($1,380).

2.
A. $75
B. $100; $100
C. The party. Because it is too late to sell his ticket to the party, the $50 he paid for the ticket is a sunk cost and should not be considered in the decision. Manuel's reservation price for the party is $110, which is greater than his reservation price (opportunity cost) of $75 for the game. Thus, he should attend the party if he can not get a refund on the party reservation.
D. The game. Because he can get a full refund for his ticket to the party, Manuel's reservation price for the party is $60 ($110 - $50). His reservation price for the game is $75. Therefore, he should attend the game because his reservation price for the game is greater when he can get a full refund for the party.

3.

A, B.

Number of sellers	Total Revenue in Centerville	Average Revenue	Marginal Revenue	Total Revenue in Outerville	Average Revenue	Marginal Revenue
0	$0	XXXX	XXXX	$0	XXXX	XXXX
1	30	$30	$30	$50	$50	$50
2	55	22.50	25	65	32.50	15
3	75	25	20	75	25	10
4	90	22.50	15	80	20	5
5	100	20	10	80	16	0

C. No; 4; 2

By shifting one seller from Outerville to Centerville Seth will decrease his revenue in Outerville by $10, but will increase his revenue in Centerville by $15, resulting in a net benefit of $5. At this allocation the marginal benefit of the last seller employed in each town is equal to $15 and, thus, his resources are allocated efficiently.

D. 3; 1

His first seller would be deployed in Centerville where the marginal revenue (benefit) of the first seller is highest, and the next three would be deployed in Centerville because the marginal benefit of sellers 1,2, and 3 is greater than that of the second seller in Outerville. The sellers are imperfectly divisible and, thus, this is the most efficient allocation possible with four sellers.

Chapter 3
Comparative Advantage: The Basis for Exchange

Key Point Review

Economies can be based on specialization and the exchange of goods and services or on generalization and self-sufficiency in the production of goods and services. Economic systems that are based on specialization and exchange are generally far more productive than those lacking specialization. The benefits of specialization derive from what economists call comparative advantage. A person has a **comparative advantage** over another if that person's opportunity cost of performing a task is lower than another person's opportunity cost. This concept is so fundamental to economics that the authors have identified it as a core idea of the course. The Principle of Comparative Advantage asserts that everyone does best when each person (or each country) concentrates on the activities for which his or her opportunity cost is lowest. The sources of comparative advantage come from inborn talent, education, training and experience on the individual level, and from differences in natural resources, society and culture at the national level.

Comparative advantage is distinguished from absolute advantage. A person has an **absolute advantage** over another if she takes fewer hours to perform a task than the other person. One need not have an absolute advantage in the production of a good in order to have a comparative advantage. The benefits from specialization and exchange are greatest, however, when people (or nations) have an absolute and comparative advantage in the production of the goods and services that they specialize in producing, and when the differences in opportunity cost are more pronounced. In addition to the gains achieved through preexisting differences, specialization deepens individuals' skills through practice and experience and eliminates the switching and start up costs of moving back and forth among numerous tasks, thus providing further economic benefits. Despite the significant gains that derive from specialization, specialization can be taken to far, resulting in mind-numbing repetitive work.

The production possibilities curve can be used to demonstrate the benefits of producing in accordance with comparative advantage. The **production possibilities curve** is a graph that describes the maximum amount of one good that can be produced for every possible level of production of the other good. Points that lie on the production possibilities curve are both **efficient points** and **attainable points**, while points that lie below the curve are only **attainable points**. Points that lie outside the production possibilities curve represent combinations of goods that cannot be produced using the currently available resources and are **unattainable points**. Any combination of goods for which currently available resources enable an increase in the production of one good without a reduction in the production of the other good represent **inefficient points**. An individual's production possibilities curve is linear (a straight line). The production possibilities curve is downward-sloping, reflecting the principle of scarcity (the idea that, because our resources are limited, producing more of one good generally means producing less of another good). The slope of the production possibilities curve represents the opportunity cost of producing additional units of one good measured in terms of the amount of production of the other good that is foregone.

The same logic that leads individuals in an economy to specialize and exchange goods with one another also leads nations to specialize and trade among themselves. The production possibilities curve for two or more people, however, is bowed outward because of individual differences in opportunity costs. When the production possibilities curve is bowed outward, the slope increases as you move along the curve, indicating that the opportunity cost increases as additional units of a good are produced. This **principle of increasing opportunity cost** (also called "the low hanging fruit principle") states that in expanding the production of any good, first employ those resources with the lowest opportunity cost, and only afterward turn to resources with higher opportunity costs. The patterns of international trade today reflect the benefits shown in the production possibilities analysis. Despite the aggregate gains that derive from specialization and international trade, not everyone benefits, and this has often led to strong opposition to free trade agreements.

Knowledge and Skills

The student must master the knowledge and skills listed below each number topic.	Key Terms	Multiple-Choice Questions	Short Answer/ Problems
1. Comparative and Absolute Advantage			
A. Define comparative and absolute advantage	2, 6		
B. Calculate opportunity costs to determine comparative and/or absolute advantage		1, 12	2
C. Explain the Principle of Comparative Advantage		2, 9	
D. Discuss the sources of comparative advantage		3, 8, 13	
2. Comparative Advantage and Production Possibilities			
A. Define production possibilities curve	4		
B. Draw a production possibilities curve			1, 2, 3
C. Identify attainable, unattainable, efficient, and inefficient points on a production possibilities curve	1, 3, 5, 7	14	1

The student must master the knowledge and skills listed below each number topic.	Key Terms	Multiple-Choice Questions	Short Answer/ Problems
D. Explain why the production possibilities curve is downward sloping		4, 6	
E. Calculate the slope of a production possibilities curve		5, 15, 16	1
F. Explain the Principle of Increasing Opportunity Cost (aka "The Low-Hanging-Fruit Principle")		17	2
3. Comparative Advantage and Specialization of Labor			
A. Discuss the conditions that result in the greatest benefits from specialization		7	
B. Identify the benefits derived from specialization		8, 18	2, 3
C. Discuss why more specialization is not always better		19	
4. Comparative Advantage and International Trade			
A. Explain how trade expands a nation's menu of possibilities		10, 20	3
B. Discuss why some people oppose free trade agreements		11	

Self-Test: Key Terms

Use the terms below to complete the following sentences. (Answers are given at the end of the chapter.)

absolute advantage
attainable point
comparative advantage
efficient point
inefficient point
production possibilities curve
unattainable point

1. A combination of goods represented by a point on a production possibilities curve is an efficient point and a(n) _____ .
2. Jean's opportunity cost of cooking gourmet dinners is lower than Bill's opportunity cost. Jean, therefore, has a _____ vis-à-vis Bill in cooking gourmet dinners.
3. If a movement from combination A to combination B requires a reduction in the production of one good in order to increase the production of the other good, the point representing combination A is a(n) _____ .
4. A graph that describes the maximum amount of one good that can be produced for every possible level of production of the other good is a _____ .
5. Any combination of goods that cannot be produced using the currently available resources is a(n) _____ .

6. Juan takes fewer hours to create a web page than does Simon. Juan, therefore, has a
   _____ vis-à-vis Simon in the creation of web pages.
7. If a movement from combination A to combination B does not requires a reduction in the
   production of one good in order to increase the production of the other good, the point
   representing combination A is a(n) _____ .

Self-Test: Multiple-Choice Questions
Circle the letter that corresponds to the best answer. (Answers are given at the end of the
chapter.)

1. Jane can produce 50 pizzas or 100 hamburgers per day, while Sam can produce 30 pizzas or
   90 hamburgers per day. Jane has an
   A. absolute advantage in the production of pizzas, but not hamburgers, and has a
      comparative advantage in the production of pizzas.
   B. absolute advantage in the production of hamburgers, but not pizzas, and has a
      comparative advantage in the production of hamburgers.
   C. absolute advantage in the production of hamburgers, and pizzas, as well as a comparative
      advantage in the production of hamburgers.
   D. absolute advantage in the production of hamburgers, and pizzas, as well as a comparative
      advantage in the production of pizzas.
   E. absolute advantage in the production of hamburgers, and pizzas, as well as a comparative
      advantage in the production of hamburgers and pizzas.

2. When each individual concentrates on performing the tasks and producing the goods for
   which he or she has the lowest opportunity cost, they are producing in accordance with the
   principle of
   A. increasing opportunity cost.
   B. decreasing opportunity cost.
   C. comparative advantage.
   D. scarcity
   E. low hanging fruit.

3. At the individual level, comparative advantage results from
   A. differences in natural resources.
   B. cultural differences.
   `. language differences.
   D. amount of resources available.
   E. differences in education or training.

4. Production possibilities curves are downward sloping, reflecting the principle of
   A. scarcity.
   B. comparative advantage.
   C. increasing opportunity cost.
   D. absolute advantage.
   E. low hanging fruit.

5. Maria can produce 100 pounds of tomatoes or 25 pounds of squash in her garden each summer, while Tonya can produce 50 pounds of tomatoes or 25 pounds of squash. The absolute values of the slope of Maria's and Tonya's production possibility curves, respectively, are
   A. 1/4 and 1/2.
   B. 1/2 and 1/4.
   C. 4 and 2.
   D. 2 and 4.
   E. 100 and 50.

6. A country's production possibilities curve is concave to the origin (i.e., bowed outward) because
   A. of the principle of scarcity.
   B. the production of a good is expanded by first employing those resources with an absolute advantage.
   C. the production of a good is expanded by first employing those resources with the lowest opportunity cost.
   D. there is a tradeoff that requires a decrease in the production of one good in order to increase the production of another good.
   E. of the principle of absolute advantage

7. The gains from specialization and exchange are greatest when individuals or nations
   A. have a comparative and absolute advantage in the goods they produce, and the differences in opportunity costs are minimal.
   B. have a comparative and absolute advantage in the goods they produce, and the differences in opportunity costs are large.
   C. have only a comparative advantage in the goods they produce, and the differences in opportunity costs are minimal.
   D. have only an absolute advantage in the goods they produce, and the differences in opportunity costs are large.
   E. have neither a comparative nor absolute advantage in the goods they produce, but the differences in opportunity costs are large.

8. Specialization of labor not only results in the ability to produce a larger amount of goods due to innate differences in people's skills, but also by
   A. rigidly segmenting work.
   B. switching back and forth among numerous tasks.
   C. breaking a task down into mind-numbing repetitive tasks.
   D. deepening skills through practice and experience.
   E. eliminating the need to train and educate the workers to perform different tasks.

9. Professor N. Gregory Mankiw has a comparative advantage in the production of economics textbooks and a neighbor's child has a comparative advantage in mowing the lawn. Professor Mankiw
   A. should never mow his own lawn.
   B. should only write economics textbooks.
   C. may be better off mowing his lawn if he felt like taking a break from writing textbooks.
   D. will always be better off hiring the neighbor's child to mow his lawn.
   E. may be better off hiring the neighbor's child to write his economics textbook if his lawn needs mowing.

10. By specializing in accordance with its comparative advantage and trading with other nations, the small nation of Islandia will benefit
    A. less than larger nations.
    B. more than larger nations.
    C. only if it's trading partners suffer losses.
    D. more or less, depending on the combination of goods it chooses to consume.
    E. regardless of the combination of goods it chooses to consume.

11. Despite the benefits of specialization and exchange indicated in the theory of comparative advantage, some groups have opposed free trade agreements because
    A. wealthier economies gain, but poor nations lose from free trade.
    B. in order for one nation to gain from trade, another nation must lose.
    C. they don't understand the theory of comparative advantage.
    D. every individual does not gain from trade.
    E. contrary to the theory of comparative advantage, evidence suggests that there are few benefits from free trade.

12. Yolanda can produce 2 dresses or 4 shirts in 8 hours of work, while Sandra can produce 3 dresses or 7 shirts in the same amount of time. Yolanda has a(n)
    A. absolute advantage in producing dresses and shirts, and a comparative advantage in producing dresses, while Sandra has a comparative advantage in producing shirts.
    B. comparative advantage in producing shirts, while Sandra has an absolute advantage in producing dresses and shirts, and a comparative advantage in producing dresses.
    C. comparative advantage in producing dresses, while Sandra has an absolute advantage in producing dresses and shirts, and a comparative advantage in producing shirts.
    D. absolute advantage in producing dresses and shirts, and a comparative advantage in producing shirts, while Sandra has a comparative advantage in producing dresses.
    E. absolute advantage and a comparative advantage in producing dresses and shirts.

13. One of the major factors contributing to the United States achieving a global comparative advantage in producing movies, books and popular music is because
    A. the United States has more capital used in the production of mass media than other nations.
    B. the United States has more entrepreneurs than other nations.
    C. the United States has a better educational system than other nations.
    D. English is the native language of the United States and the de facto world language.
    E. the United States has more writers with an innate superiority over writers in other nations.

14. A point on Joseph's production possibilities curve represents 6 music CDs and 2 videos produced in a week. A combination of 4 music CDs and 2 videos is a(n)
    A. efficient and attainable point.
    B. efficient but not attainable point.
    C. attainable and inefficient point.
    D. unattainable point.
    E. unattainable and inefficient point.

15. The slope of an individual's production possibilities curve
    A. decreases as more units of a particular good are produced.
    B. is negative and constant along the entire curve.
    C. is positive and constant along the entire curve.
    D. varies as the amount of output changes.
    E. is the same for all individuals.

16. Point A on a production possibilities curve represents a combination of 10 bicycles and 4 tricycles, and point B represents 6 bicycles and 6 tricycles. The absolute value of the slope of the production possibilities curve between points A and B equals
    A. 2
    B. 4
    C. 1/2
    D. 1/4
    E. 6

17. In a two-person economy, Little Joe can trap a maximum of 6 rabbits or catch 10 fish a week, while his father can trap 12 rabbits or catch 15 fish per week. If their family wants to consume 20 fish per week while maximizing their joint production
    A. the father should specialize in producing only fish, and Little Joe should produce both fish and rabbits.
    B. Little Joe should specialize in producing only fish, and his father should produce both fish and rabbits.
    C. Little Joe should specialize in producing fish, and his father should produce rabbits.
    D. Little Joe should specialize in producing only rabbits, and his father should produce fish.
    E. each should produce both fish and rabbits.

18. When individuals or groups specialize in producing those goods for which they have a comparative advantage and exchange those goods with one another
    A. those with an absolute advantage will gain the most, while those without an absolute advantage will lose.
    B. those with a comparative advantage will gain the most, while those without a comparative advantage will lose.
    C. total production will be greater than it would be without specialization, but would be the greatest if they produced those goods in which they only have an absolute advantage.
    D. total production will be less than it would be without specialization.
    E. total production will be the greatest that they can achieve given the available resources.

19. Increased specialization in the production of goods
    A. always increases net benefits.
    B. never increases net benefits.
    C. has benefits, but no costs.
    D. has costs, but no benefits.
    E. has costs and benefits.

20. The opportunity for a small nation to trade with an economic superpower
    A. will increase the consumption possibilities for the small nation and the economic superpower.
    B. will increase the consumption possibilities for the small nation only.
    C. will increase the consumption possibilities for the economic superpower only.
    D. will increase the consumption possibilities for the economic superpower, but will decrease the consumption possibilities for the small nation.
    E. will increase the consumption possibilities for the small nation, but will decrease the consumption possibilities for the economic superpower.

Self-Test: Short Answer/Problems
(Answers and solutions are given at the end of the chapter.)

1. Production Possibilities Curve for an Individual

A. If Ian allocates all of his resources he can write 4 short stories in a month, or he can allocate all his resources to crafting 20 leather belts. Draw his production possibilities curve, measuring the production of leather belts on the vertical axis, and short stories on the horizontal axis, on the graph below (be sure to label the axis!).

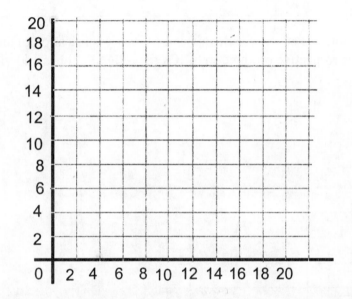

B. Ian is currently allocating all of his resources to producing leather belts. If he decides to reallocate his resources so as to produce 1 short story, he will incur an opportunity cost of

    _____.

C. Based on your answer to Question 1B, the absolute value of the slope of Ian's production possibilities curve equals _____ .

D. On the graph above, draw a point representing the combination of 12 leather belts and 4 short stories (label it A). Point A is a(n) _____ point.

E. On the graph above, draw a point representing the combination of 5 leather belts and 3 short stories (label it B). Point B is a(n) _____ and
    _____ point.

F. On the graph above, draw a point representing the combination of 2 leather belts and 2 short stories (label it C). Point C is a(n) _____ point.

2. Production Possibilities and Comparative Advantage

Sean and Shirley are proprietors of small fabrication plants that design and manufacture integrated chips (ICs) for specialized electronic products. The table below shows their respective productivity for ICs used in cellular phones and video-game machines.

	Time to design and manufacture ICs for cellular phone	Time to design and manufacture ICs for video-game machines
Sean's plant	4 days	4 days
Shirley's plant	1 day	2 days

A. Draw the production possibilities curves for Sean's and Shirley's fabrication plants on the graph below showing their respective production of ICs for cellular phones and video-game machines in 40 days.

ICs for
Game
Machines

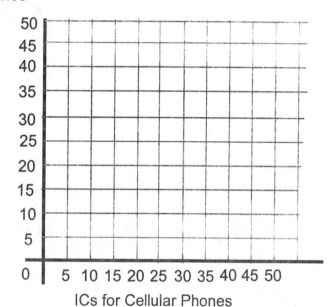

ICs for Cellular Phones

B. Sean's plant has an opportunity cost of producing ICs for cellular phones of _____ and for producing ICs for video-game machines of _____ . Shirley's plant has an opportunity cost of producing ICs for cellular phones of _____ and for producing ICs for video-game machines of _____ .

C. _____ has an absolute advantage in producing ICs for cellular phones and video-game machines.

D. _____ has a comparative advantage in producing ICs for cellular phones and _____ has a comparative advantage in producing ICs for video-game machines.

E. In order to maximize the total production of ICs for cellular phones and video-game machines, Sean should specialize in the production of ICs for _____ and Shirley should specialize in the production of ICs for _____ .

F. As the demand for its ICs for cellular phones increased to 45 per month, Shirley buys Sean's fabrication plant. Draw the production possibilities curve showing the combined maximum production of the two fabrication plants.

ICs for
Game
Machines

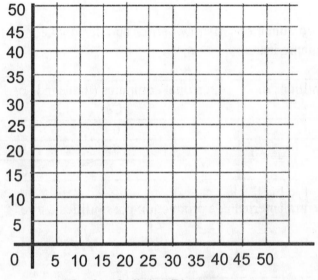

ICs for Cellular Phones

G. Prior to the merger of the fabrication plants and specialization, the slopes of Shirley's and Sean's PPCs were (constant/decreasing/increasing) _____. After the merger and specialization, the slope of the combined plants PPC (is constant/ decreases/increases) _____ after _____ ICs for cellular phones are produced , reflecting the Law of _____ (also called the _____).

H. In order to maximize production of ICs and produce 45 ICs for cellular phones per month, _____ fabrication plant should completely specialize in producing ICs for cellular phones, and _____ fabrication plant should produce ICs for cellular phones and video-game machines.

I. Your answers to Questions 2G and 2H imply that in order to maximize production of ICs while producing 45 ICs for cellular phones, they must allocate 3/4 of the combined production time of the two plants (i.e., 40 days of production in Shirley's fab plus 20 days of production in Sean's fab = 60 days divided by 80 of combined production days). The remaining 1/4 of the combined time would be allocated to producing ICs for video-game machines. If prior to the buyout, each fabrication plant had allocated 3/4 of its time (i.e., 30 days) to producing ICs for cellular phones, Shirley's fabrication plant would have produced _____ ICs and Sean's fabrication plant would have produced _____

ICs. Similarly, if each fabrication plant had allocated 1/4 (i.e., 10 days) of its time producing ICs for video-game machines, Shirley's fabrication plant would have produced _____ ICs and Sean's fabrication plant would have produced _____ ICs.

J. Based on your answer to Question 2I, the total number of ICs that would have been produced prior to the merger and specialization would have equaled _____ ICs, but after the merger and specialization the two fabrication plants would produce _____ ICs.

K. Based on your answers to Question 2J, the gains from specialization would equal _____ ICs.

3. Gains from Trade

The following table shows the combinations of strawberries and personal computers (PCs) that can be produced by Centralamericana.

Strawberries (millions of tons)	Personal computes (thousands of PCs)
8	0
6	8
0	12

A. On the graph below, plot Centralamericana's production possibilities curve.

Strawberries
(mil. tons)

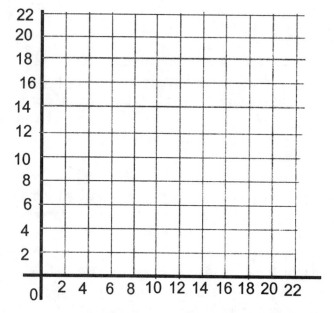

Personal Computers (1,000s)

B. The economy of Centralamerican is closed (i.e., no trade is allowed) and it has chosen to produce a combination of 6 million tons of strawberries and 8,000 PCs. Identify this combination on the above graph by labeling it point A.

C. By means of an international treaty, the economy of Centralamericana is opened to international trade. The prevailing exchange rate is 1 million tons of strawberries for 1,000 PCs. On the graph above, draw Centralamericana's new PPC after opening its economy to international trade, assuming it is producing at point A and could exchange as much of its strawberry and PC production as it chooses to at the prevailing exchange rate.

D. What combination of consumption of strawberries and PCs would not result in gains from international trade for Centralamericana? _____ million tons of strawberries and _____ PCs.

E. If Centralamericana started at Point A and chose to sell 4,000 PCs (at the prevailing exchange rate), it would then be able to consume _____ million tons of strawberries and _____ PCs. Label this point B. As a result of trade, it would have increased its consumption of strawberries by _____ millions tons compared to what it would have been able to produce without trade.

F. If Centralamericana started at Point A and chose to sell 3 million tons of strawberries at the prevailing exchange rate), it would then be able to consume _____ million tons of strawberries and _____ PCs. Label this point C. As a result of trade, it would have increased its consumption of PCs by _____ millions tons compared to what it would have been able to produce without trade.

Solutions
Self-Test: Key Terms

1. attainable point
2. comparative advantage
3. efficient point
4. production possibilities curve
5. unattainable point
6. absolute advantage
7. inefficient point

Self-Test: Multiple-Choice Questions

1. D Jane can produce more pizzas and hamburgers than Sam and, thus, has an absolute advantage in producing both. Jane's opportunity cost of producing pizzas is 2 hamburgers, while Sam's opportunity cost of producing pizzas is 3 hamburgers. Since Jane's opportunity cost of producing pizzas is less than Sam's, she has a comparative advantage in producing pizzas.
2. C
3. E
4. A
5. C The slope of Maria's PPC equals 100/25 = 4 and Tonya's equals 50/25 = 2.
6. C By exploiting the lowest cost production first the opportunity cost of producing additional units of a good increases and, thus, the slope of PPC increases (i.e., it is bowed outward).
7. B
8. D
9. C We can only be certain that Professor Mankiw will be better off writing his textbook rather than mowing his lawn if he is equally happy doing either.
10. D
11. D
12. C Yolanda's opportunity cost of producing dresses is 2 shirts, while Sandra's opportunity cost of producing dresses is 2 1/2 shirts. Since Yolanda's opportunity cost of producing dresses is less than Sandra's, she has a comparative advantage in producing dresses. Sandra can produce more dresses and shirts than Yolanda and, thus, has an absolute advantage in producing both. Sandra's opportunity cost of producing a shirt is 3/7 of a dress; while Yolanda's is 1/2 dress. Thus, Sandra has a comparative advantage in producing shirts.
13. D
14. C The combination of 4 CDs and 2 videos produced would lie below Joseph's production possibilities curve and, thus, would be attainable, but would also be inefficient.
15. B The individual's PPC is downward sloping (i.e., negative) and a straight line (i.e., constant).
16. A The slope equals the absolute value of (10 − 6) divided by (4 − 6), or 4/2 which equals 2.

17. B Litle Joe's opportunity cost of catching a fish is 3/5 rabbit, while his father's is 4/5 fish. Little Joe has a comparative advantage in catching fish and, thus, should specialize in fishing to catch his 10 fish. The father should catch the additional 10 fish and his remaining time spent trapping rabbits.
18. E
19. E
20. A

Self-Test: Short Answer/Problems

1.
A.
Leather
Belts

Short Stories

B. 5 leather belts
C. 5

D.

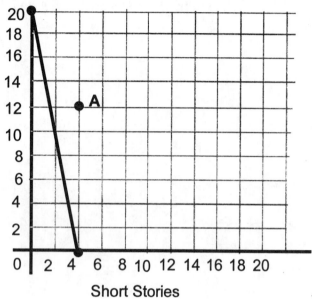

; unattainable

E.

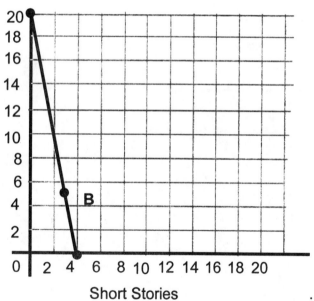

; attainable; efficient

F.

Leather
Belts

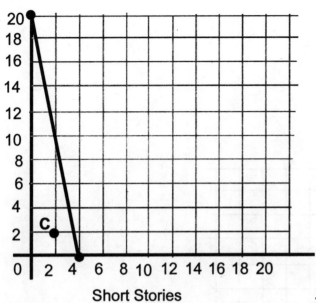

Short Stories   ; inefficient

2.

A.

ICs for
Game
Machines

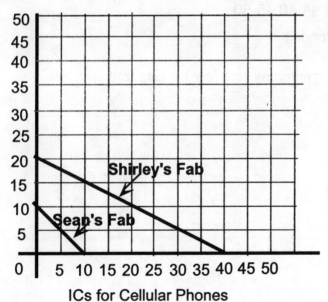

ICs for Cellular Phones

B. 1 IC for video-game machines; 1 IC for cellular phones; 1/2 IC for video-game machines; 2 ICs for cellular phones

C. Shirley

D. Shirley; Sean

E. video-game machines; cellular phones

F.

ICs for Game Machines

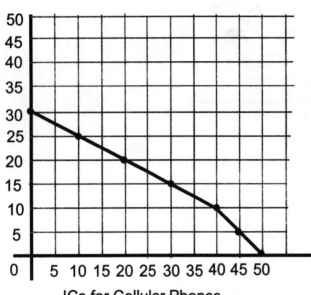

ICs for Cellular Phones

G. constant; increases; 40; increasing opportunity cost; low-hanging fruit principle

H. Shirley's; Sean's

I. 30; 7 1/2; 5; 2 1/2

J. 45; 50

K. 5

3.

A.

Strawberries
(mil. tons)

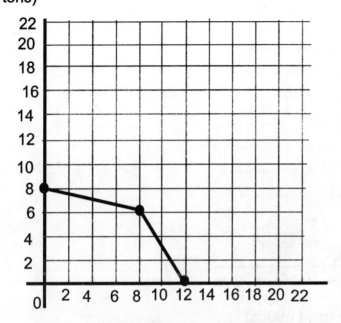

Personal Computers (1,000s)

B.

Strawberries
(mil. tons)

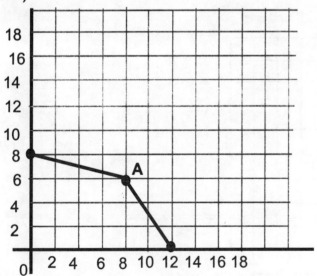

Personal Computers (1,000s)

C.
Strawberries
(mil. tons)

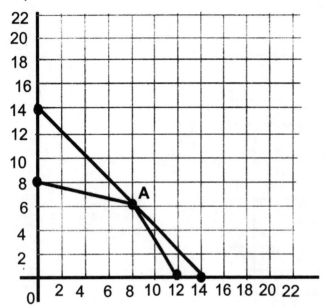

Personal Computers (1,000s)

D. 6; 8
E. 10; 4,000;   ; 3
Strawberries
(mil. tons)

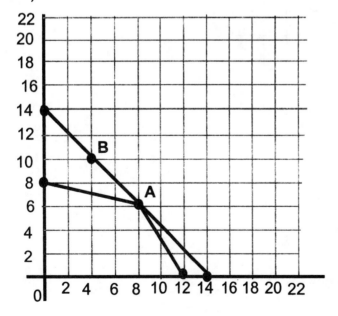

Personal Computers (1,000s)

F. 3; 11;   ; 1

**Strawberries
(mil. tons)**

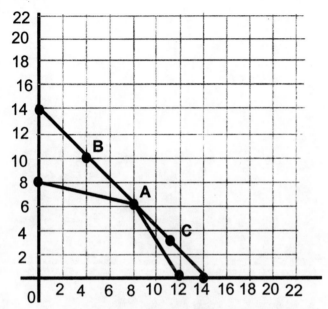

Personal Computers (1,000s)

Chapter 4
Supply and Demand: An Introduction

Key Point Review

An old joke asks "How do you make an economist? You teach a parrot to say 'Supply and Demand,' 'Supply and Demand.'" Indeed, economists return again and again to the tools of supply and demand to understand how the world works and to make predictions concerning the consequences of changes in the state of the world. The importance of understanding supply and demand, both for success in the classroom as well as the business and political environment, can not be over stressed.

A **market** consists of all the buyers and all the sellers of a particular good or service. Early economists clearly understood what a market was; there was considerably more debate on how the market determined the price of the particular good or service. Adam Smith and others believed that price was determined by the cost of production. Later economists, like Stanley Jevons, focused on the value consumers attached to a good or service as the basis for its price. Neither view was entirely satisfactory. Alfred Marshall, working in the late nineteenth century, provided the complete picture: costs and value interact together to determine the price of a good and the amounts that will be bought and sold.

The **supply curve** of a good is a curve that relates the total quantity of the good producers are willing and able to sell at each possible price. It is based on the assumption that producers will be willing to sell the good as long as the price they receive is sufficient to cover their opportunity costs. Since some people have low opportunity costs, other have moderate opportunity costs, and still others have high opportunity costs, supply curves must slope upward. At low prices, only the low-opportunity-cost individuals will find it worthwhile to produce the good. To acquire more of the good, more individuals must be drawn into production. These are the people with moderate opportunity costs. Only with a higher price will the moderate-opportunity-cost individuals find it beneficial to become producers. To induce the high-opportunity-cost individuals to join the market, an even higher price must be forthcoming. Thus, a positive or direct relationship is thought to exist between price and the quantity supplied.

The **demand curve** of a good shows the total quantity of the good buyers are willing and able to purchase at each possible price. The nature of the relationship between the price of a good and the quantity we wish to purchase is well know to all of us from practical experience. At higher prices, we wish to buy less and at lower prices, we wish to buy more. The demand curve is, therefore, downward sloping. A negative or inverse relationship exists between price and the quantity supplied.

The idea of **equilibrium**, when the forces within a system cancel each other out, resulting in an unchanging situation, appears in both the physical and social sciences. In economics, the forces are supply and demand and the system is the marketplace. The **equilibrium price** and **equilibrium quantity** of a good are determined at the point where the demand curve intersects the supply curve. A **market equilibrium** occurs when all buyers and sellers are satisfied with their respective quantities at the market price. Satisfied does not mean that buyers would not like a lower price or that sellers would be displeased with a higher price. It simply means those buyers willing to pay the equilibrium price can acquire exactly the amount they wish. Likewise, sellers who are willing to accept the equilibrium price can sell the exact amount they wish.

At prices above the equilibrium price, buyers wish to acquire a relatively small amount of a good but many suppliers can cover their opportunity costs so a large amount of the good is produced. When quantity supplied exceeds quantity demanded, the market experiences **excess supply** or a **surplus**. Since suppliers are unable to sell all they have produced, they are dissatisfied with the current market situation. Conversely, at prices below the equilibrium price, buyers wish to acquire a relatively large amount of the good, but few suppliers can cover their opportunity costs so only a small amount of the good is produced. When quantity demanded exceeds quantity supplied, the market experiences **excess demand** or a **shortage**. Since buyers are unable to acquire all they wish at the going price, they are unhappy with the current market situation. Both circumstances represent disequilibrium. Will the market naturally right itself and establish the equilibrium price and quantity?

Fortunately, and remarkably, the answer is yes. In the case of excess supply, suppliers will be dissatisfied with their unsold output. When searching for ways to correct the problem, the most obvious solution is to lower price. Lowering the price will induce some consumers to make purchases that were passed over at the higher price. Similarly, the lower price means some firms will no longer cover their opportunity costs and will leave the market. The net result is for price to be lower and the difference between quantity supplied and quantity demanded to narrow. Firms will continue to reduce price until excess supply is zero. At this point firms will have reached the equilibrium price and will be satisfied with the market situation. For excess demand, a similar process is at work. Consumers are dissatisfied; some are unable to acquire the good at the going price. These unfulfilled consumers have an incentive to offer a higher price to enlarge the chance they will receive some of the production. The higher price will drive some of the consumers out of the market while encouraging new suppliers to join the market. The net result is for price to be higher and the difference between quantity demanded and quantity supplied to shrink. Consumers will continue to offer higher prices until excess demand is zero. When this point is reached, the equilibrium price will have been achieved and consumers will be satisfied with the market situation. The market then has a tendency to move toward the equilibrium price regardless of whether the price is initially above or below the equilibrium value.

Sometimes markets are not allowed to function on their own. For a variety of political reasons, government sets prices in some markets. Your textbook discusses the example of rent controls in New Your City. Rent controls are a specific example of a **price ceiling**, a maximum allowable price set by law. Of course, the price ceiling must be set below the equilibrium price to have any effect on the market. The consequence of government setting the price below the equilibrium value is the same as when the price just happens to be below the equilibrium: excess demand. The difference is that in the market with a price ceiling, price is not allowed to rise as it would in an unregulated market. Excess demand will become chronic with demanders searching in vain for adequate amounts of the good while suppliers will have no incentive to produce more. Depending on the specific good, a host of ills will develop as consumers attempt to secure the good and suppliers come to recognize they are insulated from competition.

When a particular market is in equilibrium, the outcome is optimal in that the difference between the total benefits and total costs experienced by the buyers and sellers is maximized. When a market is in disequilibrium or the total benefits or total costs are not completely accounted for, the outcome is less than optimal. In the case of market disequilibrium, as happens with a price ceiling, it is always possible to identify mutually beneficial exchanges—there is "cash on the table." When price is below equilibrium, it will always be possible for a supplier to produce an additional unit at a cost lower than what buyers are willing to pay. Indeed, this is precisely the dynamic that leads price up toward the equilibrium in an unregulated market. In equilibrium, no mutually beneficial trades remain and there is no cash left on the table.

The **socially optimal quantity** of any good or service is the amount that maximizes the total economic surplus. When the socially optimal quantity is not produced, a rearrangement of production will result in a greater economic surplus. **Efficiency** occurs when all goods and services are produced and consumed at their socially optimal quantities. Efficiency is a significant social goal; failure to reach it means the size of the economic surplus is smaller than it could have been. The Efficiency Principle, one of the core principles, states that efficiency is an important social goal because when the economic pie is growing, everyone can have a larger slice.

For total economic surplus to be maximized, all the costs of producing and all the benefits of consuming the good must be counted. If all the costs are directly borne by the sellers and all the benefits are directly borne by the consumers, then the equilibrium is socially optimal. In some cases, however, the costs borne by sellers do not completely reflect the costs to society. The classic example is a manufacturing plant that produces air pollution in addition to the good it sells to the public. The seller's costs do not include the cost of the air pollution (e.g., increased medical care costs due to a higher incidence of lung disease). As a result, the equilibrium price is lower and the equilibrium quantity is larger than would be if the costs of the air pollution were included. The above example illustrates some market equilibriums are "smart for one but dumb for all." That is, the producers and consumers are behaving rationally ("smart for one") yet unexploited opportunities for gain from a social view remain ("dumb for all"). Collective action is usually required to tap into the unexploited social opportunities. The Equilibrium Principle, another of the core principles, reveals that a market in equilibrium leaves no unexploited opportunities for individuals, but may not exploit all gains achievable through collective action.

To successfully apply the tools of supply and demand analysis, one very important distinction must be clear in your thinking: movement along a curve versus a shift in the curve. A **change in quantity demanded** is a movement along a demand curve in response to a change in the price of the good. A **change in demand** occurs when the entire demand curve shifts. Similar terms exist for the supply curve. A **change in quantity supplied** is a movement along a supply curve in response to a change in the price of the good. A **change in supply** describes a shift of the entire supply curve.

Shifts of the supply curve are cause by two different variables. The first is the price of input used in the production of the good. All firms make use of some labor input so wages are the most common input price. If wages rises, the cost of producing the good will rise. This means that a higher price will be required in order for firms to continue producing as much as they were before the wage increase. Alternatively, at the same price as before the wage increase, fewer units will be supplied. In either case, the previous relationship between price and quantity supplied has been altered; at any price, firms are willing and able to produce less of the good. A decrease in supply has occurred and the entire supply curve has shifted to the left. The second factor that causes supply to shift is technological change. Technological change reduces the cost of production in some fashion. As a result, firms can receive a lower price and continue to make as much as they were prior to the technological change. If firms were to receive the same price as they were before the change, they will now produce more. An increase in supply has occurred and the entire supply curve has shifted to the right.

The list of variables that cause a shift in the demand curve is somewhat longer. Income obviously influences the amount of a good that consumers wish to purchase. A **normal good** is one for which demand increases (shifts to the right) when consumer incomes rise. Most, but not all, goods and services follow this pattern. An **inferior good** is one for which demand decreases (shifts to the left) when consumer incomes rise. Prices of related goods will also affect consumer demand for a particular good. Two different goods, M and N, can be related in one of two ways: substitutes or complements. Substitutes means M and N are similar can be used in place of one another. Dell computers and Compaq computers are substitutes. Formally, two goods are classified as **substitutes** if an increase in the price of one causes an increase in demand (rightward shift) for the other. If Dell raises the price of its computers, demand for Compaq computers will shift to the right. Complements means M and N are typically used together. VCRs and TVs are complements. Two goods are considered **complements** if an increase in the demand for one causes a decrease in demand (leftward shift) for the other. If the price of TVs increases, consumers will purchase fewer TVs and, as a result, demand fewer VCRs regardless of price of VCRs.

The goal of a model building exercise is to understand how the world works and then to predict how the world will react to changes. The supply and demand model allows four strong statements to be made about the direction of changes in the equilibrium price and quantity when supply and demand shift. If demand increases (rightward shift) and supply is constant, then the equilibrium price and quantity will rise. If demand decreases (leftward shift) and supply is constant, then the equilibrium price and quantity will fall. On the other hand, if supply increases (rightward shift) and demand is constant, the equilibrium price will fall and the equilibrium quantity will rise. But if supply decreases (leftward shift) with demand constant, the equilibrium price will rise and the equilibrium quantity will fall. Finally, when both supply and demand shift at the same time, the direction of change will be known for only price or quantity but not both. For example, if both supply and demand increase (rightward shift), it is certain that the equilibrium quantity will rise. But the new equilibrium price could be higher, lower, or unchanged. Which of the three possibilities for price will come to bear depends on the relative magnitudes of the supply and demand shifts. If the supply increases is very small and the demand increase is quite large, then the new equilibrium price will be higher. As another example, suppose demand decreases and supply increases. The new equilibrium price must be lower but the new equilibrium quantity could be larger, smaller, or unchanged. It again depends on the relative size of the supply shift compared to the demand shift. A small decrease in demand coupled with a large increase in supply would produce a new equilibrium quantity larger than the original.

Knowledge and Skills

The student must master the knowledge and skills listed below each numbered topic.	Key Terms	Multiple-Choice Questions	Short Answer/ Problems
1. The Demand Curve			
A. Define a demand curve	4		1
B. List the five factors that cause a change in demand and illustrate the effect when one of them changes	3, 11, 13, 16	1, 2, 8, 10	2
C. Explain the difference between changes in quantity demanded and changes in demand	2, 12	7, 9	3
2. The Supply Curve			
A. Define a supply curve	9		1
B. List the two factors that cause a change in supply and illustrate the effect when one of them changes		11, 14	2
C. Explain the difference between changes in quantity supplied and changes in supply	5, 14	5, 18	3
3. Workings of a Market			
A. Define a market	7		
B. Discuss what equilibrium means in an economic context	1, 8, 15, 17	3, 19	
C. Explain how prices of goods and services are determined		6, 12	1, 4
D. Calculate the amount of either excess supply or excess demand in a market	6, 10, 18, 21	23	1, 4
E. Explain the "No Cash on the Table" principle	19, 22	15	
F. Explain the "Smart for One, Dumb for All" principle		17	
G. Explain the impact of price controls	20	20	4
4. Market Adjustment			
A. Illustrate the impact of a change in demand on the equilibrium price and quantity		4, 21	3
B. Illustrate the impact of a change in supply on the equilibrium price and quantity		13, 22	3
C. Illustrate the impact of a change in both demand and supply on the equilibrium price and quantity		16	3

Self-Test: Key Terms
Use the terms below to complete the following sentences. (Answers are given at the end of the chapter.)

change in demand
change in quantity demanded
change in supply
change in quantity supplied
complements
demand curve
efficiency
equilibrium
equilibrium price
equilibrium quantity
excess demand
excess supply
inferior good
market
market equilibrium
normal good
price ceiling
shortage
socially optimal quantity
substitutes
supply curve
surplus

1. The _____ is the amount of a good or service that will be exchanged when quantity demanded equals quantity supplied.
2. When consumers are willing and able to purchase more of a good or service at each price then a(n) _____ has occurred.
3. If an increase in income causes consumers to purchase more of a particular good, then that good is classified as a(n) _____.
4. The total quantity consumers are willing and able to purchase of a good or a service at each price is illustrated by a(n) _____.
5. When the price of a good or service changes, a firm reacts to this through a(n) _____.
6. _____ occurs when the price of a good or service is below the equilibrium price.
7. The set of all buyers and sellers of toothpaste constitutes the _____ for toothpaste.
8. When all of the forces that influence a system are canceled by each other, resulting in a stable situation, the system is said to be in a state of _____.
9. The _____ shows the total quantity of a good or service that sellers are willing to make available at each price.
10. When the price of a good is above the equilibrium price, _____ results.

11. As incomes grow, consumers purchase fewer used cars at each price. Used cars are therefore a(n) _____.

12. When consumers alter their purchases of a good or service because the price of the good or service has changed, this is termed a(n) _____.

13. When the price of good X increases, consumers purchase less of service Y. Good X and service Y must therefore be _____.

14. A change in the price of labor will cause a(n) _____.

15. A _____ is achieved when all buyers and sellers of a good or service are satisfied with their respective quantities at the market price.

16. Goods A and B are classified as _____ if, as the price of good A rises, demand for good B increases.

17. The price that results from the intersection of the supply and demand curves is referred to as the _____.

18. A(n) _____ occurs when the price of a good or service is below the equilibrium price.

19. The amount of a good that results in the maximum possible economic surplus from producing and consuming the good is termed the _____.

20. When government sets the price of a good or service below the equilibrium, it is called a

    _____.

21. A(n) _____ develops when quantity supplied exceeds quantity demanded.

22. When all goods and services are produced and consumed at their respective socially optimal levels _____ has been achieved.

Self-Test: Multiple-Choice Questions
Circle the letter that corresponds to the best answer. (Answers are given at the end of the chapter.)

1. If the price of tea increases and the demand for sugar decreases, then
   A. tea and sugar are complements.
   B. tea is a normal good and sugar is inferior.
   C. tea and sugar are substitutes.
   D. tea is an inferior good and sugar is normal.
   E. tea and sugar are unrelated to each other.

2. If the demand for a good increases as consumer's incomes rise, the good is termed a(n)
   A. inferior good.
   B. complement good.
   C. normal good.
   D. substitute good.
   E. typical good.

3. Which of the following is not a characteristic of a market in equilibrium?
   A. Quantity demanded equals quantity supplied.
   B. Excess supply is zero.
   C. All consumers are able to purchases as much as they wish.
   D. Excess demand is zero.
   E. The equilibrium price is stable, i.e., there is no pressure for it to change

4. An increase in the demand for coal with no concurrent change in the supply of coal will
   result in a(n) _____ equilibrium price and a(n) _____ equilibrium quantity.
   A. higher; lower
   B. lower; lower
   C. higher; unchanged
   D. higher; higher
   E. lower; higher

5. As the price of cookies increases, firms that produce cookies will
   A. increase the supply of cookies.
   B. increase the quantity of cookies supplied.
   C. decrease the supply of cookies.
   D. decrease the quantity of cookies supplied.
   E. leave their production unchanged.

6. The equilibrium price and quantity of any good or service is established by
   A. only demanders.
   B. only suppliers.
   C. government regulations.
   D. both demanders and suppliers.
   E. custom and tradition.

7. Suppose the price of gasoline increases. We would expect
   A. the demand for gasoline to decrease.
   B. the demand for Sport Utility Vehicles (SUVs) to decrease.
   C. the demand for SUVs to increase.
   D. the quantity of gasoline demanded to increase.
   E. the quantity of SUVs demanded to decrease.

8. If, when the price of X increases, the demand for Y increases we can conclude that
   A. X and Y are complements.
   B. X and Y are substitutes.
   C. X and Y are normal.
   D. X and Y are inferior.
   E. X and Y are superior.

9. At the beginning of the fall semester, college towns experience large increases in their populations, causing a(n)
   A. increase in the quantity of apartments demanded.
   B. increase in the supply of apartments.
   C. increase in the demand for apartments.
   D. decrease in the quantity of apartments supplied.
   E. decrease in the supply of apartments.

10. An increase in the price of Tomko toothpaste, a substitute for Durrell toothpaste, will cause
   A. the quantity of Durrell toothpaste demanded to increase.
   B. the quantity of Tomko toothpaste demanded to increase.
   C. the demand for Tomko toothpaste to decrease.
   D. the demand for Tomko toothpaste to increase.
   E. the demand for Durrell toothpaste to increase.

11. Which of the following would not shift the supply curve for Pentium III processors?
   A. A decrease in the price of silicon wafers.
   B. An increase in the demand for Pentium III processors.
   C. An improvement in the technology used to make processors.
   D. An increase in the wage rate paid to "clean room" workers.
   E. An earthquake centered in Silicon Valley.

12. In a free market, if the price of a good is below the equilibrium price, then
   A. government needs to set a higher price.
   B. suppliers, dissatisfied with growing inventories, will raise the price.
   C. demanders, wanting to ensure they acquire the good, will bid the price higher.
   D. government needs to set a lower price.
   E. suppliers, dissatisfied with growing inventories, will lower the price.

13. A decrease in supply, holding demand constant, will always result in a(n)
   A. higher equilibrium price.
   B. lower equilibrium price.
   C. larger equilibrium quantity.
   D. larger quantity demanded
   E. indeterminate change in the equilibrium quantity.

14. Increases in the prices firms pay for inputs causes a(n)
   A. decrease in quantity supplied.
   B. increase in supply.
   C. increase in quantity supplied.
   D. decrease in supply.
   E. output prices to fall.

15. When a market is not in equilibrium then
    A. it is always possible to identify unexploited opportunities.
    B. demanders are dissatisfied with the market.
    C. suppliers are dissatisfied with the market.
    D. government intervention is necessary.
    E. it will have a tendency to remain in disequilibrium.

16. If a market is at point of equilibrium and then demand increases while supply decreases, the change in the equilibrium price is _____ and the change in the equilibrium quantity is _____.
    A. positive; positive
    B. positive; negative
    C. positive; indeterminate
    D. indeterminate; positive
    E. negative; negative

17. If the full marginal costs of producing a certain good are greater than the seller's marginal costs, then
    A. the market will produce the socially optimal outcome.
    B. the equilibrium price will reflect the true cost of production.
    C. too little of the good will be produced.
    D. too much of the good will be produced.
    E. the total economic surplus will be maximized.

18. When the demand for a good increases, firms respond by
    A. increasing their supply.
    B. decreasing their costs.
    C. increasing their price.
    D. increasing their quantity supplied.
    E. decreasing their supply.

19. A market in equilibrium would feature
    A. excess supply.
    B. unexploited opportunities.
    C. excess demand.
    D. wild variation in price.
    E. no tendency to change.

20. Suppose we know two facts: first, the market for hair-restoring tonics experiences chronic shortages and second, government sets the price of hair restoring tonics. We can conclude
    A. government has set the price too high.
    B. government has set the price above the equilibrium price.
    C. government has set the price too low.
    D. government has set the price below the equilibrium price.
    E. firms are not manufacturing enough hair-restoring tonics.

21. We observe that the equilibrium price of coffee falls and the equilibrium quantity falls. Which of the following best fits the observed data?
    A. An increase in demand with supply constant.
    B. An increase in demand coupled with a decrease in supply.
    C. An increase in demand coupled with an increase in supply.
    D. A decrease in demand with supply constant.
    E. Constant demand and an increase in supply.

22. Suppose that the equilibrium price of pickles falls while the equilibrium quantity rises. The most consistent explanation for these observations is
    A. a decrease in demand for pickles with no change in supply.
    B. an increase in demand for pickles with no change in supply.
    C. an increase in the supply of pickles and a decrease in the demand for pickles.
    D. a decrease in the supply of pickles with no change in demand.
    E. an increase in the supply of pickles with no change in demand.

23. Suppose that at a price of $5, quantity demanded is 300 units and quantity supplied is 700 units. This market will experience _____ of _____ units.
    A. excess demand, 400 units
    B. excess supply, -400 units
    C. excess demand, -400 units
    D. excess supply, 400 units
    E. a shortage, 400 units

Self-Test: Short Answer/Problems
(Answers and solutions are given at the end of the chapter.)

1. Demand, Supply, and Market Equilibrium.
The following question tests your understanding of quantity demanded, quantity supplied, and market equilibrium applied to the market for memory chips used in personal computers.

Price of a 128 MB SDRAM Memory Chip	Quantity of 128 MB SDRAM demanded (in millions)	Quantity of 128 MB SDRAM supplied (in millions)
$75	45	6
$100	21	11
$150	15	15
$200	7	23
$225	4	36

A. As the price of 128 MB memory chips rises, quantity demanded (rises/falls) _____.
When the price of memory chips falls, quantity supplied (increases/decreases) _____.

B. In this market, an equilibrium occurs at a price of _____. At this price, (quantity demanded/demand) _____ equals (quantity supplied/supply) _____ with _____ million units exchanged.

C. At a price of $225, (supply/quantity supplied) _____ exceeds (demand/quantity demanded) _____ by an amount equal to _____ units. The market is thus experiencing (excess supply/excess demand) _____. As a result, (producers/consumers) _____ will (lower/raise) _____ the price of memory chips.

D. At a price of $100, (demand/quantity demanded) _____ exceeds (supply/quantity supplied) _____ by an amount equal to _____ units. The market is thus experiencing (excess supply/excess demand) _____. As a result, (producers/consumers) _____ will (lower/raise) _____ the price of memory chips.

2. Graphical Analysis of Demand and Supply Curve Shifts

Understanding which variables cause shifts in the demand curve or the supply curve and how these shifts are illustrated in a graph is a major objective of the chapter. The following question helps to assess your comprehension of demand and supply shifts.

A. A shift from demand curve D_1 to D_2 indicates that (demand/quantity demanded) _____ has (increased/decreased)_____. This shift could be caused by an increase in the price of a (substitute/complement) _____.

B. A shift from supply curve S_2 to S_1 indicates that (supply/quantity supplied) _____ has (increased/decreased)_____. This shift could be caused by an increase in the (price of an input/quality of technology) _____.

3. Changes in Demand/Supply versus Changes in Quantity Demanded/Supplied

To fully understand how markets function, the difference between "changes in demand" and "changes in quantity demanded" must be clear in your mind. A similar distinction applies to supply and must be clear as well. A graph of a market shows the difference most plainly and also allows predictions to be made about market adjustments.

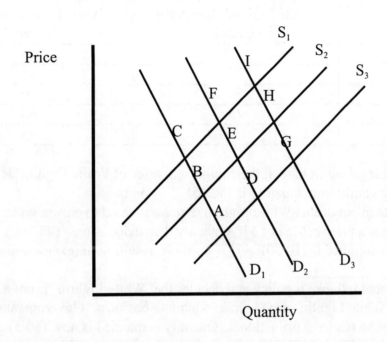

A. Assume the market is in equilibrium at point E with D_2 and S_2. Suppose the market equilibrium changes to point B. This change reflects a (decrease in demand/decrease in quantity demanded) _____ coupled with a (decrease in supply/decrease in quantity supplied) _____.

B. Assume the market is in equilibrium at point E with D_2 and S_2. Suppose the market equilibrium changes to point D. This changes stems from an (increase in demand/increase in quantity demanded) _____ combined with an (increase in supply/increase in quantity supplied) _____.

C. Assume the market is in equilibrium at point H with D_3 and S_2. If demand remains constant and supply decreases, the new equilibrium price will (higher/lower) _____ and the new equilibrium quantity will be (smaller/larger) _____.

D. Assume the market is in equilibrium at point E with D_2 and S_2. A simultaneous decrease in supply and an increase in demand would move the market to a new equilibrium at point (F/H/I) _____. The equilibrium price (falls/rises) _____ and the equilibrium quantity (falls/rises) _____. Without the aid of the above graph, only the (price/quantity) _____ change is certain to occur.

4. Price Controls and Market Equilibrium

The final problem focuses on your understanding of price controls and the effect they have on the marketplace. Consider the following market data for White Lightin,' a famous type of moonshine.

Price of a 32 oz jug of White Lightin'	Quantity of 32 oz jugs of White Lightin' demanded (thousands)	Quantity of 32 oz jugs of White Lightin' supplied (thousands)
$1	100	10
$2	75	35
$3	50	50
$4	25	65
$5	5	95

A. In an unregulated legal environment, the equilibrium price of White Lightin' is ($4/$3) _____ and the equilibrium quantity is (50/65) _____ units.

B. Suppose the government deems White Lightin' a necessity and to ensure widespread access to it imposes a price ceiling of $1. Quantity demanded is now (75/100) _____ units and quantity supplied is (10/50) _____ units, resulting in (excess supply/excess demand) _____.

C. Suppose government rethinks it policy and decides that White Lightin' is not a necessity but producers of White Lightin' need help to remain in business. Government now imposes a price of $5 (called a price floor). Quantity demanded is now (50/5) _____ units and quantity supplied is (95/65) _____. The market will now experience (excess supply/excess demand) _____.

Solutions
Self-Test: Key Terms

1. equilibrium quantity
2. change in demand
3. normal good
4. demand curve
5. change in quantity supplied
6. excess demand
7. market
8. equilibrium
9. supply curve
10. excess supply
11. inferior good
12. change in quantity demanded
13. complements
14. change in supply
15. market equilibrium
16. substitutes
17. equilibrium price
18. shortage
19. socially optimal quantity
20. price ceiling
21. surplus
22. efficiency

Self-Test: Multiple-Choice Questions

1. A As the price of tea increases, the quantity of tea demanded falls. Since sugar is frequently added to tea, the reduced consumption of tea means less sugar will be consumed regardless of the current price of sugar.
2. C
3. C The proper statement is "all consumers *willing and able to pay the equilibrium price* are able to purchase as much as they wish."
4. D
5. B
6. D
7. B A change in the price of gasoline never cause a change in the *demand* for gasoline; only a change in the *quantity demanded*. However, since gasoline is a complement to SUVs, the higher price of gasoline will decrease demand for SUVs.
8. B
9. C
10. E
11. B An increase in demand for PIIIs causes the price of PIIIs to rise, stimulating an increase in the quantity of PIIIs supplied. All the other answers cause a shift in the supply curve of PIIIs.

12. C
13. A
14. D
15. A Answers D and E are never true. For answers B or C to be correct, one must know if the price is above equilibrium (suppliers are dissatisfied) or below (demanders are dissatisfied). However, when a market is in disequilibrium, one side will be dissatisfied and can identify unexploited opportunities.
16. C When both supply and demand shift simultaneously, one can predict either the change in the equilibrium price or the equilibrium quantity but not both. In this question the price change is positive but the quantity change could be positive, negative, or zero. If you are still having difficulties with this topic, see Short Answer Question 3 for further practice.
17. D The supply curve, which includes all costs, will be to the left of the supply curve that includes only the seller's costs. As a result, the equilibrium price will be lower than the socially optimal price and the equilibrium quantity will be larger than the socially optimal amount.
18. D
19. E
20. D A shortage is evidence of a price that is below the equilibrium. In an unregulated market, price would rise to the equilibrium price thus eliminating the shortage. However, since the shortage is chronic, government must have set the regulated price below the equilibrium price.
21. D If you are having trouble with this question, try drawing a graph.
22. E If you are having trouble with this question, try drawing a graph.
23. D Excess supply = (quantity supplied –quantity demanded) = (700 –300) = 400.

Self-Test: Short Answer/Problems

1. Market equilibrium.
   A. falls; decreases.
   B. $150; quantity demanded; quantity supplied; 15.
   C. quantity supplied; quantity demanded; (36 – 4) = 32; excess supply; producers; lower.
   D. quantity demanded; quantity supplied; (21 – 11) = 10; excess demand; consumers; raise.
2. Shifting the demand and supply curves.
   A. demand; increased; substitute.
   B. supply; decreased; price of an input.
3. Market adjustments.
   A. decrease in demand; decrease in quantity supplied.
   B. increase in quantity demanded; increase in supply.
   C. higher; smaller.
   D. I; rises; rises; price (remember, when both curves shift, only one of the changes must occur-- in this case, starting at point E and moving to point I, price must rise but quantity could have increased, decreased, or remain constant).
4. Price controls.
   A. $3; 50.
   B. 100; 10; excess demand.
   C. 5; 95; excess supply

Chapter 5
Macroeconomics: The Bird's-Eye View of the Economy

Key Point Review

This chapter introduces the subject matter of macroeconomics and the issues that are central to macroeconomics, as well as the basic tools of macroeconomics. Macroeconomics is the study of the performance of national economies and the policies governments use to try to improve that performance. Among the issues macroeconomists study are the sources of long-run economic growth and living standards. By standard of living, economists mean the degree to which people have access to goods and services that make their lives easier, healthier, safer, and more enjoyable. People with a higher standard of living have more goods to consume, but even the wealthiest people are subject to the principle of scarcity. Standard of living is inextricably linked to economic growth because the more we produce, the more we can consume. The high standard of living that contemporary Americans enjoy, for example, is the result of several centuries of economic growth in the U.S. Economic growth is a process of increasing the quantity and quality of goods and services that an economy can produce. Two questions economist try to answer are, what causes economic growth to fluctuate over time, and why does economic growth and the standard of living vary among countries. One factor related to economic growth is the growth in population and hence the number of workers available to produce the goods and services. Increases in population allow the total output of goods and services to increase, but because the goods and services must be shared among a larger population it does not necessarily equate with a higher standard of living. Because of changes in population over time, output per person (output divided by the number of people in an economy) is a much better indicator of living standards than total output. Macroeconomists also study the relationship between **average labor productivity**, or output divided by the number of employed workers, and living standards. Because of the connection between production and consumption, average labor productivity is closely related to output per person and living standards.

Economies do not, however, always grow steadily; they go through periods of unusual strength and weakness. Periods of rapid economic growth are called expansions, and when an expansion is particularly strong it is called a boom. Slowdowns in economic growth are called recessions, and particularly severe slowdowns (for example, during the 1930s) are referred to as depressions. These fluctuations in the rate of economic growth cause changes in the unemployment rate, the fraction of people who would like to be employed but can't find work. Unemployment tends to rise during recessions and fall during expansions. But even during the "good times" some people are unemployed. Questions that macroeconomists try to answer include: Why does unemployment rise during periods of recession; why are there always unemployed people, even when the economy is booming; and why do unemployment rates sometimes differ markedly from country to country.

Inflation is another important macroeconomic variable. Inflation is the rate at which prices in general are increasing over time. Inflation imposes a variety of costs on the economy and, thus, macroeconomists are interested in understanding the causes of inflation. Two questions that macroeconomists try to decipher the answers to are why the rate of inflation varies from one period to another, and what causes the rate of inflation to differ markedly from country to country. Inflation and unemployment are often linked in policy discussions because it is often argued that unemployment can only be reduced if the inflation rate is allowed to rise. Macroeconomists have studied this issue to provide a better understanding of this policy debate.

While macroeconomics focuses on national economies, macroeconomists recognize that national economies do not exist in isolation. They are increasingly interdependent. The international flows of goods and services are both an economic issue and a political issue. Trade imbalances, which occur when the quantity of goods and services that a country sells abroad (its exports) differ significantly from the quantity of goods and services its citizens buy from abroad (its imports), often cause economic and political problems. When a nation exports more than it imports, it runs a trade surplus, while the reverse results in a trade deficit. Macroeconomists try to determine the causes of trade surpluses and deficits, and determine whether they are harmful or helpful.

In addition to analyzing the factors that affect the performance of the national economies, macroeconomists also study **macroeconomic policy**. Understanding the effects of various policies and helping government officials develop better policies are important objectives of macroeconomics. There are three major types of macroeconomic policy: monetary policy, fiscal policy, and structural policy. **Monetary policy** refers to the determination of the nation's money supply. In virtually all countries monetary policy is controlled by the central bank. **Fiscal policy** refers to decisions that determine the government's budget, including the amount and composition of government expenditures and government revenues. When government expenditures are greater than government revenues, the government runs a deficit, and when government revenues are greater than government expenditures, the government runs a surplus. The term **structural policy** includes government policies aimed at changing the underlying structure, or institutions, of the nation's economy. Macroeconomists are often called upon to analyze the effects of a proposed policy. An objective analysis aimed at determining only the economic consequences of a particular policy is called **positive analysis**, while a **normative analysis** includes recommendations on whether a particular policy should be implemented. Positive analysis is supposed to be objective and scientific, but normative analysis involves the values of the person or organization doing the analysis. Economists generally agree on issues related to positive analysis, but often disagree on normative analysis.

Although macroeconomics take a "bird's eye" view of the economy and microeconomics work at the ground level, the basic tools of analysis are much the same. They apply the same core principles in their efforts to understand and predict economic behavior. Because the national economy is much bigger, however, macroeconomists use aggregation to link individual behavior to national economic performance. **Aggregation** is the adding up of individual economic variables to obtain economy-wide totals.

Knowledge and Skills

The student must master the knowledge and skills listed below each numbered topic.	Key Terms	Multiple-Choice Questions	Short Answer/ Problems
1. The Major Macroeconomic Issues			
A. Explain economic growth and standard of living		1, 2	
B. Calculate output per person and average labor productivity	2	3, 17	1
C. Define recession, depression, expansion and boom		4	
D. Define unemployment rate and explain its relationship to recessions and expansions		5, 6	
E. Define inflation		7	
F. Define trade deficit and trade surplus		8, 18	
2. Macroeconomic Policy			
A. Define macroeconomic policy	7	9	
B. Define monetary, fiscal and structural policy	1, 5, 8	10, 11, 13	
C. Explain budget deficit and budget surplus		12, 19	
D. Identify normative and positive statements	3, 6	14, 20	2
3. Aggregation			
A. Define aggregation		15	
B. Discuss the strengths and weaknesses of aggregation	4	16	
C. Explain how economists aggregate units of goods that aren't comparable			3

Self-Test: Key Terms
Complete each sentence below by choosing the correct key term(s) from the following list.

aggregation
average labor productivity
fiscal policy
macroeconomic policy
monetary policy
normative analysis
positive analysis
structural policy

1. Decisions related to the amount and composition of government expenditures and government revenues determine a nation's _____ .
2. Output divided by the number of employed workers equals _____ .
3. An objective analysis aimed at determining only the economic consequences of a particular policy is called _____ .
4. An important tool that macroeconomists use to link individual behavior to national economic performance is _____ .
5. A nation's central bank can alter the amount of the economy's money supply through its control of _____ .
6. Economists often disagree on issues related to _____ .
7. An important objective of macroeconomics is helping government officials develop better

    _____ .
8. The move away from government control over the economy and toward a more market-oriented approach in countries such as Poland, the Czech Republic, and Hungary, is a large-scale example of _____ .

Self-Test: Multiple-Choice Questions
Answer each of the following multiple-choice questions by choosing the best response from the list of alternatives.

1. Economic growth is defined as a process of
    A. steady increase in the price of goods and services produced in the economy.
    B. steady increase in the quantity and quality of goods and services the economy can produce.
    C. constant increase in the quantity and quality of goods and services the economy can produce.
    D. constant increase in the price and quality of goods and services the economy can produce.
    E. constant increase in the number of jobs needed to produce the goods and service in the economy.

2. Our standard of living is directly tied to economic growth because
   A. everyone in society shares equally in the fruits of economic growth.
   B. the two terms are synonymous.
   C. in most cases economic growth brings an improvement in the average person's standard of living.
   D. the government can only improve people's standard of living if the economy is growing.
   E. a higher standard of living causes an increase in economic growth.

3. Microland has a population of 50 people and 40 of them worked last year with a total output of $200,000. The average labor productivity of Microland equaled
   A. $200,000.
   B. $200.
   C. $4,000.
   D. $40,000.
   E. $5,000.

4. During the 1930s, economies around the world were in a(n)
   A. recession.
   B. depression.
   C. expansion.
   D. boom.
   E. aggregation.

5. The unemployment rate is the
   A. percentage of people who would like to be employed but can't find work.
   B. number of people who would like to be employed but can't find work.
   C. fraction of people who are not working.
   D. number of people who are not working.
   E. the number of unemployed people.

6. The unemployment rate increases during
   A. expansions and booms.
   B. expansions and recessions.
   C. booms and recessions.
   D. recessions and depressions.
   E. booms and depressions.

7. The inflation rate
   A. was higher in the 1990s than during the 1970s.
   B. increases the standard of living for people on fixed incomes.
   C. is the rate at which prices in general are increasing over time.
   D. is roughly equal in most countries.
   E. rises during recessions along with the unemployment rate.

8. If a country imports more than it exports, it has a
   A. trade balance.
   B. trade deficit.
   C. trade surplus.
   D. budget deficit.
   E. inflation.

9. Government policies that affect the performance of the economy as a whole are called
   A. positive analysis.
   B. normative analysis.
   C. aggregation.
   D. microeconomic policy.
   E. macroeconomic policy.

10. Monetary policy
    A. refers to decisions that determine the government's budget.
    B. is controlled by a government institution called the Congressional Budget Office.
    C. is aimed at changing the underlying structure, or institutions, of the nation's economy.
    D. refers to the determination of the nation's money supply.
    E. can result in a budget deficit or budget surplus.

11. The amount and composition of government expenditures and government revenues is
    determined by
    A. fiscal policy.
    B. monetary policy.
    C. structural policy.
    D. normative analysis.
    E. positive analysis.

12. When a government collects more in taxes than it spends , it runs a(n)
    A. trade deficit.
    B. trade surplus.
    C. budget deficit.
    D. budget surplus.
    E. trade imbalance.

13. Supporters of structural policy argue that economic growth can be stimulated and living
    standards improved if
    A. the money supply is controlled by the central bank.
    B. the underlying structure, or institutions, of a nation's economy are changed.
    C. positive analysis is used to determine macroeconomic policy.
    D. normative analysis is used to determine macroeconomic policy.
    E. the federal budget is balanced.

14. Normative analysis differs from positive analysis in that
   A. normative analysis is limited to determining the consequences of a particular policy, while positive analysis includes recommendations on the desirability of the policy.
   B. positive analysis is limited to determining the consequences of a particular policy, while normative analysis includes recommendations on the desirability of the policy.
   C. normative analysis is supposed to be objective and scientific, while positive analysis involves values of the person or organization doing the analysis.
   D. economists typically agree on normative analysis, but often disagree on positive analysis.
   E. liberal economists use positive analysis, while conservative economists use normative analysis.

15. When macroeconomists add together the purchases of houses, cars, food, clothing, entertainment, and other goods and services by households in an economy, they are using
   A. normative analysis.
   B. positive analysis.
   C. aggregation.
   D. macroeconomic policy.
   E. fiscal policy.

16. The strength of aggregation is that it helps to reveal the "big picture," but it's weakness is that it
   A. adds together "apples and oranges."
   B. involves the values of the person doing the analysis.
   C. gives excessive importance to the details.
   D. adds together data on different individuals.
   E. may obscure important details.

17. Microland has a population of 50 people and 40 of them worked last year with a total output of $200,000. The output per person of Microland equaled
   A. $200,000.
   B. $200.
   C. $4,000.
   D. $40,000.
   E. $5,000.

18. If Macroland sells more goods to foreign buyers than it purchases from them, it will have a
   A. trade balance.
   B. trade deficit.
   C. trade surplus.
   D. budget deficit.
   E. budget surplus.

19. When a government's expenditures are greater than its' revenues, it has a
    A. budget deficit.
    B. budget surplus.
    C. trade deficit.
    D. trade surplus.
    E. trade imbalance.

20. In debating a government program for agriculture, Senator Agus from Kansas stated that the spending should be increased because many farmers have suffered crop losses in the last year. Senator Scrimp from New York replied that his analysis indicates that an increase in spending for the program will increase the budget deficit. Senator Agus' statement is based on
    A. aggregation, while Senator Scrimp's statement is based on disaggregation.
    B. disaggregation, while Senator Scrimp's statement is based on aggregation.
    C. positive analysis, while Senator Scrimp's statement is based on normative analysis.
    D. normative analysis, while Senator Scrimp's statement is based on positive analysis.
    E. positive analysis, as is the statement of Senator Scrimp.

Self-Test: Short Answer/Problems
1. Economic Growth and Standard of Living
Use the data in the following table on output, employment, and population in the United States and Canada during 1999 to answer the questions below.

Economic variable	United States	Canada
Output (GDP)	$9,190,400,000,000	$624,000,000,000
Population	284,286,070	31,820,500
Employed persons	133,492,000	14,531,200

A. Output per person in the United States during 1999 equaled _____ and in Canada equaled _____ .
B. The average labor productivity in the United States during 1999 equaled _____ and in Canada equaled _____ .
C. Based on the data in the table above, which country had the highest standard of living during 1999? _____

2. Normative and Positive Analysis
In the blank following each statement, write an N if the statement is based on normative analysis, or a P if the statement is based on positive analysis.

A. The U.S. Energy Department stated that "increased production of oil in April and May 2000 will result in lower gasoline prices in the summer of 2000." _____
B. Alan Greenspan, Chairman of the Board of Governors of the Federal Reserve System, stated in March 2000 that "the stock prices should rise no faster than household income."

_____

C. In April 2000, William Sullivan, chief economist at Morgan Stanley Dean Witter, stated, "the retrenchment in equity [stock] prices will undoubtedly affect the economy later in the year." _____

D. On April 4, 2000 in an article published in *The Wall Street Journal*, Brian Blackstone and Jonathan Nicholson wrote, "The National Association of Purchasing Management monthly index, a broad measure of the health of the manufacturing sector, slipped a bit to 55.8 in March from 56.9 in February. That corresponds to a 4.8% annualized growth in gross domestic product." _____

E. In an article published on the Dismal Science web site, entitled, "Krugman vs. Republican Gas Tax Relief," Michael Boldin analyzed a tax policy proposed by the Republican Party congressional leaders. He states, "the Republican plan to immediately repeal the 4.3 cents per gallon federal surcharge that was added in 1993 and suspend the larger 18.4 cents per gallon federal tax if gasoline hits $2 per gallon is both untimely and unwise as a basic policy. For one it would hurt the highway fund that is a direct beneficiary of the tax. Worse yet, it would encourage gas consumption at a time when OPEC is keeping to a tight supply schedule and domestic inventories are dwindling." _____

F. In response to the question, what is the best Fed monetary policy course at this time (March 2000), Kevin Hassett, Resident Scholar at the American Enterprise Institute, responded, "The best Fed move right now would be no move, but it is a close call." _____

G. In an article published on the Dismal Science web site, entitled, "The New Economy's Dark Side," Mark Zandi states, "Families in the top 20% of the wealth distribution own well over 80% of the nation's wealth, while the top 5% of families own 60% of the wealth."

_____

3. Aggregation
Use the data in the following table on production in Macrolandia to answer the questions below.

Product	Price per unit	Units produced in 1999	Units produced in 2000
Clothing	$5	1000	600
Food	$2	5000	4000
Houses	$100	250	800

A. Macrolandia's total output in 1999 equaled _____ and in 2000 equaled

_____

B. Based on your answer to Question 3A, in 2000 Macrolandia produce (more/less) _____ output than in 1999.

C. The change in output from 1999 to 2000 would suggest the Macrolandia economy experienced _____ and, thus, one could deduce that the Macrolandian standard of living had (improved/worsened) _____ .

D. The workers of Macrolandia are equally divided into three groups who each specialize in producing a single good (i.e., clothing, food, or houses). Calculate the output produced by each group in 1999 and 2000. The clothing workers produced _____ output in 1999 and _____ in 2000, the food workers produced _____ output in 1999 and _____ in 2000, and the housing workers produced _____ output in 1999 and _____ in 2000.

E. Thus, the output and standard of living of the (clothing/food/housing) _____ workers of Macrolandia's increased, while the output and standard of living of (clothing/food/housing) _____ and (clothing/food/housing) _____ workers of Macrolandia's decreased .

F. Thus, the aggregation in Question 3A obscures the fact that a majority of Macrolandia workers output and standard of living (decreased/increased) _____ in 2000 compared to 1999.

Solutions
Self-Test: Key Terms

1. fiscal policy
2. average labor productivity
3. positive analysis
4. aggregation
5. monetary policy
6. normative analysis
7. macroeconomic policy
8. structural policy

Self-Test: Multiple-Choice Questions

1. B
2. C
3. E Average labor productivity = output/number of employed workers, (i.e., $200,000/40 = $5,000)
4. B
5. A
6. D
7. C
8. B
9. E
10. D
11. A
12. D
13. B
14. B
15. C
16. E
17. C Output per person = output/number of people in the economy, (i.e., $200,000/50 = $4,000)
18. C
19. A Senator Agus' statement refers to the desirability of the policy, while Senator Shrimps' statement only refers to the effect of the policy on the government's budget.
20. D

Self-Test: Short Answer/Problems

1.

A. Output per person = Output divided by population $32,328.00; $19,610.00

B. Average labor productivity = Output divided by the number of employed persons $68,846.07;
$42,942.08

C. The United States has the highest standard of living because both output per person and
average labor productivity are higher than in Canada.

2.

A. P because the analysis is a prediction based on an application of the supply and demand
model.

B. N because the analysis is based on his values (key word is "should")

C. P because the analysis is a statement of the effect of the change in stock market prices on the
economy

D. P because it only indicates the statistical analysis

E. N because it is a statement of the desirability of the policy based on his values

F. N because it is a statement of the desirability of the policy based on his values

G. P because it only indicates the statistical findings of the economic analysis

3.

A. (1,000 x$5) + (5,000 x $2) + (250 x $100) = $17,500; (600 x $)5 + (4,000 x $2) + (800 x
$100) = $21,000

B. more

C. economic growth; improved

D. 1,000 x $5 = $5,000; 600 x $5 = $3,000; 5,000 x $2 = $10,000; 4,000 x $2 = $8,000; 250 x
$100 = $2,500; 800 x $100 = $8,000

E. housing; clothing; food

F. decreased

Chapter 6
Measuring Economic Activity:
GDP and Unemployment

Key Point Review

Economists depend on economic data to make accurate diagnoses; political leaders and policymakers also need economic data to help them in their decisions and planning. This chapter explains how economists measure two basic macroeconomic variables, gross domestic product (GDP) and the rate of unemployment. It also discusses how the measures are used, and provides some insight into the debates over the accuracy of the measures.

The **gross domestic product (GDP)** is the market value of the final goods and services produced in a country during a given period. To calculate GDP, economists aggregate, or add up, the market values of the different goods and services the economy produces. Economists, however, do not include the value of all goods and services in the calculation. Only the market values of **final goods and services**, the goods or services consumed by the ultimate user, are counted as part of GDP. The market values of **intermediate goods and services**, those used up in the production of final goods and services, are not included when calculating GDP because they are already included in the market value of the final goods and services. The distinction between final and intermediate goods is difficult to determine for some goods, e.g., capital goods. **Capital goods** are long-lived goods that are used to produce other goods and, thus, are not exactly final goods but neither are they intermediate goods. To overcome this difficulty, economists have conventionally classified newly-produced capital goods as final goods for the purposes of calculating GDP. Because GDP is a measure of domestic production, only goods and services produced within a nation's borders are included in its calculation. Similarly, because GDP is measured for a given period, only goods and services produced during the current year (or the portion of the value produced during the current year) are counted as part of the current year's GDP.

There are three methods for measuring GDP: (1) by aggregating the value added by each firm in the production process, (2) by adding up the total amount spent on final goods and services and subtracting the amount spent on imported goods and services, and (3) by adding labor income and capital income. The **value added** by any firm equals the market value of its product or service minus the cost of inputs purchased from other firms. The value added by each firm represents the portion of the value of the final good or service that the firm creates in its stage of the production process. Summing the value added by all firms in the economy yields the total value of final goods and service, or GDP. An advantage of the value-added method is that it eliminates the problem of dividing the value of a final good or service between two periods.

To calculate GDP using the expenditure method, economic statisticians add together consumption expenditures, investment, government purchases, and net exports. **Consumption expenditure (C)** is spending by households on goods and services. Consumption spending can be divided into three subcategories; (1) consumer durables, long-lived consumer goods such as cars and furniture; (2) consumer nondurables, shorter-lived goods like food and clothing; and (3) services, including everything from haircuts to taxi rides to legal, financial and educational services. **Investment (I)** is spending by firms on final goods and services, primarily capital goods and housing. Investment is also divided into three subcategories: (1) business fixed investment, the purchase of new capital goods such as machinery, factories and office buildings; (2) residential investment, the construction of new homes and apartment buildings; and (3) inventory investment, the addition of unsold goods to company inventories. **Government purchases (G)** are purchases of final goods by federal, state, and local governments. Government purchases do not include transfer payments (payments made by the government in which no current goods or services are received), or interest paid on the government debt. In the foreign sector, **net exports (NX)** equal exports minus imports. Exports are domestically produced final goods and services that are sold abroad. Imports are purchases by domestic buyers of goods and services that were produced abroad. Using symbols for each of the components, the algebraic equation for calculating GDP (Y) is written: $Y = C + I + G + NX. \rightarrow (M - IM)$

The third method of calculating GDP is to sum total labor and capital incomes. Labor income, before taxes includes wages, salaries, and the income of the self-employed. It represents about 75% of GDP. Capital income is made up of payments to the owners of physical capital (factories, machines, and office buildings) and intangible capital (such as copyrights and patents), and it represents about 25% of GDP. The components of capital income include such items as pre-tax profits earned by business owners, the rents paid to owners of land or buildings, interest received by bondholders, and the royalties received by holders of copyrights or patents.

As a measure of the total production of an economy during a given period, GDP is useful in comparisons of economic activity in different places, but cannot be used to make comparisons over time. To make comparisons of production in an economy over time, GDP must be adjusted for inflation. To adjust for inflation economists differentiate between nominal GDP and real

GDP. **Nominal GDP** measures the current dollar value of production, in which the quantities of final goods and services produced are valued at current-year prices. **Real GDP** measures the actual physical volume of production, in which the quantities of final goods and services produced are valued at the prices in a base year. To compare a nation's production over time, economists use real GDP.

While economists and policymakers often assume that a higher GDP is better, real GDP is not the same as economic well-being. With the major exception of government-produced goods and services, real GDP captures only those goods and services that are priced and sold in markets. There are many factors that contribute to people's economic well-being that are not priced and sold in markets. Thus, at best, it is an imperfect measure of economic well-being. Some important factors that are excluded from real GDP are leisure time; environmental quality; resource depletion; nonmarket activities such as volunteer services, home-grown foods, homemaker services, and underground economic activities from informal babysitting to organized crime; "quality of life" issues such as crime, traffic congestion, civic organization, and open space; and income inequality. Clearly, in evaluating the effects of a proposed economic policy, considering only the likely effects on GDP is not sufficient. The correct way is to apply the cost-benefit principle. Nevertheless, real GDP per person does tend to be positively associated with many things people value, including a high material standard of living, better health and life expectancies, and better education.

A second macroeconomic measure that receives a great deal of attention from economists and policymakers, as well as the general public, is the rate of unemployment. In the United States, the unemployment rate is calculated by the Bureau of Labor Statistics (BLS) by means of a monthly survey of approximately 60,000 households. Each person in those households who is 16 years or older is placed in one of three categories: employed, unemployed, or out of the labor force. A person is employed if he or she worked full time or part time during the week preceding the survey, or is on vacation or sick leave from a regular job. A person is unemployed if he or she did not work during the week preceding the survey, but made some effort to find work during the previous four weeks. All other persons are considered out of the labor force. To calculate the unemployment rate, the BLS first calculates the total number of employed and unemployed people in the economy to determine the size of the **labor force**. The **unemployment rate** is then defined as the number of unemployed people divided by the labor force and expressed as a percentage. Another useful statistic calculated by the BLS is the **participation rate**, or the percentage of working-age population that is in the labor force.

Unemployment imposes economic, psychological, and social costs on a nation. The main economic cost, borne by both the unemployed individuals and society, is the output that is lost because the work force is not fully utilized. The psychological costs of unemployment are felt primarily by the unemployed workers and their families, and include a loss of self-esteem, feelings of loss of control over one's life, depression, and suicidal behavior. The social costs, borne by both the unemployed individuals and society, include increases in crime, domestic violence, drug abuse, and other social problems. In assessing the impact of unemployment on jobless people, economists estimate how long individual workers have been without work. The BLS asks respondents how long they have been continuously unemployed to determine the **unemployment spell**. The length of an unemployment spell is called its **duration**. The duration of unemployment rises during recessions and falls during expansions.

The are some criticisms of the techniques used by the BLS to measure the rate of unemployment. One criticism is that the official unemployment rate understates the true extent of unemployment because of so-called discouraged workers and involuntary part-time workers. **Discouraged workers** are people who say they would like to have a job, but have not made an effort to find one in the past four weeks. Some observers have suggested that treating discouraged workers as unemployed would provide a more accurate picture of the labor market. Involuntary part-time workers are people who say they would like to work full time but are able to find only part-time work.

Knowledge and Skills

The student must master the knowledge and skills listed below each number topic.	Key Terms	Multiple-Choice Questions	Short Answer/ Problems
1. Gross Domestic Product (GDP)			
A. Define GDP	15	1,2	
B. Identify the components of the value-added, expenditure, and income methods of measuring GDP	1, 3, 8, 11, 13, 13, 14	3,4,5,6,7	
C. Calculate GDP using the value-added, expenditure, and income methods			1,2,3
D. Define nominal GDP and real GDP	4, 6, 10	8.9	
E. Calculate real GDP			3
F. Explain the relationship between GDP and economic well-being		10,11,12	
2. Unemployment			
A. Explain how the BLS measures unemployment	2, 7, 16	13,14	
B. Calculate the unemployment rate and participation rate			4
C. Discuss the costs of unemployment		15,16	
D. Explain the duration of unemployment	5, 12	17,18	
E. Discuss the criticisms of the unemployment rate	9	19,20	

Self Test: Key Terms
Use the terms below to complete the following sentences. (Answers are given at the end of the chapter.)

capital good
consumption expenditure
discouraged workers
duration (of an unemployment spell)
final goods and services
government purchases
gross domestic product (GDP)
intermediate goods and services
investment
labor force
net exports
nominal GDP
participation rate
real GDP
unemployment rate
unemployment spell
value added

1. Purchases of final goods by federal, state, and local governments are included in the expenditure method of calculating GDP as _____ .
2. Dividing the number of people in the labor force by the working-age population equals the

   _____ .
3. Exports minus imports equals _____ .
4. To compare a nation's production over time, economists calculate _____ .
5. By asking respondents how long they have been continuously unemployed, the BLS can determine the _____ .
6. To calculate GDP, economists include the market value of _____, but exclude the market value of _____ .
7. The BLS adds together the total number of employed and unemployed people in the economy to determine the size of the _____
8. The market value of a firm's product or service minus the cost of inputs purchased from other firms equals the firm's _____ .
9. Some critics have argued that a more accurate picture of the labor market would be achieved if _____ were counted as unemployed.
10. When valuing the quantities of final goods and services produced in an economy at current-year prices, we are calculating _____ .
11. In the expenditure method of calculating GDP, inventory investment is included as _____ spending.
12. A period during which an individual is continuously unemployed is called a(n)

   _____ .
13. The largest component in the expenditure method of calculating GDP is _____ .

14. Despite the fact that it is not exactly a final good nor an intermediate good, economists conventionally classify a newly-produced _____ as a final good for the purpose of calculating GDP.
15. The market value of the final goods and services produced in a country during a given period is the definition of _____ .
16. The number of unemployed people divided by the labor force equals the

_____ .

Self-Test: Multiple-Choice Questions
Circle the letter that corresponds to the best answer. (Answers are given at the end of the chapter.)

1. Which of the following would be included in the calculation of GDP for 1996?
    A. the price of a home built in 1991 and sold in 1996
    B. the price of 100 shares of Exxon stock purchased in 1996
    C. the price of a classic 1960 Thunderbird purchased in 1996
    D. the price of a new punch press built and purchased in 1996 to replace a worn out machine
    E. the price of a used bicycle purchased at a garage sale in 1996

2. Which of the following is an intermediate good and, therefore, would be excluded from the calculation of GDP?
    A. a new set of tires sold to a car owner
    B. a new set of tires purchased by Ford to install on a new Explorer
    C. 100 shares of stock in Microsoft
    D. a new home
    E. a preowned automobile

3. The value-added method eliminates the problem of
    A. differentiating between final and intermediate goods and services.
    B. inflation when comparing GDP over time.
    C. determining whether capital is a final good or intermediate good.
    D. dividing the value of a final good or service between two periods.
    E. aggregation.

4. Consumption expenditure is subdivided into three categories, including
    A. consumer durables, consumer nondurables, and new homes.
    B. consumer services, consumer durables and new homes.
    C. consumer durables, consumer nondurables, and services.
    D. exports, imports, and services.
    E. consumer durables, consumer nondurables, and net exports.

5. Which of the following is included when using the expenditure method to measure GDP?
    A. corporate profits
    B. gross private domestic investment
    C. capital income
    D. net interest on the government debt
    E. labor income

6. Which of the following is included when using the labor and capital income method to measure GDP?
    A. government purchases of goods and services
    B. net exports of goods and services
    C. household consumption expenditures
    D. gross private domestic investment
    E. business profits

7. If the value of imports is greater than the value of exports, then
    A. net exports are negative.
    B. net exports are positive.
    C. net exports are zero.
    D. net exports are not, under such circumstances, included in the calculation of GDP.
    E. net exports cannot be determined from the information provided.

8. To calculate nominal GDP, the quantities of goods and services are valued at prices in the _____ year, but to calculate real GDP they are valued at _____-year prices.
    A. current, base
    B. base; current
    C. current; current
    D. base; base
    E. current; last

9. Real GDP is GDP adjusted for
    A. changes in the quality of goods and services.
    B. value added during a previous year.
    C. inflation.
    D. imports.
    E. changes in the cost of intermediate goods and services.

10. One shortcoming of GDP as an indicator of economic well-being is that it fails to measure the
    A. growth in productivity.
    B. increase in the quantity of goods.
    C. nonmarket production.
    D. change in the price level.
    E. increase in the number of imported goods.

11. GDP would be a better measure of economic well-being if it included
    A. the costs of education.
    B. the total value of intermediate goods.
    C. the market value of final goods.
    D. the sales of corporate stock.
    E. leisure.

12. Despite some problems with equating GDP with economic well-being, real GDP per person does imply greater economic well-being because it tends to be positively associated with
    A. crime, pollution, and economic inequality.
    B. better education, health, and life expectancy.
    C. poverty, depletion of nonrenewable resources, and congestion.
    D. unemployment, availability of goods and services, and better education.
    E. the total quantity of goods and services available.

13. The official unemployment rate is calculated as
    A. the number of working-age people 16 years or older who are employed divided by the number of people in the labor force.
    B. all people 18 years of age or older who are employed, plus all those unemployed who are actively seeking work.
    C. the percentage of the working-age population 16 years or older who are not working but are actively seeking work.
    D. the number of people 16 years or older who are not employed and are actively seeking work divided by the number of people in the labor force.
    E. all people 16 years of age or older who are employed, plus all those unemployed who are actively seeking work, divided by the number of people in the labor force.

14. In the monthly survey conducted by the Bureau of Labor Statistics, a person who was not working during the previous week and was not actively seeking work during the last four weeks is classified as
    A. employed.
    B. unemployed.
    C. underemployed.
    D. part-time employed.
    E. not a member of the labor force.

15. From an economic perspective, the main cost of unemployment is
    A. increased crime, domestic violence, alcoholism, and drug abuse.
    B. a loss of output and income because the labor force is not fully employed.
    C. increased stress, loss of self-esteem and deterioration in the workers skills from lack of use.
    D. workers' loss of income and control over their lives.
    E. the increase in the cost of social programs to combat increased crime, alcoholism, drug abuse, and other social problems.

16. The cost of unemployment that is almost exclusively borne by workers and their families is the
    _____ cost.
    A. economic
    B. social
    C. psychological
    D. historical
    E. total

17. An unemployment spell begins when a worker
    A. losses his/her job and ends when he/she finds a new job.
    B. losses his/her job and ends when he/she finds a new job or leaves the labor force.
    C. starts to actively look for employment and ends when he/she finds a new job.
    D. is not working and starts to actively look for employment and ends when he/she finds a new job or leaves the labor force.
    E. becomes discouraged and stops seeking employment and ends when he/she begins to actively look for employment.

18. The duration of unemployment
    A. rises during recessions.
    B. falls during recessions.
    C. is a period during which an individual is continuously unemployed.
    D. is shorter for the chronically unemployed than it is for the long-term unemployed.
    E. is of less importance to macroeconomics than the costs of unemployment.

19. The accuracy of the official unemployment rate is criticized because
    A. unemployed homemakers and students who are not actively seeking employment are not included in the number of unemployed people.
    B. people who would like to work but have given up trying to find work are not included in the number of unemployed people.
    C. it fails to indicate how many people work at more than one job.
    D. people less than 16 years of age and over 70 years of age are excluded from the data.
    E. the BLS survey does not include all the households in the United States.

20. In recent years, the Bureau of Labor Statistics has released special unemployment rates that include estimates of the number of discouraged and part-time workers that indicate the number of
    A. discouraged workers is insignificant, but the number of part-time workers is significant.
    B. part-time workers is insignificant, but the number of discouraged workers is significant.
    C. part-time workers and discouraged workers is insignificant.
    D. discouraged workers and part-time workers is fairly significant.
    E. discourage workers and part-time workers is decreasing.

Self-Test: Short Answer/Problems
(Answers and solutions are given at the end of the chapter.)

1. The Expenditure Approach to GDP
This problem will give you practice calculating GDP using the expenditure method. Use the data in following table to answer the questions below.

Expenditure Components	4th Quarter, 1999 ($ Bil.)
Business fixed investment	1,190.0
Durable Goods	782.1
Exports	1,039.5
Federal government purchases	593.6
Imports	1,329.6
Inventory investment	69.1
Nondurable goods	1,905.8
Residential investment	416.7
Services	3,746.2
State and local government purchases	1,094.4

Source: U.S. Department of Commerce, Bureau of Economic Analysis. <u>Survey of Current Business</u>, Summary Tables – National Data, Table 1.1 Gross Domestic Product

A. Total consumption spending in the U.S. economy during the fourth quarter of 1999 equaled
    $_____ billion.
B. Total investment spending in the U.S. economy during the fourth quarter of 1999 equaled
    $_____ billion.
C. Net export spending in the U.S. economy during the fourth quarter of 1999 equaled
    $_____ billion.
D. Total government purchases in the U.S. economy during the fourth quarter of 1999 equaled
    $_____ billion.
E. The expenditure method of calculating indicates that gross domestic product for the U.S. economy during the fourth quarter of 1999 equaled $ _____ billion.

2. The Income Approach to GDP

This problem will give you practice calculating GDP using the labor and capital income method. Use the data in following table to answer the questions below.

Income Components	4th Quarter, 1999 ($ Bil.)
Compensation of employees	_ 5,448.3
Corporate profits	2,062.7
Net interest	491.0
Proprietor's income	1,447.2
Rental income	147.3

Source: U.S. Department of Commerce, Bureau of Economic Analysis. Survey of Current Business, Summary Tables – National Data, Compiled from Tables 1.9 and 1.14 Gross Domestic Product

A. Total incomes received by the owners of capital during the fourth quarter of 1999 equaled $_____ billion.
B. Total incomes received by labor during the fourth quarter of 1999 equaled $ _____ billion.
C. The income method of calculating indicates that gross domestic product for the U.S. economy during the fourth quarter of 1999 equaled $ _____ billion.

3. Nominal and Real GDP

This problem will give you practice calculating GDP using the value-added method and adjusting nominal GDP to calculate real GDP.

A. Mr. Jones harvested logs (with no inputs from other companies) from his property in Northern California that he sold to a Nevada Mill for $1,500. The Nevada Mill cut and planed the logs into lumber and sold it for $4,000 to the Mesa Company, to be used to build tables. The Mesa Company used the lumber in producing 100 tables that they sold to customers for $70 each. Complete the table below to calculate the value added by each firm.

Company	Revenues	Cost of purchased inputs	Value added
Mr. Jones			
Nevada Mill			
Mesa Company			

B. The total value added in the production of the tables equals $_____ . This is equal to the _____ of the 100 tables.

C. If Mr. Jones had harvested the logs in October of 2000 but did not sell them to the Nevada Mill until January 2001, which then sold the lumber to Mesa Company that produced the tables in June 2001, the contribution to GDP in 2000 would equal $ _____ and in 2001 would equal $ _____ .

D. The nation of Mandar specializes in the production of vehicles. The table below provides data on the prices and quantities of the vehicles produced in 2001 and in 2005. Assume that 2001 is the base year. In 2001, nominal GDP equals $_____ and in 2005 it equals $_____ . In 2001, real GDP equals $_____ and in 2005 it equals $_____ .

	Bicycles		Automobiles		Trucks	
Year	Quantity	Price	Quantity	Price	Quantity	Price
2001	1,000	$50	100	$10,000	400	$15,000
2005	1,500	$60	50	$12,500	500	$15,000

4. Measures of Employment

This problem will give you practice in calculating employment measures. Use the data in following table to answer the questions below.

Year	Employed	Unemployed	Not in Labor Force	Working Age Population	Labor Force	Unemployment rate (%)	Participation rate (%)
1994	123,060	7,996	65,758				
1995	124,900	7,404	66,280				
1996	126,708	7,236	66,647				
1997	129,558	6,739	66,837				
1998	131,463	6,210	67,547				

Source: *Economic Report of the President,* February 1999, Table b-35

A. Calculate the working age population for 1994 through 1998 to complete column 5 of the table.

B. Calculate the size of the labor force for 1994 through 1998 to complete column 6 of the table.

C. Calculate the official unemployment rate for 1994 through 1998 to complete column 7 of the table. (Round your answers to the nearest tenth of a percent.)

D. Calculate the participation rate for 1994 through 1998 to complete column 8 of the table. (Round your answers to the nearest tenth of a percent.)

Solutions
Self-Test: Key Terms

1. government purchases
2. participation rate
3. net exports
4. real GDP
5. duration (of an unemployment spell)
6. final goods and services; intermediate goods and services
7. labor force
8. value added
9. discouraged workers
10. nominal GDP
11. investment
12. unemployment spell
13. consumption expenditure
14. capital good
15. gross domestic product (GDP)
16. unemployment rate

Self-Test: Multiple-Choice Questions

1. D The punch press is newly produced capital
2. B The set of tires was purchased to be used in the production of an Explorer (i.e., an intermediate good) and, therefore, is not included in GDP.
3. D
4. C
5. B
6. E Profit is a component of capital income.
7. A
8. A
9. C
10. C
11. E
12. B
13. D
14. B
15. B
16. C
17. D An unemployment spell begins when a person becomes unemployed and ends when they either become employed or leave the labor force.
18. A
19. B
20. C

Self-Test: Short Answer/Problems

1.

A. $782.1 + 1,905.8 + 3,746.2 = \$6,434.1$ billion

B. $1,190.0 + 416.7 + 69.1 = \$ 1,675.8$ billion

C. $ 1,039.5 – 1,329.6 = \$-290.1$ billion

D. $593.6 + 1,094.4 = \$1,688.0$ billion

E. $6,434.1 + 1,675.8 + 1,688.0 + (-290.1) = \$9,507.8$ billion

2.

A. $2,062.7 + 147.3 + 491.0 = \$ 2,701.0$ billion

B. $5,448.3 + 1,447.2 = \$6,895.5$ billion

C. $2,701.0 + 6,895.5 = \$ 9,596.5$ billion [The difference between the answer in 2C and 1E is attributable to some technical adjustments that are necessary to accurately calculate GDP that are ignored in the capital and labor income method presented in the textbook.]

3. A.

Company	Revenues	Cost of purchased inputs	Value added
Mr. Jones	$1,500	$0	1,500
Nevada Mill	$4,000	$1,500	$2,500
Mesa Company	$7,000	$4,000	$3,000

B. $7,000; total market value

C. $1,500; $2,500 + $3,000 = $5,500

D. 1,000 x $50 + 100 x $10,000 + 400 x $15,000 = $7,050,000; 1,500 x $60 + 50 x $12,500 + 500 x $15,000 = $8,215,000; 1,000 x $50 + 100 x $10,000 + 400 x $15,000 = $7,050,000; 1,500 x $50 + 50 x $10,000 + 500 x $15,000 = $8,075,000

4.

A. Working age population = number of persons employed + number of persons unemployed + number of persons not in the labor force (for example, 1994: 123,060 + 7,996 + 65,758 = 196,814)

B. Labor force = number of persons employed + number of persons unemployed (for example, 1994: 123,060 + 7,996 = 131,056

C. Unemployment rate = (number of persons unemployed divided by number of persons not in the labor force) times 100 (for example, 1994: (7,996/131,056) x 100 = 6.1%

D. Participation rate = (number of persons not in the labor force divided by Working age population) times 100 (for example, 1994: (65,758 / 123,060) x 100 = 66.6%

Year	Employed	Unemployed	Not in Labor Force	Working Age Population	Labor Force	Unemployment Rate (%)	Participation Rate (%)
1994	123,060	7,996	65,758	196,814	131,056	6.1	66.6
1995	124,900	7,404	66,280	198,584	132,304	5.6	66.6
1996	126,708	7,236	66,647	200,591	133,944	5.4	66.8
1997	129,558	6,739	66,837	203,134	136,297	4.9	67.1
1998	131,463	6,210	67,547	205,220	137,673	4.5	67.1

Chapter 7
Measuring the Price Level and Inflation

Key Point Review

This chapter continues the study of the construction and interpretation of macroeconomic data. The topics discussed are measuring prices and inflation, adjusting dollar amounts to eliminate the effects of inflation, using a price index to maintain the constant real value of a variable, the costs of inflation, and the relationship between inflation and interest rates.

The basic tool economists use to measure the price level and inflation in the U.S. economy is the consumer price index, or CPI. The CPI is a **price index**, a measure of the average price of a given class of goods or services relative to the price of the same goods and services in a base year. The **consumer price index** measures the cost, for any period, of a standard basket of goods and services relative to the cost of the same basket of goods and services in a fixed year, called the base year. The Bureaus of Labor Statistics (BLS) determines the goods and services to include in the standard basket through the Consumer Expenditure Survey. Then each month BLS employees survey thousands of stores to determine the current prices of the goods and services. The formula for calculating the CPI is "cost of the base-year basket of goods and services in the current year" divided by the "cost of the base-year basket of goods and services in the base year."

Inflation measures how fast the average price level is changing over time. The **rate of inflation** is defined as the annual percentage rate of change in the price level, as measured, for example, by the CPI. To calculate the inflation rate, the increase in the price level from one time period to another time period is divided by the price level in the initial time period. **Deflation** is a situation in which the prices of most goods and services are falling over time, so that the rate of inflation is negative. The CPI not only allows us to measure changes in the cost of living, but can also be used to adjust economic data to eliminate the effects of inflation, a process called deflating. To adjust **nominal quantity**, a quantity that is measured at its current dollar value, we divide the nominal quantity by a price index for the period. The adjusted value is called a **real quantity**, that is, a quantity measured in physical terms. Such real quantities are also sometimes referred to as inflation-adjusted quantities. For example, nominal wages for two different periods can be adjusted using the CPI to determine the change in real wages over time. The **real wage** is the wage paid to workers measured in terms of real purchasing power. To calculate the real wage we divide the nominal (dollar) wage by the CPI for that period. The CPI can also be used to convert real quantities to nominal quantities. The practice of increasing a nominal quantity according to changes in a price index in order to prevent inflation from eroding purchasing power is called **indexing**. For example, some labor contracts provide for indexing of wages, using the CPI, in later years of a contract period.

Using the CPI to measure inflation has not been without controversy. Because the CPI has been used to index Social Security benefits, the U.S. government commissioned a report on the subject. The Boskin Commission concluded that the official CPI inflation overstates the true inflation rate by as much as one to two percent per year. The CPI may overstate inflation because of the quality adjustment bias and the substitution bias. Despite the fact that the findings of the Boskin commission have been controversial, the BLS has recently made significant effort to improve the quality of the data it uses to calculate the CPI and, hence, the inflation rate.

To understand the costs of inflation, we need to distinguish between the price level and the relative price of a good or service. The **price level** is a measure of the overall level of prices in the economy at a particular point in time, as measured by a price index (e.g., the CPI). The **relative price** of a specific good or service is its price in comparison to the prices of other goods and services. Inflation is an increase in the overall price level, not an increase in the relative price of a good or service. When an economy suffers from inflation, the cost of holding cash rises causing consumers and businesses to make more frequent trips to the bank, and to purchase cash-management systems. Banks will, therefore, hire more employees to handle the increased transactions. These costs of economizing on cash have been called shoe-leather costs. Inflation also creates "noise" in the price system that obscures the information transmitted by prices, reduces the efficiency of the market system, and imposes costs on the economy. Similarly, inflation produces unintended changes in the tax people pay and distorts the incentives in the tax system that may encourage people to work, save, and invest. Another concern about inflation is that, if it is unanticipated, it arbitrarily redistributes wealth from one group to another (e.g., between lenders and borrowers, and workers and employers). As a result, a high inflation economy encourages people to use resources in trying to anticipate inflation to protect themselves against losses of wealth. The fifth cost of inflation is its tendency to interfere with the long-run planning of households and firms. While any inflation imposes some costs on the economy, **hyperinflation**, a situation in which the inflation rate is extremely high, greatly magnifies the costs.

Another important aspect of inflation is its effect on interest rates. To understand the relationship between inflation and interest rates, economists differentiate between the nominal interest rate and the real interest rate. The **nominal interest rate** (also called the market interest rate) is the annual percentage increase in the nominal value of a financial asset. The **real interest rate** is the annual percentage increase in the purchasing power of a financial asset, and is equal to the nominal interest rate minus the inflation rate. To obtain a given real interest rate, lenders must charge a higher nominal interest rate as the inflation rate rises. This tendency for nominal interest rates to rise when the inflation rate increases is called the **Fischer effect.**

Knowledge and Skills

The student must master the knowledge and skills listed below each number topic.	Key Terms	Multiple-Choice Questions	Short Answer/ Problems
1. Price Level and Inflation			
A) Define price index, consumer price index, inflation and deflation	4, 10, 14	1, 5, 18	
B) Explain how the Consumer Price Index is measured	9	8, 11	
C) Calculate a price index and the rate of inflation		2	1
D) Define indexing and deflating	1, 5, 6, 11, 12	4, 12	
E) Calculate a real quantity from a nominal quantity and vice versa			1, 2
F) Explain the causes and effects of the CPI overstating the true inflation		3, 13	
4. The Costs of Inflation			
A) Define price level and relative price	3	14	
B) Discuss the five costs of inflation		6, 9, 15, 19	
C) Define hyperinflation and explain its effects	8	10	
5. Inflation and Interest Rates			
6. Define nominal and real interest rates	7, 13	16, 20	
7. Calculate the real interest rate			3
8. Discuss the relationship between the inflation rate and interest rates	2	7, 17	

Self-Test: Key Terms
Use the terms below to complete the following sentences. (Answers are given at the end of the chapter.)

consumer price index (CPI)
deflating (a nominal quantity)
deflation
Fisher effect
hyperinflation
indexing
nominal interest rate
nominal quantity
price index
price level
rate of inflation
real interest rate
real quantity
real wage
relative price

1. The wage paid to workers measured in terms of real purchasing power is the
    _____ .
2. The tendency for nominal interest rates to rise when the inflation rate increases is called the
    _____ .
3. Inflation is an increase in the overall _____, not an increase in the
    _____ of a good or service.
4. When the rate of inflation is negative, there is _____ .
5. Some labor contracts provide for the _____ of wages, using the CPI, in later
    years of a contract period.
6. An inflation-adjusted quantity is a quantity measured in physical terms and is referred to as a
    _____ .
7. The real interest rate is equal to the _____ minus the inflation rate.
8. The costs of inflation are greatly magnified when an economy experiences an extremely high
    inflation rate called _____ ,.
9. The cost, for any period, of a standard basket of goods and services that the typical household
    purchases relative to the cost of the same basket of goods and services in the base year is
    measured by the _____ .
10. The Bureau of Labor Statistics calculates the annual percentage rate of change in the price
    level as measured, for example, by the CPI to determine the _____ .
11. Indexing is the practice of increasing a _____ according to changes in a
    price index in order to prevent inflation from eroding purchasing power.
12. A worker's money wages for two different periods can be adjusted using the CPI to
    determine his/her real wages by _____ the money wage.
13. The annual percentage increase in the real purchasing power of a financial asset is the
    _____ .

14. Economists measure the change in the average price of a given class of goods or services relative to the price of the same goods and services in a base year by calculating a

_____.

Self-Test: Multiple-Choice Questions
Circle the letter that corresponds to the best answer. (Answers are given at the end of the chapter.)

1. Inflation exists when
   A. and only when the prices of all goods and services are rising.
   B. the purchasing power of money is increasing.
   C. the average price level is rising, although some prices may be falling.
   D. the prices of basic necessities are increasing.
   E. wages and the price of oil are rising.

2. If the CPI is 125 at the end of 2000 and equals 150 at the end of 2001, then the inflation rate for 2001 would equal
   A. 15 percent.
   B. 20 percent.
   C. 25 percent
   D. 125 percent.
   E. 150 percent.

3. If the Consumer Price Index (CPI) overstates the true rate of inflation, the use of the CPI to adjust nominal incomes results in
   A. understating gains in real incomes.
   B. overstating gains in real incomes.
   C. an accurate statement of gains in real incomes.
   D. nominal values equaling real values.
   E. an arbitrary redistribution of income.

4. Which of the following statements is true about the relationship between a nominal quantity and a real quantity?
   A. A real quantity indicates the amount of money received, while a nominal quantity indicates the real quantity's purchasing power.
   B. A nominal quantity is measured in current dollar values, but a real quantity is measured in terms of physical quantity.
   C. A nominal quantity is adjusted for inflation; a real quantity is not.
   D. A real quantity minus a nominal quantity equals purchasing power.
   E. There is no difference; nominal quantity and real quantity are two different terms for the purchasing power of money.

5. If the Consumer Price Index (CPI) decreases
    A. the purchasing power of money decreases.
    B. a dollar will buy fewer goods and services.
    C. real income equals nominal income.
    D. there is inflation.
    E. there is deflation.

6. If you borrow money at what you believe is an appropriate interest rate for the level of expected inflation, but the actual inflation rate turns out to be much higher than you had expected
    A. you will be paying the loan back with dollars that have much less purchasing power than you had expected.
    B. you will be paying the loan back with dollars that have much higher purchasing power than you had expected.
    C. you will be paying the loan back with dollars that have the same purchasing power as the dollars you borrowed.
    D. you, the borrower, will gain from an intended redistribution of wealth.
    E. you, the borrower, will unintentionally redistribute wealth to the lender.

7. If, in a given period, the rate of inflation turns out to be lower than lenders and borrowers anticipated, the effect is that
    A. the real payments by the borrowers will be lower than expected.
    B. the nominal income of lenders will be higher than expected, but their real income will be lower than expected.
    C. the nominal income of the lenders will be as expected, but their real income will be higher than expected.
    D. both the nominal and real income of lenders will be higher than expected.
    E. the real income of lenders will be higher than expected, but their nominal income will be lower than expected.

8. The Consumer Price Index is a measure of the change in prices of
    A. a standard basket of all goods and services.
    B. a standard basket of goods determined by the Consumer Expenditure Survey.
    C. a standard basket of agricultural goods determined by the Consumer Expenditure Survey.
    D. a standard basket of selected items in wholesale markets.
    E. a standard basket of machinery, tools, and new plant.

9. "Shoe leather" costs of inflation refer to the
    A. difficulty of interpreting the price signals in an inflationary environment.
    B. unintended changes in taxes caused by inflation.
    C. arbitrary redistribution of wealth from one group to another.
    D. costs of economizing on holding cash.
    E. interference of inflation on the long-run planning of households and businesses.

10. A currency board introduced in 1991 in Argentina mandated that the Argentine government exchange Argentine pesos for dollars at a one-to-one rate. The goal of introducing the currency board was to
    A. expand foreign trade between Argentina and the United States.
    B. begin the change toward dollarization and eventually replace the Argentine peso with the U.S. dollar.
    C. overcome the problem of the illegal use of dollars in the Argentine economy.
    D. reduce the Argentine government's cost of printing pesos.
    E. overcome the hyperinflation of the 1980s and ensure a strong, stable domestic currency.

11. The CPI for a given year measures the cost of living in that year relative to
    A. what it was in the base year.
    B. what it was in the previous year.
    C. the cost of the basic goods and services need to sustain a typical household.
    D. the amount spent on goods and services by the randomly selected families in the Consumer Expenditure Survey.
    E. the cost of the basic goods and services in the base year.

12. When comparing the money wages of today's workers to money wages workers earned 10 years ago, it is necessary to adjust the nominal wages by
    A. indexing the money wages in each period to today's price index.
    B. deflating the money wages in each period with today's price index.
    C. indexing the money wages in each period with the price indexes of the respective periods.
    D. deflating the money wages in each period with the price indexes of the respective periods.
    E. deflating the money wages in each period with the price index of the past period.

13. The Boskin Commission reported that the official inflation rate, based on the CPI, might overstate true inflation. It identified two reasons, including the
    A. quality adjustment bias and the indexing bias
    B. quality adjustment bias and the substitution bias.
    C. substitution bias and the indexing bias.
    D. quality adjustment bias and the deflation bias.
    E. indexing bias and deflation bias.

14. During the last half of 1999 and first quarter of 2000, the members of the Organization of Petroleum Exporting Countries (OPEC) negotiated reductions in the global production of oil. As a result, the price of heating oil and gasoline increased dramatically in the United States during that period. This led some analysts to predict an increase in the inflation rate in the United States. Drawing such a conclusion results from confusing
    A. inflation with indexing.
    B. inflation with deflation.
    C. a change in the relative price of a good with a change in the price level.
    D. a change in the relative price level with a change in the absolute price level.
    E. indexing with deflating.

15. Inflation creates static or "noise" in the price system, making it difficult for
    A. businesses and households to make long-term plans.
    B. lenders and borrowers to determine an appropriate level of nominal interest rate on loans.
    C. employers and workers to determine the appropriate level of money wages to be paid.
    D. businesses to interpret the information being transmitted by price changes.
    E. households and businesses to hold cash.

16. The real interest rate can be written in mathematical terms as
    A. $r = i - \pi$
    B. $r = \pi - i$
    C. $r = i + \pi$
    D. $r = \pi + i$
    E. $r = i / \pi$

17. In the United States during the 1970s, nominal interest rates were
    A. falling and real interest rates were falling.
    B. rising and real interest rates were rising.
    C. falling and real interest rates were rising.
    D. rising and real interest rates were falling.
    E. rising and real interest rates became negative.

18. If the Consumer Price Index is 135 at the end of 2001 and, at the end of 2002, it is 142, then
    during 2002 the economy experienced
    A. deflation
    B. inflation
    C. hyperinflation
    D. indexing
    E. deflating

19. Mr. Long is considering the purchase of a corporate bond with a yield (interest rate) of 6%
    per year, and he expects the inflation rate will average 4% per year during the period that he
    would hold the bond. Mr. Long has decided to purchase the bond only if the real rate of
    return is positive on the investment. If the tax rate on the interest income is
    A. greater than 33.3%, he should buy the bond.
    B. greater than 50%, he should buy the bond.
    C. less than 33.3%, he should buy the bond.
    D. less than 50%, he should buy the bond.
    E. less than 33.3%, he should not buy the bond.

20. Ms. Savior bought 300 shares of stock in the Dot.com Company in 2000 for $1,000. In 2002 she sold the shares for $1,050, earning $50 in capital gains. She must pay a 20% capital gains tax, leaving her with a net gain of $40. During the two years that she held the stock the price level rose by 4%. As a result her real return on the stock was
   A. positive.
   B. negative.
   C. zero.
   D. greater than the nominal yield (interest rate).
   E. equal to the nominal yield (interest rate).

Self-Test: Short Answer/Problems
(Answers and solutions are given at the end of the chapter.)

1. Consumer Price Index and Inflation
The data in the following table are taken from the U.S. Consumer Expenditure Survey conducted by the Bureau of Labor Statistics. The "Average Annual Expenditure" refers to the cost of purchasing the standard market basket of goods and services by the typical household in the United States in each year.

Year	Average Annual Expenditure	Consumer Price Index	Inflation rate (%)	After-tax Income	After-tax Real Income
1998	$35,535			$38,358	
1997	34,819			36,584	
1996	33,797			34,864	
1995	32,264			33,864	
1994	31,731			33,098	

A. Using 1995 as the base year, complete column three of the table by calculating the Consumer Price Index for 1994-98.

B. Complete column 4 of the table by calculating the inflation rates for 1995-98.

C. In the same survey, the BLS provides the average nominal income after paying taxes of the typical household, shown in column 5 of the table. Complete column 6 of the table, using the CPI to adjust the nominal income to calculate after-tax real income of the typical household.

D. In which of the years from 1994-98 was the typical household in the United States economically best off? _____ . In which of the years from 1994-98 was the typical household in the United States economically worst off? _____

2. Costs of Higher Education

Deloitte and Touche, LLP (an accounting firm) estimated the average cost of college during 1994-95 for four-year public and private institutions. The data is shown in the table below.

Categories	Public Colleges	Private Colleges
Tuition and fees	$2,686	$11,709
Books and Supplies	578	585
Room and Board	3,826	4,976
Transportation	592	523
Other	1,308	991
Total Cost	**$8,990**	**$18,784**

A. In the year 2000-01, it has also estimated that the total cost of attending a public college was $14,266 and a private college was $33,277. Using 1994-95 as the base year calculate the price index for attending public and private colleges. Price index for public college 1994-95 _____ ; price index for private college 1994-95 _____; price index for public college 2000-01_____; price index for public college 2000-01 _____ .

B. What was the percentage increase in the cost of attending a public college between 1994-95 and 2000-01? _____ percent. What was the percentage increase in the cost of attending a private college between 1994-95 and 2000-01? _____ percent.

C. Sam attended a public college in his home state beginning in 1994-95 and graduated in 2000-01. He paid the cost of his college education by working part time and summers as a firefighter. When he entered college his nominal (money) income was $13,000 and the year he graduated his nominal income had risen to $15,500. Because the cost of college includes all his living expenses, the price index for attending a public college represents his cost of living index. Thus, his real income (measured in 1994-95 dollars) in 1994-95 was $_____ and in 2000-01 it was $_____ .

D. Was Sam economically better off during the year he graduated or the first year he entered college? Explain your answer. _____

E. Sue attended a private college outside of her home state beginning in 1994-95 and she also graduated in 2000-01. She paid the cost of her college education by working part time and summers as a consultant to businesses designing web pages. When she entered college her nominal (money) income was $40,000. Because the cost of college includes all her living expenses, the price index for attending a private college represents her cost of living index. If her real income was to remain constant from 1994-95 through 2000-01, her nominal income in 2000-01 would have had to rise to $_____ .

3. Nominal and Real Interest Rates

Answer the questions below based on the data in the following table. The table shows the inflation rate in the United States, measured by the GDP deflator index, and nominal interest rates, measured by the yield on the 30-year Treasury bond.

Year	Inflation rate	Interest rate
1980	9.23	9.29
1984	3.77	11.18
1988	3.65	8.58
1992	2.75	8.14
1996	1.88	6.88

A. In what year was the real interest rate on the 30-year Treasury bond the highest? _____
B. In what year did the financial investors who bought the 30-year Treasury bonds get the best deal? _____
C. In what year was the real interest rate on the 30-year Treasury bond the lowest, but still positive? _____
D. In what year did the financial investors who bought the 30-year Treasury bonds get the worst deal? _____
E. What was the real interest rate on the 30-year Treasury bond in 1996? _____ %

Solutions
Self-Test: Key Terms

1. real wage
2. Fisher effect
3. price level; relative price
4. deflation
5. indexing
6. real quantity
7. nominal interest rate
8. hyperinflation
9. consumer price index (CPI)
10. rate of inflation
11. nominal quantity
12. deflating (a nominal quantity)
13. real interest rate
14. price index

Self Test: Multiple Choice Questions

1. C
2. B The inflation rate = (150 − 125)/125 = 25/125 = .20 or 20%
3. A If the true inflation rate is less than the official measure of inflation, then the real income would be greater than the official data would suggest.
4. B
5. E
6. A Inflation reduces the value of a dollar. Thus, if the inflation rate is greater than expected the
   dollars paid back are worth less than expected.
7. C
8. B
9. D
10. E
11. A
12. D
13. B
14. C The changes in the prices of gasoline and heating oil are changes in relative prices, not changes in the price level that would indicate inflation.
15. D
16. A r = real interest rate; i = nominal, or market, interest rate; and π = inflation rate
17. E
18. B

19. C If the tax rate is 33.3% or greater, Mr. Long will pay the equivalent of 2% or more in income taxes, leaving him an after-tax nominal return of 4% or less. Subtracting the 4% expected inflation would result in a zero or negative real return on the investment. Since he decided to only invest if the real return was positive he should only buy the bond if the tax rate is less than 33.3%.
20. C The $40 after-tax return divided by the $1,000 price of the bond equals a nominal rate of return of 4%. Subtracting the inflation rate of 4% would give her a real return of zero.

Self-Test: Short Answer/Problems

1.
A. CPI = (cost of the base-year basket of goods and services in the current year) divided by (cost of the base-year basket of goods and services in the base year) . For example, 1998 CPI = $35,535 / 32,264 = 1.10
B. inflation rate = (CPI in year – CPI in previous year) / CPI in previous year. For example, 1998 inflation rate = (1.10 – 1.08) / 1.08 = 2.06%
C. real income = nominal income / price index. For example, 1998 After tax real income = $38,358 / 1.10 = $34,827.14

Year	Average Annual Expenditure	Consumer Price Index	Inflation Rate (%)	After-Tax Income	After-Tax Real Income
1998	$35,535	1.10	2.06%	$38,358	$34,827.14
1997	34,819	1.08	3.02%	36,584	$33,899.49
1996	33,797	1.05	4.75%	34,864	$33,282.60
1995	32,264	1.00	1.68%	33,864	$33,864.00
1994	31,731	0.98		33,098	$33,653.96

D. 1998; 1996

2.
A. price index = $8.990/$8,990 = 1.00; $14,266/$8,990 = 1.59; 1.00; 1.77
B. percentage change = ($14,266- $8,990)/ $8,990 =58.7%; 77.2%
C. real income = $13,000 / 1.00 = $13,000; $9,767.63
D. during his first year
E. To determine how much her income would need to rise by, you need to index her income during the first year of school by multiplying it times the price index for private college during year she graduated, (i.e., $40,000 x 1.77 = $70,862.44).

3.
A. 1984
B. 1984
C. 1980
D. 1980
E. 5% (= 6.88 – 1.88)

Chapter 8
Economic Growth, Productivity,
and Living Standards

Key Point Review

Over the past two centuries a radical transformation has occurred in the living standards of people in the industrialized countries that has resulted from a remarkable rise in the economic growth rates of those nations. This chapter explores the sources of economic growth and rising standards of living in the modern world. Secondary issues discussed include government policies to promote economic growth, the costs of rapid economic growth, and whether there may be limits to economic growth.

Despite the recognition that it is an imperfect measure, economists have focused on real GDP per person as a key measure of a country's living standard and stage of economic development. As discussed in Chapter 18, real GDP per person is positively related to a number of pertinent variables, such as life expectancy, infant health, and literacy. During the 19th century, the annual percentage change in real GDP per person began to increase in a number of industrializing countries, and during the latter half of the 20th century the rate of economic growth increased again. As a result of the power of compound interest, real GDP in these countries is anywhere from 4 to 25 times greater than it was a century ago. However, since 1973 there has been a slowdown in the growth rates that has puzzled economists and policymakers alike.

The increases in the growth rates of real GDP during the last half of the 20th century were relatively small in comparison to the previous 80 years, but the power of compound interest resulted in large changes in real GDP over time. **Compound interest** is the payment of interest not only on the original deposit, but also on all previously accumulated interest. This is distinguished from simple interest in which interest is paid only on the original deposit. When interest is compounded, small differences in interest rates or growth rates matter a lot. As in the case of the industrializing countries during the late 19th and 20th centuries, relatively small differences in growth rates, among the countries and during different time periods ultimately produced very different living standards.

The rate of economic growth over time is an extremely important variable, and, therefore, understanding the sources of economic growth is very important. Real GDP per person can be expressed as the product of two terms: average labor productivity and the share of the population that is working. Real GDP per person can only grow if there is growth in worker productivity and/or the fraction of the population that is employed. In the United States, for example, during 1960-99 the fraction of the population employed increased as women entered the labor force in greater proportions, and as the coming of age of the "baby boomers" increased the share of the population that was of working age. This contributed to the increased growth in real GDP per capita in the United States during that time. In the long run, however, it is unlikely that this trend will continue as demographic changes take place. Average labor productivity is, therefore, the more important determinant of increases in living standards in the long run. In simple terms, the more people produce, the more they can consume.

There are six factors that appear to account for the major differences in average labor productivity between countries and between generations. Human capital, the talents, education, training and skills of workers, is the *first* factor that affects average labor productivity. In general, people acquire additional education and skills when the difference in the additional wages paid (marginal benefit) to skilled workers is greater than the marginal cost of acquiring the skills. A *second* determinant of average labor productivity is physical capital, machines, equipment and buildings. More capital generally increases average labor productivity. There are, however, **diminishing returns to capital** (i.e., if the amount of labor and other inputs employed is held constant, then the greater the amount of capital already in use, the less an additional unit of capital adds to production). Diminishing returns to capital is an illustration of the principle of increasing opportunity cost. The *third* determinant of average labor productivity is the availability of land and other resources. In general, an abundance of natural resources increases the productivity of the workers who use them. Because resources can be obtained through trade, countries need not possess large quantities of them within their own border to achieve economic growth.

A *fourth*, and possibly the most important, determinant is technology. A country's ability to develop and apply new, more productive, technologies will increase its workers' productivity. Entrepreneurship and management are a *fifth* determinant of average labor productivity. **Entrepreneurs** are people who create new enterprises and who are critical to the introduction of new technologies into the production of goods and services. Managers also play an important role in determining average labor productivity as they work to introduce new technologies to better satisfy customers, organize production, obtain financing, assign workers to jobs and motivate them to work hard and effectively. Government, a *sixth* determinant, also has a role to play in fostering improved productivity. A key contribution of government is to provide a political and legal environment that encourages people to behave in economically productive ways. A stable government and well-defined property rights and free markets are important determinants of a nation's average labor productivity.

While economic growth provides substantial benefits to society, it is not without costs. The high rate of investment in new physical and human capital requires that people save and, thus, consume less in the present. Also, reduced leisure time and, possibly, reduced workers' health and safety must be sacrificed in the present for workers to acquire the education and skills to build the capital infrastructure. The fact that a higher living standard tomorrow must be purchased at the cost of current sacrifices is an example of the scarcity principle. The cost-benefit principle suggests that a nation should pursue additional growth only if the marginal benefits outweigh the marginal costs.

If a society decides to try to increase its rate of economic growth, policymakers can help to achieve the goal by providing education and training programs or by subsidizing the provision of such programs by the private sector. In addition, governments can encourage high rates of saving and investment in the private sector through tax incentives. Governments can also directly contribute to capital formation through public investment in infrastructure. Government financing of research and development activities, especially in the area of basic scientific knowledge, and sharing the fruits of applied research in military and space applications can promote a higher rate of economic growth. Government also plays an essential role in providing the framework within which the private sector can operate productively, an area in which the poorest countries of the world lack adequate structural macroeconomic policies

While economic growth accelerated during the 19th and 20th centuries, an influential book, *The Limits to Growth*, published in 1972 reported the results of computer simulations that suggested continued growth would deplete natural resources, drinkable water, and breathable air. Critics of the limits to growth thesis point out that its underlying assumption is that growth implies producing more of the same type of goods. A second criticism is that it overlooks the fact that increased wealth expands a society's capacity to safeguard the environment. Additionally, it is argued that markets and government action can deal with the depletion of natural resources through new sources and conservation. Despite these shortcomings of the "limits to growth" perspective, most economists would agree that not all the problems created by economic growth can be dealt with effectively. Global environmental pollution will remain a problem unless international mechanisms are developed to deal with them. In particular, given that the relationship between pollution and real GDP per person is shaped like an inverted **U**, it is likely that as poorer countries become middle-income countries they will continue to pollute more until they become sufficiently wealthy to have the luxury of a clean environment.

Knowledge and Skills

The student must master the knowledge and skills listed below each number topic.	Key Terms	Multiple-Choice Questions	Short Answer/ Problems
1. The Rise in Living Standards			
A. Compare rates of growth in real GDP per person among countries during the 19th and 20th centuries		1	
B. Define compound and simple interest	3	2	
C. Calculate the effects of compound interest		3	

The student must master the knowledge and skills listed below each number topic.	Key Terms	Multiple-Choice Questions	Short Answer/ Problems
2. Determinants of a Nation's Economic Growth Rate			1
A. Discuss the relationship of real GDP per person to average labor productivity and share of working population		4	2
B. Discuss the determinants of average labor productivity	1, 2	5, 6, 7, 8, 9, 10	
C. Explain the slowdown in productivity after 1973		11	
3. The Costs of Economic Growth			
A. Identify the costs of economic growth		12	
B. Apply the cost-benefit principle to economic growth		13	
4. Policies to Promote Economic Growth			
A. Discuss potential government policies that may promote economic growth		14, 15	
B. Identify the main constraint on the poorest countries' economic growth rates		16	
5. Limits to Growth			
A. Identify the issues raised in the book *The Limits to Growth*		17	
B. Discuss the criticisms of the "limits to growth" thesis		18, 19	
C. Explain the relationship between pollution and real GDP per person		20	3

Self-Test: Key Terms

Use the terms below to complete the following sentences. (Answers are given at the end of the chapter.)

compound interest
diminishing returns to capital
entrepreneur

1. The greater the amount of capital already in use, the less an additional unit of capital adds to production if the amount of labor and other inputs employed is held constant because of

   _____ .

2. People who create new enterprises are _____ .

3. The payment of interest on all previously accumulated interest the payment of interest and on the original deposit is called _____ .

Self-Test: Multiple-Choice Questions

Circle the letter that corresponds to the best answer. (Answers are given at the end of the chapter.)

1. The rate of growth in real GDP per person in the United States, Japan, Canada, Australia and the major European economies was highest during the period of
   A. 1870-1998.
   B. 1950-1998.
   C. 1973-1979.
   D. 1979-1997.
   E. 1960-1973.

2. Compound interest differs from simple interest in that compound interest is interest paid on
   A. the original deposit only, whereas simple interest is interest paid on not only on the original deposit but also on all previously accumulated interest.
   B. all previously accumulated interest, whereas simple interest is interest paid on not only on the original deposit but also on all previously accumulated interest.
   C. the original deposit only, whereas simple interest is interest paid only on all previously accumulated interest.
   D. the original deposit and on all previously accumulated interest, whereas simple interest is interest paid on all previously accumulated interest .
   E. the original deposit and on all previously accumulated interest, whereas simple interest is interest paid on the original deposit only.

3. If on the day you were born, your parents deposited $1,000 into a savings account that would earn an annual compound interest rate of 5 percent, what would the value of the account be on your 20th birthday?
   A. $1,100.00
   B. $2,653.30
   C. $3,325,256.73
   D. $1,500.00
   E. $1,050.00

4. The increase in average labor productivity is important to the economy because
   A. without it, real GDP per person cannot increase.
   B. without it, real GDP per person must decrease.
   C. it is a key to improving living standards in the long run.
   D. the fraction of the total population that is employed is constant over time and, thus, real GDP per person is solely dependent upon average labor productivity.
   E. it implies more resources are being employed to produce less output.

5. International data on the relationship between the amount of capital per worker and average labor productivity indicate that there is a
   A. positive relationship between the two variables.
   B. negative relationship between the two variables.
   C. no relationship between the two variables.
   D. positive relationship between the two variables for some countries, but a negative relationship between the two variables for other countries.
   E. positive relationship between the two variables for some countries, but no relationship between the two variables for other countries.

6. An abundance of natural resources, such as arable land, raw materials, and energy,
   A. within a country's borders is necessary to achieve economic growth.
   B. increases the productivity of workers who use them.
   C. results in economic growth only if the population increases at least as rapidly.
   D. results in economic growth only if an economy obtains them through international trade.
   E. seldom contribute to economic growth, as measured by percentage increases in real GDP per person.

7. The investment in human capital that contributed to the rapid economic recovery in Germany and Japan after World War II was mainly achieved through
   A. a superior system of higher education.
   B. public education.
   C. an apprentice system and on-the-job training.
   D. subsidies provided by the U.S.-funded Marshall Plan.
   E. a large wage differential paid to skilled versus unskilled workers.

8. The faster the rate of technological change, the
   A. lower the rate of growth in productivity.
   B. lower the rate of economic growth.
   C. higher the rate of unemployment.
   D. higher the rate of productivity.
   E. higher the rate of capital accumulation.

9. For a given number of workers, as the amount of capital is increased output will
   A. increase at a diminishing rate.
   B. increase at an increasing rate.
   C. increase at a constant rate.
   D. decrease at a diminishing rate.
   E. decrease at an increasing rate.

10. Entrepreneurship is
    A. easy to teach in schools and colleges.
    B. not affected by government policies.
    C. more important than management in determining average labor productivity.
    D. mainly affected by individual factors rather than sociological factors.
    E. believed to have been largely absent in medieval China.

11. Which of the following contributed to the worldwide slowdown in productivity since 1973?
    A. the increase in the price of oil that followed the Arab-Israeli war of 1973
    B. the decline the quality of public education
    C. the improvement in the measurement of productivity growth
    D. a dearth of technological innovations during the 1970s
    E. an increase in technological innovations during the 1970s

12. The scarcity principle implies that the cost of a higher economic growth rate is
    A. less future capital accumulation.
    B. less current consumption.
    C. greater future capital consumption.
    D. greater current consumption.
    E. greater future consumption.

13. The cost-benefit principle suggests that higher economic growth
    A. is always desirable.
    B. is seldom desirable.
    C. should be pursued only if the marginal benefits outweigh the marginal costs.
    D. should be pursued only if the marginal costs outweigh the marginal benefits.
    E. should be pursued only if the marginal benefits equal the marginal costs.

14. Most countries provide their citizens free public education through high school because
    A. the supply curve for education does not include all the social benefits of education.
    B. a market in equilibrium exploits all the gains achievable from collective action.
    C. the demand curve for education does not include all the social benefits of education.
    D. educational vouchers that help citizens purchase educational services in the private sector have not proven to increase human capital.
    E. direct government control over the standards and quality of education is necessary to increase human capital.

15. The U. S. government has promoted saving or investment in the economy by
    A. increasing the tax rates on Individual Retirement Accounts (IRAs).
    B. providing subsidies to the private sector to build infrastructure.
    C. reducing the amount of public investment in government-owned capital.
    D. providing funding during the early stages of the development of the internet.
    E. eliminating all taxes on Individual Retirement Accounts (IRAs).

16. In order to increase their rate of economic growth, most poor countries need to
    A. establish political stability and the rule of law.
    B. obtain greater financial support from the rich countries.
    C. extract more of the natural resources that lie within their borders.
    D. maintain the structural macroeconomic policies that they began to implement after World War II.
    E. increase regulation of private sector monopolies.

17. The general thesis of the book, *The Limits to Growth*, is that continued pursuit of economic growth will soon
    A. cease when all the workers are employed.
    B. consume all available natural resources, drinkable water, and breathable air.
    C. cause the principle of scarcity to no longer be an issue.
    D. increase the living standard of the poorest nations to that of the richest nations.
    E. limit our desire to increase the production of goods and services.

18. Critics of the "limits to growth" thesis argue that
    A. economic growth will always take the form of more of what we have now, rather than newer, better, and cleaner goods and services.
    B. the market is not capable of adjusting to shortages of resources.
    C. clean air and water is a luxury good and the more economically developed a country becomes the easier it will be to keep the environment clean.
    D. government action spurred by political pressure is the best way to avoid the depletion of natural resources and pollution of the environment that results from economic growth.
    E. all the problems created by economic growth can be dealt with effectively through the market or the political process.

19. One criticism of the "limits to growth" thesis is that the market can deal with shortages of natural resources that may result from economic growth through price changes that induce
    A. consumers to consume more and suppliers to produce less of the resources.
    B. consumers to consume less and suppliers to produce more of the resources.
    C. a slowdown in the rate of economic growth.
    D. government actions to allocate public funds to preserve open space and reduce air pollution.
    E. an optimal level of environmental quality on a global scale.

20. Empirical studies show that the relationship between pollution and real GDP per person takes the shape of an inverted **U**. This suggests that as countries move from very low levels of real GDP per person the level of pollution
    A. tends to continuously worsen.
    B. tends to continuously improve.
    C. improves, but from middle-income to high-income levels pollution worsens.
    D. worsens, but from middle-income to high-income levels pollution improves.
    E. worsens at middle-income levels, but improves at high-income levels.

Self-Test: Short Answer/Problems
(Answers and solutions are given at the end of the chapter.)

1. Compounding Economic Growth Rates

The table below shows the output per person for selected countries in 1998 and the economic growth rates of the countries for 1990-98. Use the data in the table to answer the following questions.

Country	1998 GNP per capita[1]	1990 - 1998 Growth Rate	2008 GNP per capita
Canada	$24,050	2.2%	
France	22,320	1.5%	
Germany	20,810	1.6%	
Italy	20,200	1.2%	
Mexico	8,190	2.5%	
New Zealand	15,840	3.2%	

Source: *World Development Report, 1999/2000*, Tables 1 and 11.

[1] Calculated in 1998 dollars and using the purchasing power parity method to adjust the value of output across countries.

A. Assuming that each countries' economy continues to grow at the same rate that it did during 1990-98, complete column 4 of the table by calculating the GNP per capita (person) for 2008.

B. On the graph below, plot the level of GNP per capita for the remaining countries for 10, 20, 50, and 100 years later, assuming a compound growth rate equal to that of 1990-98,

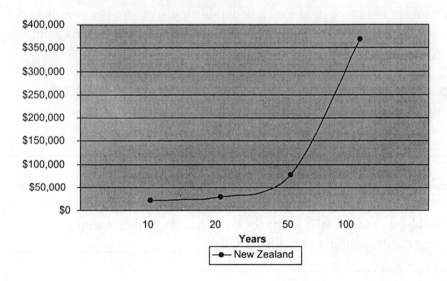

C. Approximately how many decades would it take for New Zealand's output per person to equal that of Canada's output per person? _____ decades.

D. Approximately how many decades would it take for Germany's output per person to equal that of France's output per person? _____ decades.

E. Approximately how many decades would it take for Mexico's output per person to equal that of Italy's output per person? _____ decades.

2. Why Nations Become Rich

This problem will help you understand the relationship between how much workers produce, how many people are working and the quantity of goods and services available to consume. The following table is comprised from data published by the U.S. Department of Labor' Bureau of Labor Statistics/ Office of Productivity and Technology. All data are for 1998 and the Real GDP and productivity are measured in 1998 dollars.

Country	Real GDP per person	Average Labor Productivity	Share of the population Employed
United States		$65,888	49.2
Canada	$25,496		47.5
France	$22,255	$56,722	
Japan	$24,170		51.2
Norway		$54,007	51.1

A. Complete the table above by calculating the value of real GDP per person for the United States and Norway, average labor productivity for Canada and Japan, and the share of the population employed in France during 1998.

B. The data indicate that workers in France produce considerable more output per year than do the workers in Norway, yet the average Norwegian has a higher standard of living. Explain why.

_____

C. A larger share of the population in Japan is employed than in the United States, yet the average American has a higher standard of living than the Japanese do. Explain why.

_____

_____

D. The population in Japan is aging faster than the population in Canada and, thus, by the early 21st century the share of the population employed in Japan will decline as the elderly retire. If the share of the population employed in Japan falls to the level of Canada, which country would have the higher real GDP per capita, assuming no other changes? _____
Explain your answer. _____

3. Pollution and Real GDP

This problem focuses on the relationship between real GDP per person and the level of pollution in a country. The following table shows the classification, by level of Real GDP per person, of a limited number of countries in the *World Development Report 1999/2000*.

Country	Ranking
China	Low income
Namibia	Lower middle income
Mexico	Upper middle income
Australia	High income

A. Identify each of the four countries listed in the table with one of the lettered points on the inverted **U**-shaped curve on the following graph. A _____,
B_____, C_____, and D_____ .

B. If the level of real GDP per person in Mexico increases so that it moves up to the next classification in future World Development Reports, will the amount of pollution likely increase or decrease?_____ Explain your answer. _____

_____

C. If the level of real GDP per person in China increases so that it moves up to the next classification in future World Development Reports, will the amount of pollution likely increase or decrease?_____ Explain your answer. _____

_____

Solutions
Self-Test: Key Terms

1. diminishing returns to capital
2. entrepreneur
3. compound interest

Self-Test: Multiple-Choice Questions

1. E Compare the growth rates for each of these periods in Tables 20.1 and 20.3
2. D
3. B $1,000 x 1.05^{20} = $2,653.30
4. C
5. A See Figure 20.4
6. B
7. C See Economic Naturalist 20.1
8. D
9. A
10. E
11. D
12. B
13. C
14. C
15. D
16. A
17. B
18. C
19. B
20. E

Self-Test: Short Answer/Problems

1.

A.

Country	98 GNP per capita	2008 GNP	2018 GNP
Canada	$24,050.00	$29,896.75	$37,164.90
France	$22,320.00	$25,903.27	$30,061.80
Germany	$20,810.00	$24,389.85	$28,585.53
Italy	$20,200.00	$22,759.17	$25,642.57
Mexico	$8,190.00	$10,483.89	$13,420.27
New Zealand	$15,840.00	$21,704.62	$29,740.56

B.

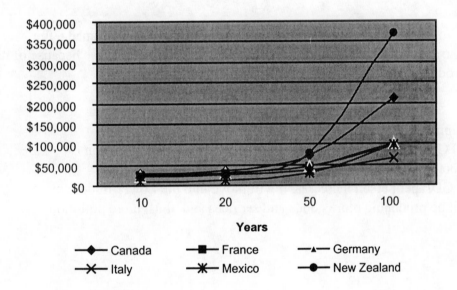

C. 5

D. 5

E. 6

2.

A.

Country	Real GDP per person	Average Labor Productivity	Share of the population Employed
US	$32,413	$65,888	49.2
Canada	$25,496	$53,702	47.5
France	$22,255	$56,722	39.2
Japan	$24,170	$47,232	51.2
Norway	$27,581	$54,007	51.1

B. Because a larger share of the population is employed in Norway than is employed in France, the average person in Norway has a higher standard of living than the French.

C. The average labor productivity in the United States is higher than that of Japan, and, thus, despite the fact that a smaller share of the population is employed in the U.S. its citizens have a higher standard of living.

D. Canada. If the share of the population employed in Japan declines to that of Canada, the standard of living for the average Canadian will be higher than that of the Japanese because of its higher average labor productivity.

3.

A. A - China, B - Namibia, C - Mexico, and D - Australia

B. Decrease. As its real GDP per person increases, it will move into the high-income classification and will better be able to afford the luxury of a clean environment.

C. Increase. As its real GDP per person increases, it will move into the Lower-middle income classification and it will be producing more goods and services and, thus, more pollution.

Chapter 9
Workers, Wages, and Unemployment
in the Modern Economy

Key Point Review

Chapter 21 is an excellent example of the applicability of the basic supply and demand model to understanding changes in the economy. The chapter begins with a presentation of five important trends of labor markets in the industrial world. First, all industrial countries have enjoyed significant growth in real wages over the entirety of the twentieth century. Second, since the early 1970s, the growth rate of real wages has slowed. Third, in recent decades, wage inequality has risen in the United States. Fourth, the number of people in the United States with jobs has grown considerably in the recent past. Finally, Western Europe has been plagued by high rates of unemployment for the past two decades.

One of the strengths of the basic supply and demand model introduced in Chapter 4 is its ability to fit many different circumstances. To understand the workings of the labor market it is unnecessary to invent a new model; reconfiguring the basic model will prove adequate. In a labor market, the price is the wage rate, the quantity is the amount of labor, individuals are the suppliers, and firms are the demanders.

The demand for labor is based on the two notions: how productive a given worker is and the value of the worker's production. As the firm hires additional workers, it is able to produce a greater amount of output. The key measure for labor demand analysis is not the total amount produced by 5 employees but the extra production associated with the hiring of the fifth worker. The extra output obtained by hiring an extra worker defines the marginal product of labor. The principle of **diminishing returns to labor** states that if other inputs like capital are fixed, the extra output from hiring an extra worker will decline at some point. However, knowing the marginal product of one's workers is not enough information to render a judgment about the optimal number to hire. In some sense, the firm cares not about the amount each worker produces but about the extra revenue the extra production will generate. The benefit of hiring an extra worker is calculated as price times marginal product and referred to as the value of marginal product. In fact, the value of marginal product is the firm's demand curve for labor. Consider a firm that discovers the value of marginal product for the fourth worker is $45. Under what conditions would the firm hire the fourth worker? Using the Cost-Benefit Principle, they will hire the fourth worker if he costs no more than $45.

Analogous to the demand curves in Chapter 4, two factors cause the labor demand curve to shift to the right or left. First, if the price of the firm's output increases, then the value to the firm of a given worker's marginal product grows, thus shifting labor demand to the right. Second, if the marginal productivity of workers rises due to technological change or training, then labor demand will increase, shifting to the right. Reductions in output price or marginal productivity cause decreases in labor demand. A decrease in the wage rate does not cause an increase in labor demand; it causes an increase in the quantity of labor demanded or a movement along the labor demand curve.

The supply of labor shows the total number of people willing to work at each real wage rate. The real wage rate represents the opportunity cost of not working, for example, if the wage is $5 and one chooses to work one less hour, one has given up $5. The plausible assumption is made that the higher the real wage rate, the greater the number of people who will be willing to work. Increases and decreases in the supply of labor stem from changes in the size of the working age population and the percentage of working-age people who seek employment.

The first three labor market trends can now be understood within the framework of a supply and demand model. The first trend, significant real wage growth over the entire twentieth century, results from sustained productivity growth. For the industrial countries, technological progress and large increases in the stock of capital caused the productivity growth. Of course, the size of the working-age population expanded (a labor supply increase), but the increase in labor demand due to greater productivity was large enough to absorb the new entrants and to drive the real wage up.

The second trend, a distinct slowdown in real wage growth during the past 30 years, comes from a slowdown in productivity growth coupled with continued growth in the working-age population, particularly the rising participation of women. Unlike the first 70 years of the century, the increases in labor demand were large enough to accommodate the new entrants but not large enough to drive the real wage up markedly.

Explaining the third trend, increased wage inequality, rests with two factors: globalization and technological change. Greater international trade encourages countries to further specialize in producing the goods for which they possess a comparative advantage, benefiting all consumers in all countries. When domestic markets are opened to trade, some markets will see an increase in demand for their output (the ones with a comparative advantage), while others will see a decrease in demand (those without a comparative advantage). As demand goes, so goes price. Thus, in the markets *lacking* a comparative advantage, the decrease in demand results in a lower price, translating into a decrease in the value for marginal product and, in turn, lower wages. In the markets *with* a comparative advantage, the reverse occurs, driving wages up. The United States enjoys comparative advantage in goods produced by highly skilled, high-wage workers but has difficulty competing with other countries in the production of goods requiring low-skilled, low-wage workers. The effects of trade then tend to drive the high wage workers' wage up further while lowering the wages of low wage workers, making wage inequality more pronounced. The free market solution involves **worker mobility,** the movement of worker's between jobs, firms, and industries. The higher wages in the high-skilled labor markets should draw new workers in while the lower wages in the low-skilled labor markets should cause workers to exit. However, the transition from one labor market to another, particularly low skilled to high skilled, does not happen instantly, so government assistance to aid the process may be justified.

The other issue propelling greater wage inequality is the nature of technological progress. While technological progress expands the size of the economic pie, it is not neutral in its influences. Unfortunately, it appears that **skill-biased technological change**–technological change favoring the marginal productivity of high skilled workers–characterizes recent decades. The effect of skill-biased technological change serves to increase the demand for high-skilled workers, resulting in higher wages for workers already receiving high wages. Wage inequality, as a consequence, worsens.

Economists have separated unemployment into three categories. **Frictional unemployment** results from the matching of workers and jobs and lasts for a relatively short period. Because workers and jobs are dissimilar or heterogeneous and the labor market is ever changing or dynamic, the process of matching workers and jobs takes time. So when a person quits one job, he or she may spend a few weeks or months finding the next one. The psychological and financial costs of frictional unemployment are relatively minor because it is short in duration. In fact, frictional unemployment is considered beneficial to the economy when a better match of worker and job occurs. Long-term and chronic unemployment that exists despite the normal operation of the economy is termed **structural unemployment**. The causes of structural unemployment take several forms: lack of skills, language barriers, or discrimination. Changes in the nature of the economy can also produce long term unemployment. For example, the United States steel industry is in decline and many former steelworkers will never again work in the steel industry. Finally, structural features of the economy can cause chronic unemployment. The costs of structural unemployment are much greater than those of frictional unemployment. When the economy suffers a recession, the additional unemployment that results is called **cyclical unemployment**. The costs of cyclical unemployment are also significant.

The structural features of the economy that contribute to the failure to reach full employment include several governmental programs. The minimum wage, as with any price floor, generates a surplus of workers, more commonly called unemployment. Unemployment insurance is a government transfer to unemployed workers, designed to lessen the burden of unemployment while searching for a new job. However, it may also lengthen the period of search and/or reduce the intensity of the search. Government regulations for workplace health and safety or discrimination tend to raise the cost of employing workers and reduce their productivity. Thus, firms wish to hire fewer workers than they would have in the absence of the regulations. Finally, labor unions "cause" unemployment by increasing the wage the firm must pay and hence the cost of hiring a worker. The issue here is not to determine if any of the features are efficient or inefficient. The point is simply that these features have implications for the labor market: more and longer unemployment.

The higher unemployment rates experienced by Western Europe over the past 20 years can be understood as a product of the structural features. Western European labor markets have a much higher degree of both government regulation and unionization compared to the United States. Globalization and skill-biased technological change, which caused low wage workers in the United States to see their wages fall, resulted in Western European employers permanently laying off workers *because wages could not fall*.

Knowledge and Skills

The student must master the knowledge and skills listed below each numbered topic.	Key Terms	Multiple-Choice Questions	Short Answer/ Problems
1. Labor Market Trends			
A. Discuss domestic and international patterns in real wages		1	
B. Discuss domestic and international patterns in unemployment and employment		2	
2. A Labor Market Model			
A. Define the marginal product of labor and diminishing returns to labor	4	3,4	1
B. Discuss the value of marginal product of labor and its relationship to labor demand.		5,6	1
C. Illustrate factors that shift the labor demand curve		7	1
D. Discuss the nature of labor supply		8	
E. Illustrate factors that shift the labor supply curve		9	
3. Application			
A. Explain the role of technological change and the size of the capital stock on real-wage growth		10,11	2, 3
B. Explain the effect of greater international trade on wage inequality		12	2, 3
C. Discuss worker mobility and other solutions to lessen the harmful impact of international trade on wage inequality	3	13	2
D. Define skill-biased technological change and explain its impact on wage inequality	1	14, 19	2, 3
E. Discuss efficient and inefficient solutions to lessen the harmful impact of technological change on wage inequality		15, 20	2
4. Unemployment			
A. Define frictional, structural, and cyclical unemployment	2, 5, 6		
B. Discuss the costs of the three types of unemployment		16	
C. List and discuss the impediments to full employment		17	
D. Explain the difference between unemployment patterns in Western Europe and the United States		18	

Self-Test: Key Terms

Use the terms below to complete the following sentences. (Answers are given at the end of the chapter.)

cyclical unemployment
diminishing returns to labor
frictional unemployment
skill-biased technological change
structural unemployment
worker mobility

1. Technological change that serves to alter the marginal productivity of higher-skilled workers differently than lower-skilled workers is termed _skill biased t-change_.

2. The additional unemployment that occurs during a recession is called _cyclical unem._.

3. _Worker mobility_ describes the movement of workers between jobs, firms, and industries.

4. The observation that if capital and other inputs are fixed, then the greater the quantity of labor already employed, the less each additional worker adds to production is known as _diminishing returns to labor_

5. The short-term unemployment associated with the process of matching workers with jobs is called _frictional unem._.

6. _structural unem._ is the long-term and chronic unemployment that exists even when the economy is producing at a normal rate.

Self-Test: Multiple-Choice Questions
Circle the letter that corresponds to the best answer. (Answers are given at the end of the chapter.)

1. Which of the following statements is *not* supported by the data presented in Chapter 21?
   A. During the twentieth century, the industrial nations have experienced sizable real-wage growth.
   B. Real wages for skilled workers have risen dramatically over the past 20 years.
   C. The differential between skilled and unskilled workers' real wages has remained constant over the twentieth century.
   D. Real-wage inequality is less pronounced in Western Europe than in the United States.
   E. The average worker in the United States in 1999 has four times the purchasing power of the average worker in 1929.

2. Which of the following statements is *not* supported by the data presented in Chapter 21?
   A. Over the past several decades, the United States economy has generated a significant number of new jobs.
   B. Western European countries have experienced lower levels of unemployment than the United States in recent years.
   C. Job creation in Western European countries has been meager over the past two decades.
   D. In 1999, more than two-thirds of the over-16 population in the United States held a job.
   E. Of late, the United States economy has created jobs at a rate exceeding the rate of growth of the over-16 population.

3. When a firm hires 3, 4, and 5 workers, it observes that total output is 15, 25, and 30 units, respectively. The marginal product of the fourth worker is thus _____ units.
   A. 40
   B. 25
   C. 15
   D. 10
   E. 5

4. Suppose the marginal products of the fifth, sixth, and seventh workers are 7, 4, and 1, respectively. One can infer that the firm
   A. is experiencing diminishing returns to labor.
   B. has hired too many workers.
   C. is profit maximizing.
   D. has selected low skilled workers.
   E. is experiencing negative returns to labor.

5. In order for a firm to determine the value of a particular worker, the firm must know
   A. the average amount of output the worker will produce.
   B. the extra amount of output the worker will produce.
   C. the price at which the output can be sold.
   D. the average amount of output the worker will produce and the price at which the output can be sold.
   E. the extra amount of output the worker will produce and the price at which the output can be sold.

6. The _____ is the firm's demand curve for labor because it illustrates the _____ for each extra worker.
   A. marginal product curve; extra output
   B. value of marginal product curve; the extra revenue
   C. value of average product curve; the average revenue
   D. value of marginal product curve; the extra profit
   E. value of marginal product curve; the extra cost

7. Which of the following events would not cause the demand curve for labor to shift?
   A. An increase in the productivity of labor.
   B. A decrease in demand for the output produced by the labor.
   C. A decrease in the wage rate paid to laborers.
   D. Introduction of new, inexpensive capital equipment designed to replace laborers.
   E. An increase in demand for the output produced by the labor.

8. The reason the labor supply curve is thought to be upward sloping is that as the real wage rate rises,
   A. the opportunity cost of not working increases.
   B. the attractiveness of working declines.
   C. the alternatives to working become more attractive.
   D. the greed of individuals becomes more obvious.
   E. more individuals are seduced into working when they would rather not.

9. The most important factor that shifts the labor supply curve is the
   A. size of the real wage rate.
   B. growth of the real wage rate.
   C. the size of the under-16 population.
   D. social norms about work.
   E. the size of the working-age population.

10. In terms of the model of labor markets, the growth of real wages in the industrial countries during the twentieth century is best explained as a(n)
    A. decrease in labor supply due to declining working-age populations.
    B. increase in labor demand due to higher prices for consumer goods.
    C. result of unions and government regulation of labor markets.
    D. increase in labor demand due to technological change and the growth of capital stocks.
    E. increase in labor supply due to increasing availability of educational opportunities.

11. The slowdown in real-wage growth that characterizes the past 30 years of the twentieth century is best explained as a(n)
    A. nearly total lack of productivity growth.
    B. combination of less rapid productivity growth and increased labor supply.
    C. increase in labor supply.
    D. combination of higher prices for consumer goods and decreased labor supply.
    E. increased government regulation of the labor market.

12. The increased wage inequality in the United States caused by increased international trade stems from
    A. foreign countries "dumping" products on the United States.
    B. increased demand for domestically produced goods requiring low-skilled labor.
    C. increased demand for domestically produced goods requiring high-skilled labor.
    D. decreased demand for domestically produced goods requiring high-skilled labor.
    E. higher productivity of foreign labor.

13. As wages in United States decline for low-skilled workers and rise for high-skilled workers due to international trade,
    A. the incentive to become a high-skilled worker is stronger, pulling more workers to the high-skill sector.
    B. the United States government should prohibit international trade.
    C. the United States government should compensate low-skilled workers with cash payments for the rest of their working life.
    D. no effective solution exists, so the growing inequality must just be accepted.
    E. allowing low-skilled workers to unionize is the only possible avenue to greater wage equality.

14. The technological change of the past 30 years seems to have
    A. benefited all workers equally.
    B. predominantly benefited low skilled workers.
    C. harmed both low- and high-skilled workers.
    D. only benefited workers in the computer sector.
    E. predominantly benefited high-skilled workers.

15. To counteract the negative effects of both international trade and skill-biased technological change on the wages of low-skilled workers, the textbook proposes
    A. an end to international trade.
    B. governmental review of technologies with a ban on those that favor the highly skilled.
    C. assistance to retrain low-skilled workers and ease their transition to new labor markets.
    D. a hike in the minimum wage.
    E. subsidies to the industries that employ large numbers of low-skilled workers.

16. Generally speaking, _____ unemployment is thought to be the least costly because
    _____.
    A. cyclical; it is just part of the business cycle
    B. structural; as economies grow, some sectors gain and others lose
    C. cyclical; most of the layoffs are short term
    D. frictional; it results in a better match of worker with job
    E. frictional; it tends to last the longest

17. Which of the following features of labor markets in the United States does *not* contribute to long-term, chronic unemployment?
    A. Minimum wage legislation.
    B. Labor unions.
    C. Job search engines on the Internet.
    D. Unemployment insurance.
    E. Health and safety regulations.

18. According to the textbook, the best explanation for the chronically higher unemployment rates in Western Europe is
    A. a lack of retraining programs.
    B. a decline in demand for low skilled workers.
    C. structural features of the labor market that retard worker mobility.
    D. excessive international trade.
    E. a combination of a decrease in demand for low-skilled workers and more limited worker mobility.

19. The combination of greater international trade and skill-biased technological change in the United States during the past 30 years has
    A. harmed low- and high-skilled workers equally.
    B. dramatically increased the degree of wage inequality because the United States has a comparative advantage in goods requiring high-skilled workers.
    C. not intensified the degree of wage inequality since the United States has a comparative advantage in goods that require both low- and high-skilled workers.
    D. harmed low-skilled workers without providing any tangible benefit to consumers.
    E. harmed low-skilled workers less than if only one of the two factors was present.

20. Which of the following proposals to assist low-skilled workers deals with the effects of international trade and skill-biased technological change would be most economically efficient?

A. A program to setup and provide access to an Internet-based job bank aimed at all industries.
B. Extension of the coverage period for unemployment insurance.
C. Tariffs on foreign goods produced using inexpensive foreign labor.
D. A public relations campaign to encourage consumers to buy American-made goods.
E. Demands that foreign countries pay their low-skilled workers more.

Self-Test: Short Answer/Problems
(Answers and solutions are given at the end of the chapter.)

1. Labor Markets
Calculation of marginal product, the value of marginal product, and determining the profit maximizing level of labor usage are reviewed in this question. The data below show the relationship between labor usage and total output for a firm.

Employee-hours	Output	Price	Marginal Product	Value of Marginal Product
0	0	$2	0	0
1	65	$2	65	130
2	105	$2	40	80
3	125	$2	20	40
4	135	$2	10	20
5	140	$2	5	10

(Handwritten annotations in Employee-hours column: 20, 40, 60, 80, 100; in Output column: 40, 80, 120, 160, 200)

A. Calculate the marginal product and the value of the marginal product for the different levels of employee-hours.
B. Suppose the price the firm receives for its output rises from $2 to $3. As a result, the (marginal product/value of marginal product) _value of M.P._ increases, implying the firm's demand for labor has (increased/decreased) _increased_.
C. Suppose that the efficiency of labor increases such that all employee-hours generate 10% more output, e.g., the first employee-hours now results in 71.5 units of output. The impact is that (only the marginal product/both the marginal product and the value of marginal product) _Both_ increase, shifting the labor demand curve to the (left/right) _right_.
D. If the firm must pay a wage of $40 per employee-hour, the profit maximizing level of labor usage is (3/4) _3_. If the wage rate were to fall to $20, the firm would increase its (labor demand/ quantity of labor demanded) _Quantity of LD_ to (3/4) _4_ hours.

1. Labor Market Dynamics I

This question assesses your ability to use the labor market model to explain the trends in wage and employment data presented at the beginning of the chapter. The graph below shows the market for two types of labor for the United States: workers A produce good X while workers B produce good Z. Presently, both occupations pay the same real wage to workers. Suppose a new trade agreement is signed to ease trading with other countries. Suppose further that in the international market, the United States has a comparative advantage in Z, but that other countries have the comparative advantage in X.

Comp. adv.

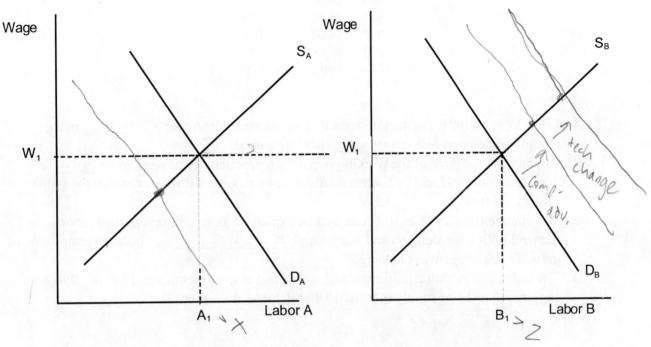

A. Illustrate the effects of the trade agreement on the wages of workers A and B.

B. Suppose that in addition to the trade agreement, recent technological innovations have favored workers B. Illustrate the effects, if any, on the wages of workers A and B.

C. A group, representing workers A, lobbies vigorously in opposition to the trade agreement on the grounds that workers would be harmed. Discuss who, if anyone, would be harmed by failing to sign the trade agreement. → workers & consumers of Z

D. Discuss an efficient way to assist workers A and have greater international trade.

1. **Labor Market Dynamics II**

This question also assesses your ability to use the labor market model to explain the trends in wage and employment, but rather than reasoning from the change to the effect, now the reasoning will run from effect to change. The table below presents imaginary data on equilibrium real wages and employment for a national labor market.

Year	Real Wage	Employment
1990	$5.00	100
1991	$5.50	120
1992	$6.00	100
1993	$6.00	130
1994	$5.75	125

A. From 1990 to 1991, the data indicate that an (increase/decrease) _increase_ in the (supply of/demand for) _demand_ labor occurred.

B. Apparently, the (size of the working population/productivity of workers) _size & W.P._ declined from 1991 to 1992, since the data are consistent with a decrease in the (supply of/demand for) _demand ~~supply~~_ labor.

C. The change from 1992 to 1993 can best be explained as an increase in (just labor demand/both labor demand and labor supply) _~~just~~ both_ because (employment grew/the real wage was unchanged) _~~employ grew~~ r.w. unchanged_

D. The reduction in both equilibrium real wages and employment from 1993 to 1994 suggests that (labor supply increased/labor demand decreased) _l.d. decre._

Solutions
Self-Test: Key Terms

1. skill-biased technological change
2. cyclical unemployment
3. worker mobility
4. diminishing returns to labor
5. frictional unemployment
6. structural unemployment

Self-Test: Multiple-Choice Questions

1. C
2. B
3. D Total output with 4 workers is 25 while total output with 3 workers is 15 so adding the fourth worker increases total output by 10 units.
4. A
5. E The firm need to know the value of the marginal product ($P*MP$) for each worker.
6. B
7. C A wage change would cause a movement along the labor demand curve.
8. A
9. E
10. D
11. B
12. C
13. A
14. E
15. C
16. D
17. C
18. E
19. B
20. A

Self-Test: Short Answer/Problems

1.

    A. See table.

Employee-hours	Output	Price	Marginal Product	Value of Marginal Product
0	0	$2		
1	65	$2	65	$130
2	105	$2	40	$80
3	125	$2	20	$40
4	135	$2	10	$20
5	140	$2	5	$10

    A. value of marginal product; increased

    B. both the marginal product and the value of the marginal product; right

    C. 3; quantity of labor demanded; 4

2.

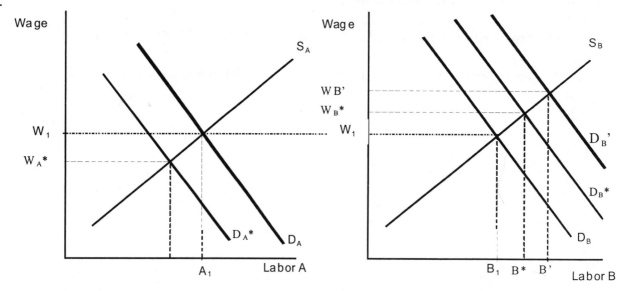

    A. The demand for good X declines due to trade and thus demand for labor A declines (D_A*), lowering employment and wages. Demand for Z increases with trade, which increases demand for B workers (D_B*) driving employment and wages up.

    B. The technological change further stimulates demand for labor B (D_B'), causing an added increase in wages and employment.

    C. Failing to sign the trade agreement harms consumers and workers producing good Z.

    D. Sign the agreement and use tax revenues to assist the unemployed laborers in A to get new training and locate new jobs.

3.

    A. increase; demand for

    B. size of the working population; supply of

    C. both labor demand and labor supply; the real wage was unchanged

    D. labor demand decreased

Saving = income - spending
S.R. = saving / income
wealth = assets - liabilities

Chapter 10
Saving and Capital Formation

Key Point Review

In this chapter, saving and its links to the formation of new capital are discussed. The concepts of saving and wealth and the connections between them are presented in the first part of the chapter. This is followed by a discussion of why people save. The chapter is completed with a discussion of national saving and its relationship to capital formation, using a supply and demand approach.

Saving by an economic unit (e.g., a household, business, or nation) is its current income minus its spending on current needs. It can be expressed as a **saving rate** by dividing the amount of saving by the amount of income. Saving by an economic unit is closely related to its **wealth**, the value of its assets minus its liabilities. **Assets** are anything of value that is owned, while **liabilities** are the debts that are owed. Accountants list the assets and liabilities of an economic unit on a balance sheet to determine its net worth. Saving and wealth are related because saving contributes to wealth. This relationship is best understood by distinguishing between stocks and flows. A **flow** is a measure that is defined per unit of time, and a **stock** is a measure that is defined at a point in time. In many cases, a flow is the rate of change in a stock. For example, the flow of saving causes the stock of wealth to change at the same rate. Higher rates of saving, therefore, lead to faster accumulation of wealth and a higher standard of living. Although saving increases wealth, it is not the only factor that determines wealth. Wealth also changes because of changes in the values of the real and financial assets owed by an economic unit. If the value of existing assets increase, the owner has a **capital gain**, but if the value of existing assets decrease, then there is a **capital loss**. In summary, changes in wealth equal the amount of saving plus capital gains minus capital losses.

People save part of their income rather than spending all they earn for three reasons. First, they save to meet certain long-term objectives, such as retirement or the purchase of a home.

This is called **life-cycle saving**. A second reason people save is called **precautionary saving**, saving to protect against unexpected setbacks. The third reason for saving is **bequest saving**, saving for the purpose of leaving an inheritance. Although most people save for one of these three reasons, the amount that they save depends on the economic environment. The economic variable that is most important in saving decisions is the real interest rate, r. The real interest rate is the reward for saving. Because of the power of compound interest in the long run, a higher real interest rate causes a dramatic increase in the real value of a saver's wealth. On the other hand, a higher real interest rate reduces the amount people need to save each year to reach a given wealth target. Nonetheless, empirical evidence suggests people are willing to save more the higher the real interest rate, all else being equal.

There are some, however, who argue that, despite these rational reasons for saving, some people lack the self-control to do what is in their own best interest. Despite having good intentions to save, for example, some lack the necessary self-control to put aside as much of their income as they would like. This so-called self-control hypothesis suggests that consumer credit arrangements that make borrowing and spending easier may reduce the amount that people save. Similarly, the demonstration effect suggests that additional spending by some people causes others to spend more to maintain a lifestyle commensurate with their peer group. These hypotheses, in addition to the generous government assistance for the elderly, may explain why household saving in the U.S. has declined recently.

The above discussion pertains to individual saving, but macroeconomists are interested primarily in saving and wealth for the country as a whole. As for any economic unit, a nation's saving equals its current income less its spending on current needs. The current income of a country is its GDP, or Y, the value of the final goods and service produced within the country's borders during the year. Identifying the part of total expenditures that corresponds to a country's current needs is more difficult. Because investment spending is done to improve the future productive capacity, it is clearly not a part of spending on current needs. For consumption and government spending, some portion is for current needs while another portion is for future needs. Determining how much should be attributed to each portion is extremely difficult. For this reason, the U.S. government statistics has for some years treated all of consumption expenditures and government spending as spending on current needs. The textbook authors follow this convention, with the caveat that this will understate the true amount of national saving. **National saving** (S), therefore, equals GDP less consumption expenditures and government purchases of goods and services, or $S = Y - C - G$ (this excludes the international sector, which is discussed in a later chapter).

To better understand national saving, one can divide it into two major components: private saving by households and businesses, and public saving by the government. To distinguish these two components, the above equation is expanded to incorporate taxes and payments made by the government to the private sector. Government payments to the private sector include transfers and interest paid to individuals and institutions that hold government bonds. **Transfers** are payments the government makes to the public for which it receives no current goods or services in return (e.g., social security benefits). If T represents taxes paid by the private sector to the government less transfer payments made by the government to the private sector, it can be called net taxes. **Private saving** can, thus, be expressed as $S_{private} = Y - T - C$, or private sector after-tax income minus its consumption spending. Private sector saving can be further broken down into household saving and business saving. **Public saving**, or saving of the government sector, is equal to net tax payments minus government purchases ($S_{public} = T - G$). A **government budget deficit**, the excess of government spending over tax collections ($G - T$), implies that public saving is negative, while a **government budget surplus**, the excess of government tax collections over spending ($T - G$), means public saving is positive.

In recent years, decreases in private household saving in the United States have been partially offset by increases in public saving. The relatively low U.S. household saving rate is not a problem from a macroeconomic perspective because national saving, not household saving, determines the capacity of an economy to invest in new capital goods and continue to improve its standard of living. Although U.S. household saving is low, saving by business firms is significant, and, during the 1990s, government budget surpluses have approximately offset the fall in household saving. Overall, despite the fact that it is low by international standards, the U.S. national saving rate has been reasonably stable and sufficient to allow it to become one of the most productive economies in the world. From a microeconomic perspective, however, the low household saving rate does exacerbate the problem of large and growing inequality in wealth among U.S. households. Saving patterns are increasing this inequality as better-off households not only save more, but, as business owners and stockholders, they also are the ultimate beneficiaries of the saving by businesses.

From the point of view of the economy as a whole, the importance of national saving is that it provides the funds needed for investment. Investment is the creation of new capital goods and housing and is critical to increasing average labor productivity and improving standards of living. Firms' willingness to invest depends on the expected cost of using the capital and the expected benefit, measured as the marginal product, of the capital. On the cost side, two important factors are the price of capital goods and the real interest rate. The more expensive the capital goods, the less willing businesses are to invest in them. The real interest rate measures the opportunity cost of a capital investment. Since an increase in the real interest rate increases the opportunity cost of investing in new capital, it lowers the willingness of firms to invest. On the benefit side, the key factor in determining business investment is the value of the marginal product of the new capital, calculated net of operating costs, maintenance expenses, and taxes paid on the revenues the capital generates. The value of the marginal product of capital is affected by several factors, including technological improvement and the relative price of the good or service that the capital is used to produce. Technological improvements and increases in the price of the good or service raise the marginal product of capital and increase the willingness of businesses to invest.

These factors can be analyzed in a supply and demand model. In an economy without international borrowing and lending, national saving must equal investment. The supply of national savings and the demand for savings are equalized through the workings of financial markets. The supply of saving shows the relationship between the real interest rate and the quantity of national saving. It is an upward-sloping curve because empirical evidence suggests that increases in the real interest rate stimulate saving, all other things equal. The demand for saving shows the relationship between the real interest rate and the quantity of investment in new capital. It is a downward-sloping curve because higher real interest rates raise the opportunity cost of capital and reduce the willingness of firms to invest, all other things equal. Holding aside the possibility of borrowing from foreigners, a country can only invest those resources that its savers make available.

In equilibrium, desired investment (the quantity demanded of saving) and national saving (the quantity supplied of saving) must be equal. Desired saving is equated with desired investment through adjustments in the real interest rate, which functions as the price of saving. Changes in factors other than the real interest rate that affect the supply of or demand for saving will shift the curves, leading to a new equilibrium in the financial market. Technological improvements and changes in the price of the good or service produced by the capital will shift the demand for saving. The supply of saving is affected by changes in private and public saving. In particular, an increase in the government budget deficit shifts the supply of saving curve to the left and the equilibrium quantity of saving and investment will decrease. This tendency of government budget deficits to reduce investment spending is called **crowding out**.

Knowledge and Skills

The student must master the knowledge and skills listed below each number topic.	Key Terms	Multiple-Choice Questions	Short Answer/ Problems
1. Saving and Wealth			
A. Define saving, saving rate, wealth, assets, liabilities, stocks, and flows	3, 10, 13, 14, 16, 17, 18		
B. Explain the link between saving and wealth		1, 9	1
C. Define capital gains and capital losses	4, 19		
D. Discuss the factors that change wealth		2, 10	
2. Why Do People Save?			
A. Identify the three broad reasons for saving	8, 12, 15	11	
B. Explain the relationship between saving and the real interest rate		3, 12	
C. Discuss the reasons why U.S. household saving rate is low		4, 13	
3. National Saving and its Components			
A. Define national saving, and transfers	2, 6		
B. Define private saving and discuss its two components	7	5, 14	
C. Define public saving, government budget deficit and surplus, and explain the relationships among them	1, 9, 11	15, 16	
D. Discuss why low U.S. household saving is not a macroeconomic problem, but may be a microeconomic concern		6,	

The student must master the knowledge and skills listed below each number topic.	Key Terms	Multiple-Choice Questions	Short Answer/ Problems
4. Investment and Capital Formation			
A. Apply cost-benefit analysis to the investment decision		7, 17	2
B. Identify the factors that affect the costs and benefits of investment		18, 19	
5. Saving, Investment, and Financial Markets			
6. Use the supply and demand model to analyze national saving		8, 20	3
7. Define crowding out	5		

Self-Test: Key Terms

Use the terms below to complete the following sentences. (Answers are given at the end of the chapter.)

assets
bequest saving
capital gains
capital losses
crowding out
flow
government budget deficit
government budget surplus
liabilities
life-cycle saving
national saving
precautionary saving
private saving
public saving
saving
saving rate
stock
transfer payments
wealth

1. The excess of government spending over tax collections (G – T) equals the _G.B.D._ .
2. Excluding the international sector, GDP less consumption expenditures and government purchases of goods and services, or Y – C – G, equals _national saving_ .
3. In accounting, the debts that one owes are recorded as _liabilities_ .
4. A decrease in the value of existing assets causes _capital losses_ .

5. The tendency of government budget deficits to reduce investment spending is called _crowding out_ .

6. Payments the government makes to the public for which it receives no current goods or services in return are _transfer payments_ .

7. Private sector after-tax income minus its consumption spending equals _private sav._

8. The type of saving that is done for certain long-term objectives, such as retirement, or the purchase of a home, is _life-cycle saving_ .

9. If public saving is positive, there is a(n) _a.b.s_ .

10. Current income minus spending on current needs represents the _saving_ of an economic unit.

11. Net tax payments minus government purchases equals _public sav._ .

12. Saving done for the purpose of leaving an inheritance is _bequest_ .

13. A measure that is defined per unit of time is a(n) _stock flow_ .

14. Dividing the amount of saving by the amount of income equals the _saving rate_ .

15. To protect against unexpected setbacks, people maintain _precautionary sav._ .

16. The value of assets minus liabilities equals _wealth_ .

17. In many cases, a flow equals the rate of change in a(n) _stock_ .

18. Anything of value that one owns is a(n) _asset_ .

19. If the value of existing assets increases, the owner has _cap. gains_ .

Self-Test: Multiple-Choice Questions
Circle the letter that corresponds to the best answer. (Answers are given at the end of the chapter.)

1. Luis had accumulated $5,000 in wealth at the end of a year. At the beginning of the next year he deposits $50 in a saving account that will earn 10% interest per year. If there are no changes in his liabilities, at the end of the next year his wealth will have
   A. increased by $50.
   B. decreased by $50.
   C. increased by $55.
   D. decreased by $55.
   E. not changed.

2. The strong U.S. bull market of the late 1990s ended (at least temporarily) in early 2000, as the stock market indexes fell 25% or more during the second quarter of 2000. As a result, many Americans
   A. suffered capital losses and increases in their wealth.
   B. suffered capital losses and decreases in their wealth.
   C. enjoyed capital gains and increases in their wealth.
   D. enjoyed capital gains and decreases in their wealth.
   E. suffered capital losses and decreases in their liabilities.

3. If the real interest rate on saving account increases from 3% to 5%, all other things equal
   A. business investment spending for new capital will increase.
   B. business investment spending for new capital will remain unchanged.
   C. people will be less willing to save.
   D. people will be more willing to save.
   E. the amount people will save will remain unchanged.

4. Which of the following hypotheses is a plausible explanation for why U.S. households save so little?
   A. Interest rates in the United States are typically lower than they are in the rest of the world.
   B. Most American already own homes and, therefore, have less need for life-cycle saving.
   C. The highly developed financial markets in the United States have reduced the need for precautionary saving by Americans.
   D. Government assistance to low-income U.S. households has increased the demonstration effects on spending by the poor.
   E. Government assistance to the elderly has reduced the need for life-cycle saving.

5. If net taxes paid by households increase,
   A. private saving will decrease.
   B. private saving will increase.
   C. public saving will decrease.
   D. transfer payments to households will decrease.
   E. transfer payments to households will increase.

6. The low and declining U.S. household saving rate is
   A. a macroeconomic problem because it reduces the amount of funds available for investment and, thus, reduces the standard of living.
   B. not a macroeconomic problem because the national saving rate has been stable and sufficient.
   C. a microeconomic problem because it reduces the amount of funds available for investment and, thus, reduces the standard of living.
   D. not a microeconomic problem because the national saving rate has been stable and sufficient.
   E. not a microeconomic problem because the booming stock market has increased the wealth of Americans and reduced income inequality.

7. Joe's Taco Hut can purchase a delivery truck for $20,000 and Joe estimates it will generate a net income (i.e., after-taxes and maintenance and operating costs) of $2,000 per year. He should
   A. purchase the truck if the real interest rate is less than 2%.
   B. not purchase the truck if the real interest rate is greater than 2%.
   C. purchase the truck if the real interest rate is greater than 10%.
   D. purchase the truck if the real interest rate is less than 10%.
   E. purchase the truck if the real interest rate is less than 3%.

8. The investment demand curve indicates that there is a(n)
    A. positive relationship between the real interest rates and the level of investment spending, all other things equal.
    B. inverse relationship between the real interest rates and the level of investment spending, all other things equal.
    C. direct relationship between the real interest rates and the level of investment spending, all other things equal.
    D. inverse relationship between the determinants of investment and the level of investment spending, holding interest rates constant.
    E. positive relationship between the determinants of investment and the level of investment spending, holding interest rates constant.

9. Rafael's current income is $100 more per month than his current consumption needs. He decides to use the $100 to reduce his credit card debt. As a result, his
    A. liabilities will decrease and his wealth will increase.
    B. liabilities and his wealth will decrease.
    C. assets will decrease and his wealth will increase.
    D. assets and his wealth will decrease.
    E. assets and his wealth will increase.

10. If, in a given year, the saving rate in an economy decreases by an amount equal to the net capital gains, the economy's
    A. wealth will decrease.
    B. wealth will increase.
    C. wealth will remain unchanged.
    D. assets will decrease.
    E. liabilities will decrease.

11. One reason that household saving in Japan is higher than household saving in the U.S. is
    A. that the average Japanese income is higher than it is in the United States.
    B. housing in the United States is more expensive and, therefore, Americans spend more of their income on housing and save less.
    C. because Japanese workers continue working until they are much older and, therefore, they can save more.
    D. the Japanese save more for precautionary reasons because they have, in general, less job security than American workers.
    E. the higher cost of housing and larger down payments required to purchase a house in Japan results in higher life-cycle saving.

12. During a conversation with her mother about her financial circumstances, Sylvia complained that she could not afford to save because she wanted to maintain a lifestyle similar to that of her friends. Her mother suggested that if she would save more now, she would not only have more wealth, but she would also have a higher standard of living than her friends in the future. Her mother's argument was
   A. incorrect, because if she saved her standard of living would be lower than that of her friends.
   B. incorrect, and probably an attempt to confuse her daughter in order to get her to begin saving some of her income.
   C. correct, because of the power of compound interest her income would increase to a level that would allow her to save and consume more.
   D. correct, because the more saving, the higher the standard of living.
   E. irrelevant, because daughters never listen to what their mother tells them.

13. Household saving in the United States
   A. is low relative to previous periods, but approximately equal to the rate in other countries.
   B. decreased through the 1990s and became negative in 1998.
   C. had decreased since the 1960s, but, because the economy was so strong during the 1990s, has recently increased.
   D. is low relative to other countries and has declined since the 1960s.
   E. is low relative to other countries, but has increased during the 1990s.

14. Private saving
   A. can be broken down into household saving and business saving.
   B. can be broken down into transfers and household saving.
   C. rises when net taxes increase.
   D. falls when income rises.
   E. rises when government spending decreases.

15. An increase in net taxes (i.e., taxes paid by the private sector to the government minus transfer payments and interest payments made by the government to the private sector) will
   A. increase private saving.
   B. decrease public saving.
   C. increase public saving.
   D. reduce investment in new capital equipment.
   E. cause crowding out.

16. Public saving is
   A. increased when the government budget deficit rises.
   B. identical to the government budget surplus.
   C. less important to national saving than private saving.
   D. more important to national saving than private saving.
   E. unimportant in determining the capacity of an economy to invest in new capital.

17. Samantha has $5,000 in a CD account paying 10% interest. It will mature in a few weeks and the bank told her that interest rates on CDs were decreasing. She is thinking of spending it on a new computer and software that she will use to start a bookkeeping service. If she were to do so, she would have to quit her job where she makes $15,000 per year in after-tax income. She has estimated that the bookkeeping service will earn a net income of $15, 250 after taxes, and maintenance and operating costs.
    A. Since the interest rate is declining, Samantha would be better off using the money to buy the computer.
    B. If the interest rate on the new CD is 7% or greater she should leave the money in the CD.
    C. If the interest rate on the new CD is 2.5% or greater she should buy the computer.
    D. If the interest rate on the new CD is 2% or less she should leave the money in the CD.
    E. If the interest rate on the new CD is 5% or greater she should leave the money in the CD.

18. As the cost of capital goods falls relative to other prices, the
    A. demand for investment in new capital will shift to the left.
    B. demand for investment in new capital will shift to the right.
    C. amount of investment in new capital will increase.
    D. amount of saving will rise.
    E. amount of saving will fall.

19. A decrease in the capital gains tax on income generated through investment in new capital will
    A. shift the demand for investment curve to the left.
    B. shift the demand for investment curve to the right.
    C. shift the supply of saving curve to the left.
    D. shift the supply of saving curve to the right.
    E. decrease real interest rates.

20. The introduction of a new technology that raises the marginal product of new capital will
    A. decrease real interest rates and increase the equilibrium quantity of saving supplied and demanded.
    B. decrease real interest rates and the equilibrium quantity of saving supplied and demanded.
    C. increase real interest rates and the equilibrium quantity of saving supplied and demanded.
    D. increase real interest rates and decrease the equilibrium quantity of saving supplied and demanded.
    E. decrease real interest rates and the equilibrium quantity of saving supplied and demanded will remain unchanged.

Self-Test: Short Answer/Problems
(Answers and solutions are given at the end of the chapter.)

1. Savings and Wealth

In this problem you will identify an individual's assets and liabilities to determine his wealth. You will also calculate the effect of saving on wealth over time.

At the end of the year 2000, Franklin prepares for the new millenium by writing down all his assets and liabilities. His list includes a car with a market value of $7,500, but with $6,000 left on the car loan; his home with a market value of $125,000 and a mortgage of $122,500; a checking account with$750 in it; a credit card balance of $1,000; 8,000 shares of the ABC Corporation with a current price of $12 per share; and a debt of $2,500 on a student loan.

A. Construct Franklin's balance sheet below, and calculate his wealth.

Franklin's Balance Sheet

Assets	Liabilities
Total	Total
	Net Worth

B. Upon returning to his job after the new year 2001, his boss informs him that he has been awarded a bonus of $1,000. He has decided he will not spend it on consumption, but rather will use it to increase his wealth. His alternatives are to put it into a CD account paying 7.5% annual interest, pay off his credit card debt that has an annual interest charge of 11%, or pay off his student loan that has a 7% annual interest charge. What would you recommend that he do with his bonus to maximize the increase in his wealth? _____
Why? _____

C. After reviewing his net worth, Franklin decides that he has insufficient wealth to achieve his goal of retiring in 20 years. He decides to begin saving $500 per year in a 401K retirement account (that is not subject to taxes until after he retires). After investigating all the options, Franklin settles on depositing his 401K funds into a money market account paying 5% annual interest. Assume that Franklin deposits $500 on the 1st of January in each year, and calculate the value of his retirement account at the end of each of the following periods: 1 year
_____, 2 years _____, 3 years _____ , 4 years _____, 5 years _____ .

D. At the end of the 5th year, Franklin reviews his retirement account and discovers that had he deposited the 401K funds in a stock fund rather than the money market account, he would have earned an average of 10% in capital gains each year. Recalculate the value that his retirement

account would have reached, if he had chosen the stock fund, at the end of 1 year _____,
2 years _____, 3 years _____, 4 years _____, and 5 years _____ .

2. Cost-Benefit Analysis for Investment Decisions

This problem focuses on the use of cost-benefit analysis in making investment decisions. You
will calculate the marginal product of capital, determine the marginal benefit and marginal cost
of capital, and decide whether to make an investment. You will also analyze the effects of
changes in taxation, the cost of capital, and expected income on the investment decision.

Thelma is thinking of going into the business of translating documents for international
businesses. In order to do so, she needs to borrow $5,000 to the buy computer equipment. She
has estimated that she will net $25,000 per year, after deducting operating and maintenance
costs. The tax rate on her business profit each year would be 15%, and the annual interest rate on
the loan would equal 12%. Her best job alternative would be teaching Spanish in high school
with an after-tax income of $20,000.

A. Assume the computer equipment does not lose value over time. Calculate the marginal
product of the computer equipment. $ _____

B. Calculate the amount of the annual interest that Thelma would have to pay on the loan.
$_____

C. Should Thelma invest in the computer equipment and start the translation business?
_____ Why or why not? _____
_____

D. If the government increases the tax rate on business profits to 19%, and the computer
equipment does not lose value over time, calculate the marginal product of the computer
equipment. $ _____

E. After the tax increase in Question D, should Thelma to buy the computer equipment and start
the translation business? _____ Why?
_____
_____

F. If the cost of the computer equipment decreased to $2,000, should Thelma buy the computer
equipment and start the translation business? _____ Why or why not? _____
_____

G. If the computer equipment was less productive than Thelma thought, so that her net income
was $22,500 per year, should Thelma buy the computer equipment and start the translation
business? _____ Why or why not?
_____

3. The Supply and Demand for Saving

In this problem you will use the supply and demand model to analyze the financial market for saving and investment. You will determine the equilibrium real interest rate and quantity of saving and determine the effects of changes in the government budget and technology on the market equilibrium.

Answer the questions below based on the following the supply and demand curves for saving.

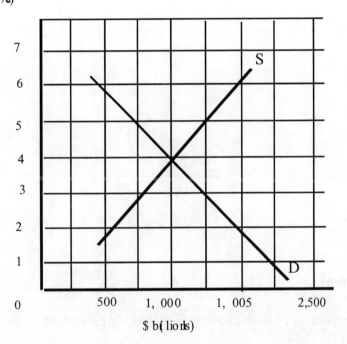

Rea Int rest
Rat (%)

$ b(lio ns)

A. The equilibrium real interest rate is _____ % and the equilibrium quantity of saving/ investment is $_____ billion.

B. An increase in the government budget surplus would cause the (supply/demand) _____ curve for saving to (increase/decrease) _____ . On the above graph, draw a new curve that would reflect the change caused by the increased government budget surplus.

C. As a result of the increased government budget surplus, the equilibrium real interest rate _____ and the equilibrium quantity of saving/investment _____ .

D. The introduction of new technologies that increase the marginal product of new capital would cause the (supply/demand) _____ curve for saving to (increase/decrease) _____ . On the above graph, draw a new curve that would reflect the change caused by the new technologies.

E. As a result of the new technologies, the equilibrium real interest rate _____ and the equilibrium quantity of saving/investment _____ .

Solutions
Self-Test: Key Terms

1. government budget deficit
2. national saving
3. liabilities
4. capital losses
5. crowding out
6. transfer payments
7. private saving
8. life-cycle saving
9. government budget surplus
10. saving
11. public saving
12. bequest saving
13. flow
14. saving rate
15. precautionary saving
16. wealth
17. stock
18. assets
19. capital gains

Self-Test: Multiple-Choice Questions

1. C His wealth increases by an amount equal to the saving plus the interest earned on the saving. Thus, $50 + $5 ($50 x .10) = $55
2. B
3. D
4. E
5. A
6. B
7. D If the interest rate is less than 10%, then the financial cost of the capital (equal to the amount of the loan times the interest rate) will be less than the financial benefit of the capital (equal to the net income earned with the capital).
8. B
9. A Debt is a type of liability, and reducing liabilities increase wealth.
10. C
11. E
12. C
13. D
14. A
15. C
16. B

17. E The financial benefit of the computer is $250. If the interest rate on the CD is less than 5%, the financial cost of the capital ($5,000 times the interest rate) would be less than the financial benefit of the computer. Therefore, if the interest rate on the CD is less than 5%, she should buy the computer.

18. A

19. B

20. C

Self-Test: Short Answer/Problems

1.

A.

Franklin's Balance Sheet

Assets		Liabilities	
Car	$7,500	Car loan	$6,000
Home	125,000	Mortgage	122,500
Checking account	750	Credit card balance	1,000
ABC Corp. shares	96,000	Student loan	2,500
Total	$ 229,250	Total	$132,000
		Net Worth	$ 97,250

B. He should pay off his credit card debt because it will reduce his liabilities and, thus, increase his wealth. The credit card debt has a higher opportunity cost (interest rate) than the student loan and he will save more in interest payments than he would earn on the CD account.

C. $525(= $500 + [$500 x.05]); $1,076.25 (= 525 + 500 + [1,025 x .05]); $1,655.06; $2,262.81; $2,900.95

D. $550; $1,155; $1,820.50; $2,552.55; $3,357.80

2.

A. $1,250 (Thelma would have to pay $3,750 [$25,000 x .15] in profit taxes, leaving her an after-tax income of $25,000 – $3,750 = $21,250. Subtracting the Spanish teacher salary [$20,000] that she must forego to start the translating business from the after-tax income [$21,250] equals the marginal product of the computer equipment.)

B. $600 (= $5,000 x .12)

C. Yes; Because the financial cost ($600 interest payment) is less than the financial benefit ($1,250 marginal product of the computer equipment).

D. $250 (The solution is the same as in 2A, except the tax rate is now .19.)

E. No; Because the financial cost ($600) is greater than the financial benefit ($250).

F. Yes; Because the financial cost ($240) is less than the financial benefit ($250).

G. No; Because the financial benefit has become negative ($ –1,775), and, therefore, is less than the financial cost.

3.

A. 4; $1,000 billion

B. supply; increase;

Rea Int rest
Rat (%)

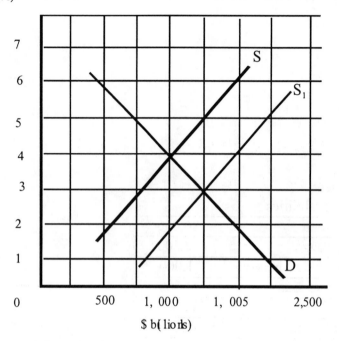

C. decreased; increased

D. demand; increase;

Rea Int rest
Rat (%)

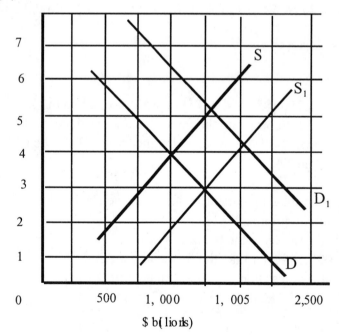

E. increased; increased

Chapter 11
Financial Markets, Money, and
the Federal Reserve

Key Point Review

The major financial markets and institutions, and their role in directing saving to productive use are discussed in the first part of this chapter. In the second part, money is introduced and measuring the quantity of money in the economy is discussed. The third part introduces the Federal Reserve and discusses some of its policy tools.

A successful economy not only saves but also uses its saving to invest in projects that are likely to be the most productive. In a market economy like that of the United States, savings are allocated by means of a decentralized, market-oriented financial system. A market-oriented financial system improves the allocation of savings by providing savers information about the uses of their funds that are most likely to prove productive, and by helping savers share the risks of individual investment projects. Three key components of a market-oriented financial system are discussed in this chapter: (1) the banking systems, (2) the bond market, and (3) the stock market.

Commercial banks are privately owned firms that accept deposits from individuals and businesses and use those deposits to make loans; they are the most important financial intermediaries in the banking system. **Financial intermediaries** are firms that extend credit to borrowers using funds raised from savers. Savers are willing to hold bank deposits because banks (and other financial intermediaries) have a comparative advantage in information-gathering about lending opportunities that results in lower costs and better results than individual savers could achieve on their own. Banks also make it easier for households and business to make payments for goods and services.

In addition to obtaining funds from banks, corporations and governments can obtain funds in the bond market. Corporations and governments frequently raise funds by issuing bonds and selling them to savers. A **bond** is a legal promise to repay a debt, usually including both the **principal amount** (the amount originally lent) and regular interest payments. The promised interest rate when a bond is issued is called the **coupon rate**, which is paid to the bondholder in regular interest payments called **coupon payments**. The coupon rate must be sufficiently attractive to savers, depending upon the term, or length of time before the debt is fully repaid, and the risk that the borrower will not repay the debt. Bonds also differ in terms of their tax treatment. The interest on municipal bonds, issued by local governments, is exempt from federal income taxes and, thus, typically pays a lower coupon rate than do other comparable bonds. Bondholders do not have to hold bonds until they are to be repaid by the issuer because they can sell them in the bond market. The price (or market value) of a bond at any point in time is inversely related to interest rates being paid on comparable newly issued bonds.

Another important way of raising funds, but one that is restricted to corporations, is by issuing stock to the public. A share of **stock**, also called equity, is a claim to partial ownership of a firm. Stockholders receive returns on their financial investment in a firm through dividend payments and capital gains (the increase in the price of the stock). A **dividend** is a regular payment received by stockholders for each share that they own, as determined by the firm's management and is usually dependent on the firm's recent profits. The price of a share of stock at any point in time depends on the expected future dividends and capital gain, adjusted for the risk premium. **Risk premium** is the rate of return that financial investors require to hold risky assets minus the rate of return on safe assets.

Like banks, bond and stock markets provide a means of channeling funds from savers to borrowers with productive investment opportunities. Savers and their financial advisors search for high returns in the bond and stock markets and, thus, provide a powerful incentive to potential borrowers to use the funds productively. The markets also give savers a means to diversify their financial investments. **Diversification** is the practice of spreading one's wealth over a variety of different financial investments in order to reduce overall risk. From society's perspective, diversification makes it possible for risky but worthwhile projects to obtain funding without individual savers having to bear too much risk. For the typical saver, a convenient way to diversify is buy stocks and bonds indirectly through mutual funds. A **mutual fund** is a financial intermediary that sells shares in itself to the public, then uses the funds raised to buy a wide variety of financial assets.

Although many people own stocks and bonds, a far greater percentage of people own money. **Money** is any asset that can be used in making purchases. Money has three principal uses: it serves as a medium of exchange, a unit of account, and a store of value. Money serves as a **medium of exchange** when it is used to purchase goods and services. Without money, all economic transactions would have to be in the form of **barter**, that is the direct trade of goods and services for other goods and services. Barter is inefficient because it requires that both parties to a trade have something the other party wants, a so-called double coincidence of wants. Money facilitates more efficient transactions and permits individuals to specialize in producing particular goods and services. As a **unit of account**, money is the basic yardstick for measuring economic value. As a **store of value** money serves as a means of holding wealth.

When measuring the quantity of money in the economy, economists vary as to how they define the concept of money. The narrowest definition of the amount of money in the United States is called **M1**, the sum of currency outstanding and balances held in checking accounts. A broader measure of the money supply is **M2**, which includes all the assets in M1 plus savings deposits, small-denomination time deposits, and money market mutual funds. Because the definition of the money supply includes both currency and bank deposits, the amount of money is the economy depends in part on the behavior of commercial banks and their depositors. When households or businesses deposit currency into a bank, the currency becomes a part of the bank reserves. **Bank reserves** are cash or similar assets held by commercial banks for the purpose of meeting depositor withdrawals and payments. When banks must keep bank reserves equal to the amount of their deposits, it is referred to as a **100% reserve banking** system. If banks can maintain a **reserve/deposit ratio** (bank reserves divided by deposits) of less than 100%, then it is referred to as a **fractional-reserve banking system**. In a fractional-reserve banking system the amount of the money supply is expanded when banks make loans in the form of new deposits.

The **Federal Reserve System**, often called the Fed, is the central bank of the United States and is responsible for monetary policy, as well as oversight and regulation of financial markets. The leadership of the Fed is provided by its **Board of Governors**, consisting of seven members appointed by the President to staggered fourteen-year terms. Decisions about monetary policy are made by the **Federal Open Market Committee** (FOMC), which is made up of the seven members of the Board of Governors, the President of the Federal Reserve Bank of New York, and four of the presidents of the other Federal Reserve Banks. The Fed's primary responsibility is making monetary policy, which involves decisions about the appropriate size of the nation's money supply. The Fed controls the money supply indirectly by changing the amount of reserves held by commercial banks. The Fed affects the amount of reserves through open-market operations, discount window lending, and changing reserve requirements.

Open-market operations, the most important tool of monetary policy, includes **open-market purchases** of government bonds from the public for the purpose of increasing the supply of banks reserves and the money supply, and **open-market sales** of government bonds to the public for the purpose of reducing bank reserves and the money supply. **Discount window lending** of reserves by the Fed to commercial banks is the second tool the Fed uses to affect bank reserves. When the Fed lends reserves the quantity of reserves in the banking system is directly increased and, ultimately, bank deposits and the money supply can increase. The **discount rate** is the interest rate the Fed charges commercial banks to borrow reserves. The Fed can also affect the amount of reserves in the banking system by changing the reserve requirements. **Reserve requirements** are the minimum values of the ratio of bank reserves to bank deposits that commercial banks are allowed to maintain. Although the Fed has the authority to change reserve requirements to affect the money supply, it seldom uses it in this way.

Besides controlling the money supply, the Fed has the responsibility (along with other government agencies) of ensuring that financial markets operate smoothly. Historically, in the United States, banking panics were the most disruptive type of recurrent financial crisis. A **banking panic** is an episode in which depositors, spurred by news or rumors of the imminent bankruptcy of one or more banks, rush to withdraw their deposits from the banking system. The Fed, established in 1913 in response to a particularly severe banking panic in 1907, was given the power to supervise and regulate banks to create greater confidence in banks, and was allowed to lend cash to banks to help them meet withdrawals during a bank panic. Following the creation of the Fed there were no bank panics until 1930. During 1930-33, however, the United States experienced the worst and most protracted series of bank panics in its history. The inability of the Fed to stop the bank panics of the 1930s caused Congress to institute a system of deposit insurance. Under a system of **deposit insurance**, the government guarantees depositors that they will get their money back even if the bank goes bankrupt, eliminating the incentive of depositors to withdraw their deposits when rumors of financial trouble are circulating.

Knowledge and Skills

The student must master the knowledge and skills listed below each number topic.	Key Terms	Multiple-Choice Questions	Short Answer/ Problems
1. The Financial System			
A. Explain how market-oriented financial systems improve the allocation of saving		1, 17	
B. Define financial intermediaries and discuss their comparative advantage	11	2	
C. Define bond, principal amount, coupon rate and coupon payment	1, 8, 21, 27		
D. Discuss the factors affecting the coupon rate and price of a bond		3, 17	1
E. Define stock dividend, and risk premium	4, 13, 25		
F. Discuss the factors affecting stock price		4	1
G. Define diversification and mutual fund	2, 16		
2. Money			
A. Define money and barter	15, 23	5	
B. Define and discuss the 3 functions of money	12, 28, 32	6, 19	
C. Identify the components of M1 and M2	7, 18	7	
D. Calculate the amount of M1 and M2			2
3. Commercial Banks and Money Creation			
A. Define bank reserves, 100% reserve banking, reserve/deposit ratio, and fractional reserve banking system	3, 19, 24, 30	8	
B. Calculate bank reserve/deposit ratio		9	3
C. Calculate the maximum amount a bank can lend and the effect of lending on M1		10	3
4. The Federal Reserve System			
A. Define the Federal Reserve System, Board of Governors, and Federal Open-Market Committee and discuss the structure of each component of the Fed	9, 14, 22		
B. Define open-market operations, open-market purchase, and open-market sale	5, 26, 31		
C. Define discount window lending and discount rate	10, 29		
D. Define reserve requirements	17		
E. Explain how the Fed uses the tools of monetary policy to change the amount of bank reserves and the money supply		11, 12, 13, 14	3

The student must master the knowledge and skills listed below each number topic.	Key Terms	Multiple-Choice Questions	Short Answer/ Problems
F. Define bank panic and deposit insurance	6, 20		
G. Explain the Fed's role in stabilizing financial markets		16, 20	

Self-Test: Key Terms

Use the terms below to complete the following sentences. (Answers are given at the end of the chapter.)

100% reserve banking
bank reserves
banking panic
barter
Board of Governors of the Federal Reserve System
bond
coupon payments
coupon rate
deposit insurance
discount rate
discount window lending
diversification
dividend
Federal Open Market Committee
Federal Reserve System
fractional-reserve banking system
M1
M2
medium of exchange
money
mutual fund
open-market operations
open-market purchase
open-market sale
principal amount
reserve requirements
reserve/deposit ratio
risk premium
stock
store of value
unit of account

1. The promised interest rate when a bond is issued is called the _Coupon Rate_ .
2. An investor can reduce the overall risk of investing through _____ .
3. Cash or similar assets held by commercial banks for the purpose of meeting depositor withdrawals and payments are called _____ .
4. The rate of return that financial investors require to hold risky assets minus the rate of return on safe assets is the _____ .
5. The most important tool of monetary policy used by the Fed is _____ .
6. The incentive for depositors to withdraw their deposits when rumors of financial trouble are circulating is eliminated when banks have _____ .
7. The sum of currency outstanding and balances held in checking accounts equals

   _____ .

8. Unlike individuals, corporations and governments can frequently raise funds by issuing a

   _____ .

9. Monetary policy, as well as oversight and regulation of the financial markets, is the responsibility of the _____ .
10. The Fed lends reserves to banks through _____ .
11. Firms that extend credit to borrowers using funds raised from savers are called

    _____ .

12. When money serves as a means of holding wealth it is serving the function of

    _____ .

13. The price of a share of stock at any point in time depends on the expected future capital gain and _____ , adjusted for the risk premium.
14. The seven members of the Fed's Board of Governors, the President of the Federal Reserve Bank of New York, and four of the presidents of the other Federal Reserve Banks make up the _____ .
15. Without money, all economic transactions would have to be in the form of

    _____ .

16. For the typical saver, a convenient way to diversify is buy stocks and bonds indirectly through a(n) _____ .
17. The Fed seldom uses_____ to alter the amount of bank reserves and the money supply.
18. The assets in M1 plus savings deposits, small-denomination time deposits, and money market mutual funds equal _____ .
19. If banks can maintain a reserve/deposit ratio of less than 100%, then the banking system is a

    _____ .

20. Historically, in the U.S., the most disruptive type of recurrent financial crisis was caused by a

    _____ .

21. The regular interest payments paid to the bondholder are called the _____ .
22. The leadership of the Fed is provided by the _____ .
23. Although many people own stocks and bonds, a far greater percentage own a type of special financial asset economists call _____ .
24. When banks must keep bank reserves equal to the amount of their deposits, it is referred to as a(n) _____ system.

25. An important way of raising funds, but one that is restricted to corporations, is by issuing _____ to the public.

26. In order to reduce bank reserves and the money supply, the Fed would complete a(n) _____ of government bonds.

27. The amount originally lent by a bondholder to a corporation or government is called the _____ .

28. When money is used to buy a car, it serves the function of _____ .

29. The interest rate the Fed charges commercial banks to borrow reserves is called the _____ .

30. Bank reserves divided by deposits equals the _____ .

31. If the Fed wants to increase the supply of bank reserves and the money supply, it should implement a(n) _____ .

32. Because money is the basic yardstick for measuring economic value is serves as a(n) _____ .

Self-Test: Multiple-Choice Questions

Circle the letter that corresponds to the best answer. (Answers are given at the end of the chapter.)

1. A market-oriented financial system is an effective mechanism for channeling funds from savers to borrowers with productive investment opportunities because it
   A. reduces the risk faced by each saver.
   B. shift the risk of investing from borrowers to savers.
   C. pools the costs of gathering information about prospective borrowers.
   D. diversifies the risk of investing.
   E. facilitates the direct lending of funds by savers to borrowers.

2. A feature common to all financial intermediaries is that they
   A. buy and sell information about savers and borrowers.
   B. have a comparative advantage in gathering and evaluating information about borrowers.
   C. act as agents for buyers and sellers in the money market.
   D. shift the risk of investing from borrowers to savers.
   E. collect funds from a few savers and distribute the funds to many borrowers.

3. In comparison to a corporate bond, a municipal bond of the same term and credit risk will have a
   A. higher risk premium.
   B. higher coupon payment.
   C. higher coupon rate.
   D. lower coupon rate.
   E. same coupon rate.

4. The price of a share of corporate stock varies over time depending upon stockholders'
    expectations about the future
    A. coupon rate, risk premium, and coupon payment.
    B. dividend, stock price, and coupon rate.
    C. coupon payment, dividend and risk premium.
    D. coupon rate, coupon premium and dividend.
    E. dividend, stock price, and risk premium

5. Double coincidence of wants is avoided if money is used as a
    A. medium of exchange.
    B. measure of value.
    C. standard of deferred payment.
    D. store of value
    E. tool of monetary policy.

6. Money serves as a basic yardstick for measuring economic value (i.e., a unit of account),
    allowing
    A. people to hold their wealth in a liquid form.
    B. governments to restrict the issuance of private monies.
    C. easy comparison of the relative prices of goods and services.
    D. goods and services to be exchanged with a double coincidence of wants.
    E. private money to be issued for local use.

7. M1 differs from M2 in that
    A. M1 includes currency and balances held in checking accounts, which are not included in
        M2.
    B. M2 includes savings deposits, small-denomination time deposits, and money market
        mutual funds which are not included in M1
    C. M2 includes small savings accounts, large time deposits, and money market mutual funds
        that are not included in M1.
    D. M1 is a broader measure of the money supply than M2.
    E. the assets in M2 are more liquid than the assets in M1.

8. When a bank makes a loan by crediting the borrower's checking account balance with an
    amount equal to the loan
    A. money is created.
    B. the bank gains new reserves.
    C. the bank immediately loses reserves.
    D. money is destroyed.
    E. the Fed has made an open-market purchase.

9. If a bank's desired reserve/deposit ratio is .33 and it has deposit liabilities of $100 million and reserves of $50 million, it
   A. has too few reserves and will reduce its lending.
   B. has too many reserves and will increase its lending.
   C. has the correct amount of reserves and outstanding loans.
   D. should increase the amount of its reserves.
   E. should decrease the amount of its reserves.

10. If the reserve/deposit ratio is .25 and the banking system receives an additional $10 million in reserves, bank deposits can increase by a maximum of
    A. $10 million.
    B. $250 million.
    C. $400 million.
    D. $4 million.
    E. $40 million.

11. The most important tool of monetary policy is
    A. reserve requirement ratios.
    B. the discount rate.
    C. open-market operations.
    D. the minimum net worth required of banks.
    E. market interest rates.

12. When the Fed sells government securities, the banks'
    A. reserves will increase and lending will expand, causing an increase in the money supply.
    B. reserves will decrease and lending will contract, causing a decrease in the money supply.
    C. reserve requirements will increase and lending will contract, causing a decrease in the money supply.
    D. reserves/deposit ratio will increase and lending will expand, causing an increase in the money supply.
    E. reserves/deposit ratio will decrease and lending will contract, causing an increase in the money supply.

13. An open-market purchase of government securities by the Fed will
    A. increase bank reserves, and the money supply will increase.
    B. decrease bank reserves, and the money supply will increase.
    C. increase bank reserves, and the money supply will decrease.
    D. decrease bank reserves, and the money supply will decrease.
    E. increase bank reserves, and the money supply will not change.

14. When banks borrow funds via the Fed's discount window
    A. interest rates rise.
    B. the reserve/deposit ratio falls.
    C. bank reserves are increased and, ultimately, bank deposits and the money supply increase.
    D. bank reserves are decreased and, ultimately, bank deposits and the money supply increase.
    E. bank reserves are increased and, ultimately, bank deposits and the money supply decrease.

15. When an individual deposits currency into a checking account
    A. bank reserves increase, which allows banks to lend more and, ultimately, increases the money supply.
    B. bank reserves decrease, which reduces the amount banks can lend thereby reducing the growth of the money supply.
    C. bank reserves are unchanged.
    D. bank reserves decrease, which increases the amount banks can lend, thereby increasing the growth of the money supply.
    E. bank reserves increase, which reduces the amount banks can lend, thereby reducing the growth of the money supply.

16. Deposit insurance for banks
    A. helped the Fed combat the bank panics of 1930-33.
    B. was first legislated by the Federal Reserve Bank Act of 1913.
    C. may induce the managers of banks to take more risks.
    D. guarantees the interest payments on depositors' checking accounts.
    E. is a perfect solution to the problem of bank panics.

17. The informational role of the stock and bond markets provides incentives for savers and their financial advisors to
    A. direct funds to those borrowers that appear to have the safest investments.
    B. direct funds to those borrowers that appear to have the most productive investments.
    C. diversify their investments by purchasing mutual funds.
    D. shift the risk of investing to the borrowers.
    E. avoid the cost of paying the financial intermediaries by going directly to the borrowers to make loans.

18. Antonio holds a two-year bond issued by the Jetson Corporation with a principal amount of $10,000. The annual coupon rate is 6 percent. He considered selling it after receiving the first coupon payment a week ago at a price of $9,390. Since that time, the coupon rate on new bond issues has risen from 6.5% to 7.0%. If he were to sell the bond today, the price would be
    A. $10,000.
    B. higher than it was a week ago.
    C. the same at it was a week ago.
    D. lower than it was a week ago.
    E. impossible to determine from the information given.

19. Holding money as a store of wealth has the advantage of being useful as a medium of exchange and being anonymous. The disadvantages of holding your wealth in the form of money are that it
   A. may be stolen or lost, and people may think you're a smuggler or drug dealer.
   B. is difficult to trace and may be lost or stolen.
   C. may be lost or stolen and usually pays no interest.
   D. pays no interest and is difficult to trace.
   E. pays no interest and people may think you're a smuggler or drug dealer.

20. During the bank panic of 1930-33, the public withdrew deposits from the bank preferring to hold currency. As a result,
   A. bank reserves decreased but were offset by an equal increase in currency, with no net effect on the money supply.
   B. bank reserves increased by less than the increase in currency, causing the money supply to decrease.
   C. bank reserves decreased by more than the increase in currency, causing the money supply to decrease.
   D. bank reserves decreased by less than the increase in currency, causing the money supply to increase.
   E. bank reserves decrease by an amount equal to the increase in currency, causing the money supply to decrease.

Self-Test: Short Answer/Problems
(Answers and solutions are given at the end of the chapter.)

1. Bond and Stock Prices
This problem will require you to calculate the effects of various factors on the price of bonds and stocks.

A. Carley has purchased a newly issued bond from the SimonSays Corp. for $10,000. The SimonSays Corp. will pay the bondholder $750 at the end of years 1-4 and will pay $10,750 at the end of year 5. The bond has a principal amount of $_____, a term of _____ years, a coupon rate of _____ %, and a coupon payment of $_____ .

B. After receiving coupon payments 1 through 4, Carley has decided to sell the bond. What price should she expect to receive if the one-year interest rate on comparable financial assets is 5%? $_____ What price should she expect to receive if the one-year interest rate on comparable financial assets is 8%? $_____

C. Justin has decided to buy 100 shares of stock in The Boot Company. He expects the company to pay a dividend of $3 per share in one year and expects the price of the shares will be $40 at that time. How much should he be willing to pay today per share if the safe rate of interest is 7% and The Boot Company carries no risk? $_____

D. How much should Justin be willing to pay today per share if the safe rate of interest is 5% and The Boot Company carries no risk? $_____

E. How much should Justin be willing to pay today per share if the safe rate of interest is 5% and he requires a risk premium of 2%? $_____

2. Measuring the Money Supply

In this problem you will practice calculating the measures of the U.S. money supply—Ml and M2.

Month/Year	Currency	Savings deposits	Demand and other Checkable deposits	Money market mutual funds	Small time deposits
1/2000	$523.0	$1735.6	$588.6	$857.7	$961.3
2/2000	517.3	1751.7	574.4	860.6	966.8
3/2000	517.1	1761.3	586.3	874.4	972.5
4/2000	518.2	1774.4	589.4	888.3	981.2

Source: Federal Reserve Bank of St. Louis. All figures are in billions of dollars.

A. Use the preceding data to complete the following table, calculating the amounts for Ml and M2 for January through April 2000.

Month/Year	M1	M2
1/2000		
2/2000		
3/2000		
4/2000		

B. (b) If the public transfers funds from their (small) savings accounts at the Township Savings and Loan Association to their checking accounts at the VillageBank, this will (increase/decrease/leave unchanged)_____ M1, and (increase/decrease/leave unchanged)_____ M2.

C. (c) If the public deposits currency into their checking accounts at VillageBank, this will (increase/decrease/leave unchanged) _____ Ml, and (increase/ decrease/leave unchanged) _____ M2.

3. Reserve/Deposit Ratio, Open-Market Operations, and Money Creation

In this problem you will calculate reserve/deposit ratios, determine how much a bank can lend based on its reserves, deposit liabilities and reserve/deposit ratio, and determine the effect of open-market sales and purchases of government securities on a bank's ability to lend and create money. Each question refers back to balance sheet of The Bank of Haute Finance show below (i.e., do not take into account the transaction indicated in Questions 3A-3C when answering Questions 3B-3D).

Balance Sheet of
The Bank of Haute Finance

Assets	Liabilities
Currency (= reserves) $10,000	Deposits $10,000

A. If The Bank of Haute Finance has a desired reserve/deposit ratio of 10%, it can make new loans of $_____ in the form of new _____. After making the new loans The Bank of Haute Finance will have total deposit liabilities of $_____ , currency (= reserves) of $_____ , and outstanding loans of $_____ . Its total assets will then equal $_____ and its total liabilities will equal $_____ .

B. If the Fed imposes a minimum reserve/deposit ratio in the form of a 20% reserve requirement, the maximum amount of new loans The Bank of Haute Finance could make would be $_____ . After making the new loans The Bank of Haute Finance would have total deposit liabilities of $_____ , currency (= reserves) of $_____ and outstanding loans of $_____ . Its total assets would then equal $_____ and its total liabilities would equal $_____ .

C. Assume the Federal Reserve System buys $3000 of government securities from Susan Slavin and she deposits the $3000 in her checking account at The Bank of Haute Finance. Following the deposit, The Bank of Haute Finance would have currency (= reserves) of $_____ and deposit liabilities of $_____ . Assuming the Fed maintains a minimum reserve/deposit ratio of 20%, The Bank of Haute Finance could make new loans of $_____ . By doing so it would (increase/decrease) _____ the money supply by $_____ .

D. Assume the Federal Reserve System sells $3000 of government securities to The Bank of Haute Finance which it pays for out of its reserves. After the sale of the government securities, The Bank of Haute Finance would have currency (= reserves) of $_____ and deposit liabilities of $_____ . Assuming the Fed maintains a minimum reserve/deposit ratio of 20%, The Bank of Haute Finance could make new loans of $_____ . By doing so it would (increase/decrease) _____ the money supply by $_____ .

E. In comparing the answers to Questions 3B and 3D, by selling $3,000 of government securities to The Bank of Haute Finance, the Fed would be able to reduce the growth in the supply of money by $_____ .

Solutions
Self-Test: Key Terms

1. coupon rate
2. diversification
3. bank reserves
4. risk premium
5. open-market operations
6. deposit insurance
7. M1
8. bond
9. Federal Reserve System
10. discount window lending
11. financial intermediaries
12. store of value
13. dividend
14. Federal Open Market Committee
15. barter
16. mutual fund
17. reserve requirements
18. M2
19. fractional-reserves banking system
20. banking panic
21. coupon payments
22. Board of Governors of the Federal Reserve System
23. money
24. 100% reserve banking
25. stock
26. open-market sale
27. principal amount
28. medium of exchange
29. discount rate
30. reserve/deposit ratio
31. open-market purchase
32. unit of account

Self-Test: Multiple-Choice Questions

1. D
2. B
3. D Because municipal bonds are exempt from federal income taxes, they have a lower coupon rate than comparable nonmunicipal bonds.
4. E
5. A
6. C

7. B
8. A
9. B With $50 million in reserves and $100 million in deposits, its reserve/deposit ratio of 1/2 is greater than its desired ratio. It would, therefore, increase its deposits to $150 million by making new loans.
10. E $10 million in new reserves divided by $40 million in new deposits equals .25 (the reserve/deposit ratio)
11. C
12. B
13. A
14. C
15. A
16. C
17. B
18. D Because the interest rate and the price of a bond are inversely related, the increase in the coupon rate on newly issued bonds causes the price of the bond to fall.
19. C
20. E Because each dollar of bank reserves translates into several dollars of money supply, the decrease in bank reserves is equal to the increase in currency caused the money supply to decrease.

Self-Test: Short Answer/Problems

1.
A. $10,000; 5; 7.5%; $750
B. $10,750 / 1.05 = $10, 238.10; $9,953.70
C. $43 / 1.07 = $40.95
D. $43 / 1.05 = $40.19
E. $43 / (1.05 + .02) = $40.19

2.
A.

Month/Year	M1	M2
1/2000	$1,111.6	$4,666.2
2/2000	$1,091.7	$4,670.8
3/2000	$1,103.4	$4,711.6
4/2000	$1,107.6	$4,751.5

B. increase; leave unchanged (because the components of M1 are also included in M2)
C. leave unchanged; leave unchanged (currency and checking deposits are included in both M1 and M2. Thus, depositing currency into a checking account does not change the amount of M1 or M2.)

3.

A. $90,000 (Because the desired reserve/deposit ratio is .10 the $10,000 in reserves can support $10,000/.10 = $100,000 in deposits. Thus, $100,000 minus the existing $10,000 in deposits = $90,000); checking deposits; $100,000; $10,000; $90,000; $100,000; $100,000

B. $40,000 (Now that the Fed has imposed a reserve requirements of .20, the $10,000 in reserves can support $10,000/.2 = $50,000. Thus, the bank can make new loan of $40,000); $50,000; $10,000; $40,000; $50,000; $50,000

C. $10,000 + $3,000 = $13,000; $13,000; $52,000 ($13,000/.2 = $65,000 from which the existing $13,000 is subtracted, allowing new loans of $52,000); increase; $52,000

D. $10,000 - $3,000 = $7,000; $7,000/.2 = $35,000 from which the existing $10,000 is subtracted, allowing new loans of $25,000; increase; $25,000

E. $50,000 - $25,000 = $25,000

Chapter 12
Short-term Economic Fluctuations:
An Introduction

Key Point Review

In the preceding section of the book, the factors that determine long-run economic growth and living standards were discussed. While long-run economic conditions are the ultimate determinant of living standards, short-run fluctuations in economic conditions are also important. The history, characteristics, and causes of the short-run fluctuations in economic conditions are discussed in this chapter.

The short-run fluctuations in economic conditions are commonly known as recessions and expansions. A **recession**, or contraction, is a period in which the economy is growing at a rate significantly below normal. An extremely severe or protracted recession is called a **depression**. A more informal definition of a recession (often used by the mass media) is a period during which real GDP falls for at least two consecutive quarters. While the "two consecutive quarters" rule would not classify a slow-growth episode as a recession, many economists would argue that a period in which real GDP growth is significantly below normal should be counted as a recession. The beginning of a recession is called a **peak**, the high point of economic activity prior to a downturn. The end of a recession, marking the low point of economic activity prior to a recovery, is called the **trough**. By far the longest and most severe recession in the United States was during 1929-33. Since World War II, U.S. recessions have generally been short, lasting between six and sixteen months. The opposite of a recession is an **expansion**; a period in which the economy is growing at a rate that is significantly above normal. A particularly strong and protracted expansion is called a **boom**. On average, expansions have lasted longer than recessions. The two longest expansions were during 1961-69, and the one following the trough of 1990-91 (in February, 2000 this boom broke the all-time record for the duration of a U.S. expansion).

Expansions and recessions are not new, as they have been a feature of industrial economies since at least the late 18th century. Short-run economic fluctuations, although they are sometimes referred to as business cycles, or cyclical fluctuations, do not recur at predictable intervals but rather are quite irregular in their length and severity. This irregularity makes it extremely hard to predict the dates of peaks and troughs. Expansions and recessions are felt throughout the economy, and even globally. Unemployment is a key indicator of short-term fluctuations, typically rising during recessions and falling (although more slowly) during expansions. Cyclical unemployment is the type of unemployment associated with recessions. In addition to rising unemployment, labor market conditions become more unfavorable during recessions, with real wages growing more slowly and workers less likely to receive promotions or bonuses. Inflation also follows a typical pattern during recessions and expansions, though not as sharply defined. Recessions tend to be preceded by increases in inflation, and followed soon after by a decline in the rate of inflation. Durable goods industries tend to be more affected by recessions and expansions, while services and nondurable goods industries are less sensitive to short-term economic fluctuations.

Economists measure expansions and recessions by determining how far output is from its normal level. The normal level of output is called **potential output** (also known as potential GDP or full-employment output): the amount of output (real GDP) that an economy can produce when using its resources, such as capital and labor, at normal rates. Actual output (real GDP) may be below or above potential output at any point in time. The difference between potential output and actual output is called the **output gap**. The output gap is expressed in symbols as Y^* - Y. A positive output gap, when actual output is below potential output and resources are not fully utilized, is called a **recessionary gap**. A negative output gap, when actual output is above potential output and resources are utilized at above-normal rates, is called an **expansionary gap**.

Recessionary gaps are associated with below normal utilization of labor resources. This is another way of saying there is extra unemployment during recessions. Specifically, in addition to the frictional and structural unemployment, which are always present in the labor market, cyclical unemployment is present during recessions. Economists call that part of the total unemployment rate that is attributable to frictional and structural unemployment the **natural rate of unemployment.** The natural rate of unemployment can vary over time because of changes in frictional and/or structural unemployment. The natural rate of unemployment is the unemployment rate that prevails when cyclical unemployment is zero. Cyclical unemployment can, therefore, be calculated as the difference between the actual unemployment rate (u) and the natural rate of unemployment (u^*). During recessions cyclical unemployment is positive, and during expansions it is negative. The relationship between the output gap and the amount of cyclical unemployment is given by Okun's Law. **Okun's Law** states that each extra percentage point of cyclical unemployment is associated with about a two-percentage point increase in the output gap. The output losses calculated according to Okun's Law suggest that recessions have significant costs (which are reflected, for example, in the importance that short-run economic fluctuations have on presidential elections in the United States).

The chapter concludes with preview of the causes of recessions and expansions, which are discussed in greater detail in the next three chapters. Briefly, in the short run, prices do not always adjust immediately to changing demand or supply as some producers vary the quantity of output rather than price, meeting the demand at a preset price. In the short run, therefore, changes in economy-wide spending are the primary cause of output gaps. In the long run, however, prices will adjust to their market-clearing levels, as producers better understand the information provided by the market, and output will equal potential output. The quantities of inputs, and the productivity with which they are used, are the primary determinants of economic activity in the long run. While total spending in the economy affects output in the short run, in the long run its main effects are on prices.

Knowledge and Skills

The student must master the knowledge and skills listed below each number topic.	Key Terms	Multiple-Choice Questions	Short Answer/ Problems
1. Recessions and Expansions			
A. Define recession, depression, expansion, boom, peak, and trough	1, 4, 6, 8, 10, 11		
B. Identify the periods and characteristics of historically important recessions and expansions		1, 10, 17	
C. Discuss the characteristics of short-term economic fluctuations		2, 11, 18	
D. Explain unemployment and inflation patterns during recessions and expansions		3, 12	
2. Measuring Fluctuations			
A. Define potential output, output gap, recessionary gap and expansionary gap	2, 5, 7, 12	14	1
B. Identify the causes of output gaps		4, 8, 13	
C. Define the natural rate of unemployment and explain its relationship to cyclical unemployment	9	19	
D. Explain why the natural rate of unemployment may change over time		5, 20	
E. Define Okun's Law	3		
F. Calculate the effect of cyclical unemployment on the output gap		6	
3. Why Short-run Fluctuations Occur			
A. Explain what "meeting the demand" means		7, 15	
B. Explain how price changes eliminate output gaps in the long run		9, 16	

Self-Test: Key Terms
Use the terms below to complete the following sentences. (Answers are given at the end of the chapter.)

boom
depression
expansion
expansionary gap
natural rate of unemployment
Okun's Law
output gap
peak
potential output
recession
recessionary gap
trough

1. A particularly strong and protracted expansion is called a _____ .
2. The amount of output (real GDP) that an economy can produce when using its resources, such as capital and labor, at normal rates is the _____ .
3. A one-percentage point increase in cyclical unemployment is associated with about a two-percentage point increase in the output gap, according to _____ .
4. An extremely severe or protracted recession is called a _____ .
5. When actual output is above potential output and resources are utilized at above-normal rates, there is a(n) _____ .
6. The end of a recession is marked by a(n) _____ .
7. The difference between potential output and actual output equals the _____ .
8. A period in which the economy is growing at a rate significantly below normal is a(n) _____ .
9. When cyclical unemployment is zero, the rate of unemployment equals the _____ .
10. The high point of economic activity prior to a downturn is called a(n) _____ .
11. A period in which the economy is growing at a rate that is significantly above normal is a(n) _____ .
12. When Y* is greater than Y, a(n) _____ exists.

Self-Test: Multiple-Choice Questions
Circle the letter that corresponds to the best answer. (Answers are given at the end of the chapter.)

1. The longest and most severe recession in the United States was during
   August 1957 to February 1961, initiating what became known as the Great Depression.
   A. November 1973 to March 1975, initiating what became known as the Great Depression.
   B. May 1937 to June 1938, initiating what became known as the Great Depression.
   C. January 1980 to November 1982, initiating what became known as the Great Depression.
   D. August 1929 to March 1933, initiating what became known as the Great Depression.

2. Short-term economic fluctuations
   A. recur at predictable intervals.
   B. have a limited impact on a few industries or regions.
   C. contain peaks and troughs that are easily predicted by the professional forecasters.
   D. are irregular in their length and severity.
   E. have little impact on unemployment and inflation.

3. Unemployment typically
   A. is unaffected by recessions and expansions.
   B. rises during recession and falls during expansions.
   C. falls during recessions and rises during expansions.
   D. rises during recessions and falls during expansions, as does inflation.
   E. falls during recessions and rises during expansions, as does inflation.

4. The Japanese economy slowed markedly during the 1990s due to
   A. faster growth in potential output combined with a significant output gap.
   B. slower growth in potential output, and actual output equal to potential output.
   C. slower growth in potential output combined with a significant output gap.
   D. faster growth in potential output, and actual output equal to potential output.
   E. normal growth in potential output combined with a significant output gap.

5. As the average age of U.S. workers has increased since 1980
   A. frictional unemployment has fallen and the natural rate of unemployment has decreased.
   B. cyclical unemployment has fallen and the natural rate of unemployment has decreased.
   C. structural unemployment has fallen and the natural rate of unemployment has decreased.
   D. frictional unemployment has risen and the natural rate of unemployment has increased.
   E. cyclical unemployment has risen and the natural rate of unemployment has increased.

6. If cyclical unemployment rises to 2.5% and potential output (GDP) equals $9,000 billion, the output gap would equal
   A. $22,500 billion.
   B. $225 billion.
   C. $9,000 billion.
   D. $8,775 billion.
   E. $9,225 billion.

7. The firm behavior known as "meeting the demand," refers to
   A. firms adjusting prices from moment to moment in response to changes in demand.
   B. firms adjusting prices continuously in order to ensure that the quantity supplied equals the quantity demanded.
   C. changes in economy-wide spending as the primary cause of output gaps.
   D. price changes that eliminate output gaps in a self-correcting market.
   E. firms adjusting prices only periodically, while in the short run varying the quantity of output.

8. A recessionary gap occurs when
   A. total spending is abnormally high.
   B. total spending is at normal levels, but potential output is growing at abnormally high levels.
   C. total spending is low for some reason.
   D. potential output is less than actual output.
   E. actual output is greater than potential output.

9. The self-correcting market mechanism eliminates output gaps over time though price
   A. decreases if demand exceeds potential output.
   B. increases if demand is less than potential output.
   C. decreases if an expansionary gap exists.
   D. decreases if recessionary gap exists.
   E. increases if recessionary gap exists.

10. The longest expansion in the U.S. economy
    A. began in August 1929, at the trough of the Great Depression.
    B. lasted 106 months.
    C. began in March 1991, at the trough of the 1990-91 recession.
    D. lasted 92 months.
    E. began in February 1961, at the trough of the 1960-61 recession.

11. On average, recessions in the United States have been
    A. shorter than expansions.
    B. longer than expansions.
    C. longer and more severe during the post-WWII period than prior to WWII.
    D. shorter but more severe during the post-WWII period than prior to WWII.
    E. equal in duration to expansions.

12. During short-term economic fluctuations, inflation tends to
    A. rise following an economic peak and fall soon after the trough.
    B. fall following an economic peak and rise soon after the trough.
    C. rise following an economic peak and rise soon after the trough.
    D. fall following an economic peak and rise soon after the trough.
    E. move in the same direction as unemployment.

13. An economy grows significantly below its normal rate when
    A. actual output is above potential output.
    B. actual output equals potential output, but potential output is growing very slowly.
    C. actual output equals potential output, but potential output is growing very rapidly.
    D. actual output is below potential output and potential output is growing very rapidly.
    E. actual output is above potential output and potential output is growing very rapidly.

14. An expansionary gap implies that resources are
    A. not being fully utilized and the unemployment rate would be above the natural rate of unemployment.
    B. being utilized at above-normal rates and the unemployment rate would be above the natural rate of unemployment.
    C. not being fully utilized and the unemployment rate would be below the natural rate of unemployment.
    D. being utilized at above-normal rates and cyclical unemployment is positive.
    E. being utilized at above-normal rates and cyclical unemployment is negative.

15. In some markets, such as the market for grain, price-setting by auction occurs, but in other markets it does not because
    A. there are not enough auctioneers to announce prices for all the markets.
    B. auctions are inefficient when there are a small number of customers and low sales volume at any given time.
    C. auctions are inefficient when a market has a large number of buyers and sellers and a large volume of standardized goods.
    D. auctions are not feasible when the goods are perishable (e.g., ice cream).
    E. the economic benefits of auctions are less than the economic costs of auctions in markets for perishable goods.

16. In the long run
    A. prices adjust to market-clearing levels, and output equals potential output.
    B. prices adjust to market-clearing levels, and output is less than potential output.
    C. prices adjust to market-clearing levels, and output is greater than potential output.
    D. output is primarily determined by economy-wide spending.
    E. the main effect of total spending is on output.

17. During the period1960-1999, inflation was at its highest level in the United States during the
    A. boom of 1961-69.
    B. expansion of 1982-90.
    C. expansion of 1990-99.
    D. recession of 1981-82.
    E. recession of 1973-75.

18. Recessions and expansions have a greater impact on
    A. inflation than on unemployment.
    B. frictional unemployment than on cyclical unemployment.
    C. structural unemployment than on cyclical unemployment.
    D. industries that produce durable goods than on service and nondurable goods industries.
    E. industries that produce services and nondurable goods than on durable goods industries.

19. The difference between the total unemployment rate and the natural rate of unemployment
    A. is positive during a recession.
    B. is negative during a recession.
    C. is positive during an expansion.
    D. represents that portion of total unemployment that economists call frictional
       unemployment.
    E. represents that portion of total unemployment that economists call structural
       unemployment.

20. Online job services have made labor markets more efficient and, thus, have contributed to
    A. a decline in cyclical unemployment.
    B. an increase in cyclical unemployment.
    C. a decline the natural rate of unemployment.
    D. an increase in the natural rate of unemployment.
    E. an increase in structural and frictional unemployment.

Self-Test: Short Answer/Problems
(Answers and solutions are given at the end of the chapter.)

1. Actual Output and Potential Output

This problem utilizes data on real GDP and potential GDP for the United States for the years 1994-1999, in billions of 1992 dollars, and will help you become more familiar with the concept of output gaps (recessionary and expansionary gaps).

Year	Real GDP	Potential GDP	Output Gap	Expansionary or Recessionary Gap?
1994	$6,611	$6,777		
1995	6,762	6,955		
1996	6,995	7,138		
1997	7,720	7,325		
1998	7,553	7,517		
1999	7,883	7,714		

A. Complete column 4 of the above table by calculating the size of the output gap for 1994 through 1999 (be sure to include a plus sign if a positive gap, or a minus sign if negative gap).
B. In column 5 of the above table, identify whether the output gap was a recessionary gap or an expansionary gap for each year.

Solutions
Self-Test: Key Terms

1. boom
2. potential output
3. Okun's Law
4. depression
5. expansionary gap
6. trough
7. output gap
8. recession
9. natural rate of unemployment
10. peak
11. expansion
12. recessionary gap

Self-Test: Multiple-Choice Questions

1. E
2. D
3. C
4. C
5. A
6. B $9,000 billion times .025 = $225 billion
7. E
8. C
9. D
10. C
11. A
12. D
13. B
14. E
15. B
16. A
17. D
18. C
19. A
20. C

Self-Test: Short Answer/Problems

1.

A., B.

Year	Real GDP	Potential GDP	Output Gap	Expansionary or Recessionary Gap?
1994	$6,611	$6,777	$166	Expansionary gap
1995	6,762	6,955	$193	Expansionary gap
1996	6,995	7,138	$143	Expansionary gap
1997	7,720	7,325	($395)	Recessionary gap
1998	7,553	7,517	($36)	Recessionary gap
1999	7,883	7,714	($169)	Recessionary gap

Chapter 13
Aggregate Demand and Output
in the Short Run

Key Point Review

In this chapter, the basic Keynesian model (also known as the Keynesian cross) is developed showing how recessions and expansions may arise from fluctuations in aggregate spending. The chapter first presents the two key assumptions of the model, then explains the important concept of aggregate demand, or total planned spending in the economy. After showing how aggregate demand helps to determine the level of output, the use of government policies to reduce or eliminate output gaps is discussed.

The Keynesian model is based on the ideas first developed by John Maynard Keynes (1883-1946) and published in *The General Theory of Employment, Interest and Money* (1936). The two key assumptions of the basic Keynesian model are (1) aggregate demand, or total planned spending in an economy, fluctuates depending on the prevailing level of real GDP (as well as other factors) and (2) in the short run, firms meet the demand for their products at preset prices. Firms change prices only if the benefits of doing so outweigh the **menu costs**, (i.e., the costs of changing prices).

The most important concept of the basic Keynesian model is aggregate demand. **Aggregate demand** (AD) is the total planned spending on final goods and services. AD is composed of four components: (1) consumer expenditures, or simply consumption (C), is spending by households on final goods and services; (2) investment (I) is spending by firms on new capital goods, residential investment, and increases in inventories; (3) government purchases (G) is spending by the federal, state and local governments on goods and services; and (4) net exports (NX), or exports minus imports, is sales of domestically produced goods and services to foreigners less purchases by domestic residents of goods and services produced abroad. Total planned spending may differ from actual spending. If, for example, a firm sells more of its output than it planned to sell, actual investment will be greater than planned investment and total actual spending will be greater than total planned spending. Assuming that actual spending for consumption, government purchases, and net exports equals planned spending, but that actual investment may not equal planned investment, the equation for aggregate demand is $AD = C + I^P + G + NX$, where I^P is planned investment spending.

Consumption, the largest component of AD, is affected by many factors, the most important being after-tax, or disposable, income. The relationship between consumption spending and its determinants, is referred to as the **consumption function** and is expressed by the equation $C = \overline{C} + c(Y - T)$, where $\overline{C}$ is a constant term intended to capture factors other than disposable income, and $(Y - T)$ represents disposable income, and c is a fixed number called the marginal propensity to consume. The **marginal propensity to consume**, or MPC, is the amount by which consumption rises when disposable income rises by one dollar, and is greater than 0 but less than 1 (i.e., $0 < c < 1$). The consumption function can also be show graphically, in which case $\overline{C}$ represents the intercept of the consumption function on the vertical axis and the MPC is the slope of the consumption function. The consumption function indicates that as disposable income rises, consumption spending will increase, but by a lesser amount.

Incorporating the consumption function into the equation for aggregate demand results in the expanded equation $AD = [\overline{C} + c(Y - T)] + I^P + G + NX$. Assuming the non-consumption components of AD are fixed quantities (denoted by an overbar), the equation can be rewritten as $AD = [\overline{C} + c(Y - \overline{T})] + \overline{I} + \overline{G} + \overline{NX}$. Grouping together those terms that depend on output (Y), and those that do not, yields the equation $AD = [\overline{C} + c\overline{T} + \overline{I} + \overline{G} + \overline{NX}] + cY$. This equation captures the key idea that as real output changes, aggregate demand changes with it, in the same direction. It also shows that aggregate demand can be divided into two parts, one portion that is determined outside the model called **autonomous aggregate demand**, and a second portion that is determined within the model (because it depends on output) called **induced aggregate demand**.

In the basic Keynesian model, the **short-run equilibrium output** is the level at which output, Y, equals aggregate demand, AD, and is the level of output that prevails during the period in which prices are predetermined. The short-run equilibrium output is determined where $Y = AD$, or equivalently $Y - AD = 0$. The short-run equilibrium output can be solved for numerically by first substituting the values for the autonomous aggregate demand and the MPC, then substituting Y for AD, and solving for Y. The short-run equilibrium output can also be determined graphically where the 45° line intersects the expenditure line. If output is less (greater) than the equilibrium level in the short run, when prices are pre-set and firms are committed to meeting their customers' demand, output will rise (fall).

A decrease in one or more of the components of autonomous aggregate demand will cause short-run equilibrium output to fall. The effect of a one-unit increase or decrease in autonomous aggregate demand on the short-run equilibrium output is called the **income-expenditure multiplier**, or the multiplier for short. In the basic Keynesian model, the multiplier equals $\dfrac{1}{1 - c}$. Because the basic Keynesian model omits some important features of the real economy, however, it tends to yield unrealistically high values of the multiplier.

According to the basic Keynesian model, inadequate spending is an important cause of recession. To fight recessions caused by insufficient aggregate demand, policymakers can use stabilization policies. **Stabilization policies** are government policies that are used to affect aggregate demand, with the objective of eliminating output gaps. There are two major types of stabilization policy, monetary policy and fiscal policy. This chapter focuses on fiscal policy, i.e., government spending and taxes. Keynes felt that changes in government spending were probably the most effective tool for reducing or eliminating output gaps. He argued that a recessionary gap could be eliminated by increases in government spending. Alternatively, a decrease in taxes (payments from the private sector to government) could eliminate a recessionary gap. Government spending can be in the form of government purchases of goods and services or transfer payments (payments from government to the private sector). Changes in government purchases directly change the amount of AD, whereas transfer payments and taxes only indirectly change AD by altering the amount of disposable income. The change in AD is equal to the change in taxes (or transfer payments) times the MPC. Because the MPC is a fraction, the change in taxes or transfer payments must be larger than the change in government purchases to cause the same change in AD.

While the basic Keynesian model suggests that fiscal policy can be used quite precisely to eliminate output gaps, in the real world it is more complicated than that. Using fiscal policy as a stabilization tool is complicated by the fact that fiscal policy may affect potential output as well as aggregate demand. Government spending, for example, on investments in public capital, (e.g., roads, airports, and schools) can play a major role in the growth of potential output. Taxes and transfer payments may affect the incentives, and thus the economic behavior, of households and firms that, in turn, affect potential output. In addition, fiscal policy is not always flexible enough to be useful for stabilization. Changes in government spending or taxation must usually go through a lengthy legislative process making it difficult to respond in a timely way to economic conditions. A second factor limiting the flexibility of fiscal policy is the fact that policymakers have many objectives besides stabilizing aggregate demand. Nevertheless, most economists view fiscal policy as an important stabilizing force in dealing with prolonged episodes of recession. The presence of **automatic stabilizers**, provisions in the law that call for automatic increases in government spending or decreases in taxes when real output declines, help to increase AD during recessions and reduce it during expansions, without the delays inherent in the legislative process.

Knowledge and Skills

The student must master the knowledge and skills listed below each number topic.	Key Terms	Multiple-Choice Questions	Short Answer/ Problems
1. The Basic Keynesian Model			
A. Explain the two key assumptions of the model		1, 13	
B. Define menu costs and discuss how they affect the decision to change prices	6	2	
C. Discuss John Maynard Keynes' contributions to economics		3	

The student must master the knowledge and skills listed below each number topic.	Key Terms	Multiple-Choice Questions	Short Answer/ Problems
2. Aggregate Demand (AD)			
A. Define aggregate demand	2		
B. Identify the components of AD		4	
C. Explain why planned spending may differ from actual spending		5, 14	
D. Define autonomous and induced aggregate demand	7, 10	15	
E. Define consumption function and marginal propensity to consume	1, 3		
F. Explain the relationship between the consumption function and aggregate demand		6, 7	1
3. Short-Run Equilibrium Output			
A. Define short-run equilibrium output	8	16, 17	
B. Explain how firms respond when output differs from the equilibrium value		8, 18	
C. Calculate the short-run equilibrium output			2, 4
D. Graphically identify the short-run equilibrium output			3
E. Numerically and graphically show how a decline in spending can cause a recessionary gap			3
F. Define the income-expenditure multiplier	5		3
G. Calculate the multiplier within the basic Keynesian model		9	
4. Stabilizing Aggregate Demand			
A. Define stabilization policy and automatic stabilizers	4, 9		
B. Discuss the use of fiscal policy to stabilize aggregate demand		10, 11, 19	
C. Calculate the effects of changes in government purchases, transfer payments and taxes on short-run equilibrium output			4
D. Discuss two qualifications related to the use of fiscal policy as a stabilization tool		12, 20	

Self-Test: Key Terms

Use the terms below to complete the following sentences. (Answers are given at the end of the chapter.)

aggregate demand
automatic stabilizers
autonomous aggregate demand *(expenditure)*
consumption function
income-expenditure multiplier
induced aggregate demand *(expenditure)*
marginal propensity to consume (MPC)
menu costs
short-run equilibrium output
stabilization policies

1. The relationship between consumption spending and its determinants, is referred to as the

   _____ .

2. The sum of consumption, investment, government purchases, and net exports equals

   _____ .

3. The slope of the consumption function is determined by the _____ .

4. To fight recessions caused by insufficient aggregate demand policymakers can use

   _____ .

5. The effect of a one-unit increase or decrease in autonomous aggregate demand on the short-run equilibrium output is called the _____ .

6. Firms change the price of a product only if the benefits of doing so outweighs the

   _____ .

7. The portion of aggregate demand that is determined outside the model is the

   _____ .

8. The level of output that prevails during the period in which prices are predetermined is the

   _____ .

9. AD increases during recessions and falls during expansions, without the delays inherent in the legislative process, because of _____ .

10. The portion of aggregate demand that is determined within the model (because it depends on output) is the _____ .

Self-Test: Multiple-Choice Questions

Circle the letter that corresponds to the best answer. (Answers are given at the end of the chapter.)

1. Which of the following is the *crucial* key assumption of the basic Keynesian model?
   A. Aggregate demand fluctuates.
   B. In the short run, firms meet the demand for their products at preset prices.
   C. In the long run, firms meet the demand for the products at preset prices.
   D. In the short run, firms adjust price to changes in aggregate demand so as to clear the market.
   E. In the long run, firms adjust price to changes in aggregate demand so as to clear the market.

2. When firms apply the core principle of cost-benefit analysis to price changing decisions, they change the prices of their goods if
   A. menu costs are greater than or equal to the benefits of changing prices.
   B. menu costs are greater than or equal to the additional revenue derived from changing prices.
   C. additional revenue derived from changing prices is less than the menu costs.
   D. additional revenue derived from changing prices is greater than the menu costs.
   E. additional revenue derived from changing prices is less than or equal to the menu costs.

3. In *The General Theory of Employment, Interest, and Money*, John Maynard Keynes explained
   A. how economies always operate at the natural rate of employment.
   B. the causes of expansionary gaps and recommended the use of monetary policy to combat the resulting high inflation.
   C. how economies can remain at low levels of output for long periods and recommended increased government spending to combat the resulting high unemployment.
   D. that attempts to extract large reparation payments from Germany after World War I would prevent economic recovery of Germany and likely lead to another war.
   E. the key elements of the post-WWII international monetary and financial institutions.

4. Aggregate demand is the sum of desired or planned
   A. consumption expenditures, investment, government purchases, and net exports.
   B. consumption expenditures, investment, government purchases, and exports.
   C. consumption expenditures, investment, government purchases, and net imports.
   D. consumption expenditures, net investment, government purchasers, and net exports.
   E. consumption expenditures, net investment, government expenditures, and net exports.

5. If a firms' actual sales are greater than expected sales
   A. actual inventories will be greater than planned inventories, and actual investment will be greater than planned investment.
   B. actual inventories will be less than planned inventories, and actual investment will be less than planned investment.
   C. actual inventories will be greater than planned inventories, and actual investment will be less than planned investment.
   D. actual inventories will be less than planned inventories, and actual investment will be greater than planned investment.
   E. planned inventories will be less than actual inventories, and planned investment will be greater than actual investment.

6. A decrease in consumers' disposable income will cause a(n)
   A. decrease in the consumption function and an increase in output.
   B. increase in the consumption function and a decrease in output.
   C. decrease in the consumption function and an increase in aggregate demand.
   D. increase in the consumption function and an increase in aggregate demand.
   E. decrease in the consumption function and a decrease in aggregate demand.

7. If autonomous consumption equals $250 billion, the marginal propensity to consume (MPC) is .6, investment equals $180 billion, government purchases equal $75 billion, taxes equal $200, and net exports equal minus $40 billion, the aggregate demand equation is
    A. AD = $250 billion + .6Y
    B. AD = $585 billion + .6Y
    C. AD = $505 billion + .6Y
    D. AD = $625 billion + .6Y
    E. AD = $345 billion + .6Y

8. If, in the short run, real output is less than the equilibrium level of output, firms will respond by
    A. increasing the price of their products.
    B. decreasing the price of their products.
    C. increasing their production.
    D. decreasing their production.
    E. producing the same amount of output.

9. If the consumption function is C= $400 + .75Y, then
    A. the MPC = .75 and the income-expenditure multiplier = .25.
    B. the MPC = .75 and the income-expenditure multiplier = 1.33.
    C. the MPC = .75 and the income-expenditure multiplier = .75.
    D. the MPC = .75 and the income-expenditure multiplier = 4.
    E. the MPC = .25 and the income-expenditure multiplier = 4.

10. John Maynard Keynes believed that the most effective stabilization policy was
    A. changes in government spending to reduce or eliminate output gaps.
    B. monetary policy to reduce or eliminate expansionary gaps.
    C. changes in government spending to reduce or eliminate recessionary gaps, but monetary policy to reduce or eliminate expansionary gaps.
    D. changes in taxes to reduce or eliminate output gaps.
    E. the self-correcting process of the market to reduce or eliminate output gaps.

11. During the 1990s, the Japanese government spent $1.9 billion to build a toll road to the northern island of Hokkaido. The purpose of the expenditure was to
    A. reduce the traffic congestion on the only other highway that goes to Hokkaido.
    B. stimulate the Japanese economy and help to bring it out of its recession.
    C. increase exports and imports between Hokkaido and Japan.
    D. reduce the size of the Japanese government's budget surplus that was acting a drag on the Japanese economy.
    E. increase the potential output of the Japanese economy.

12. The use of fiscal policy to eliminate output gaps is complicated by the fact that fiscal policy
    A. is more flexible than monetary policy.
    B. only affects aggregate demand, but has no effect on potential output.
    C. affects both aggregate demand and potential output.
    D. does not take into account the effects that automatic stabilizers have on potential output.
    E. includes not only government purchases, but also transfer payments and taxation.

13. One of the key assumptions of the basic Keynesian model is that
    A. the price level is increasing.
    B. the price level is decreasing.
    C. output is constant.
    D. income fluctuates.
    E. aggregate demand fluctuates

14. Planned spending equals actual spending for households, governments, and foreigners in the basic Keynesian model, but for businesses
    A. planned spending equals actual inventories.
    B. planned spending equals planned inventories.
    C. actual investment may differ from planned investment.
    D. actual investment is always greater than planned investment.
    E. actual investment is always less than planned investment

15. The portion of aggregate demand that is determined within the model is called induced aggregate demand and includes
    A. that part of household consumption that is dependent upon income.
    B. all of household consumption.
    C. household consumption and investment spending.
    D. household consumption, investment spending, and government purchases.
    E. household consumption, investment spending, government purchases, and net exports.

16. The short-run equilibrium in the basic Keynesian model occurs where
    A. actual inventories are greater than the level planned by businesses.
    B. actual inventories are less than the level planned by businesses.
    C. aggregate demand equals the potential output.
    D. aggregate demand equals output.
    E. aggregate demand is greater than output.

17. In the basic Keynesian model, when aggregate demand equals output
    A. inventories are zero.
    B. consumption equals investment.
    C. unplanned changes in inventories are positive.
    D. unplanned changes in inventories equal zero.
    E. unplanned changes in inventories are negative.

18. If, in the short run, output is greater than the equilibrium level of output, firms will respond by
    A. increasing the price of their products.
    B. decreasing the price of their products.
    C. producing the same amount of output.
    D. increasing their production.
    E. decreasing their production.

19. A $100 increase in transfer payments or a $100 decrease in taxes will cause
    A. a smaller increase in aggregate demand than a $100 increase in government purchases.
    B. a larger increase in aggregate demand than a $100 increase in government purchases.
    C. the same increase in aggregate demand as would a $100 increase in government purchases.
    D. a smaller decrease in aggregate demand than a $100 increase in government purchases.
    E. a larger decrease in aggregate demand than a $100 increase in government purchases.

20. Fiscal policy is not always flexible enough to be useful for economic stabilization because
    A. automatic stabilizers counteract the stabilizing features of government spending and taxation.
    B. other objectives of policymakers may conflict with the need to stabilize aggregate demand.
    C. the legislative process requires policymakers to take action quickly leaving them inadequate time to determine the economic needs for stabilizing aggregate demand.
    D. it affects both aggregate demand and potential output.
    E. the only effects of fiscal policy that matter are its effects on potential output.

Self-Test: Short Answer/Problems
(Answers and solutions are given at the end of the chapter.)

1. The Consumption Function and Aggregate demand
This problem is designed to help you understand the relationship between the consumption function and aggregate demand. You will be asked to graph the consumption function, write the algebraic equation for aggregate demand, and differentiate between autonomous and induced aggregate demand.

A. On the graph below, plot the consumption function curve for disposable income levels $0 to $700, assuming C = $175 billion, the marginal propensity to consume (MPC) equals .75, and taxes equal $100 billion.

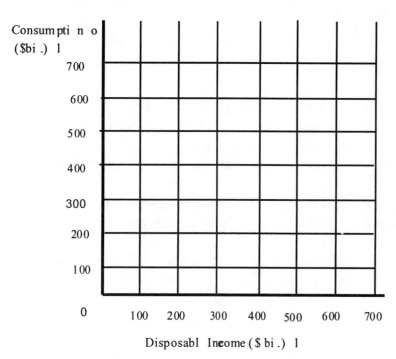

B. Assume that planned investment spending equals $50 billion, government purchases are $75 billion, and net exports equal –$75 billion. The algebraic equation for the aggregate demand curve would be AD = $ _____ billion + _____ (Y - $_____ billion) + $ _____ billion + $ _____ billion + $ _____ billion. Combining the autonomous portions of AD would result in a simplified equation, AD = $_____ billion + _____ Y.

C. Plot the aggregate demand curve on the above graph and label it AD.

D. Autonomous aggregate demand equals $_____ billion, and is graphically represented where the aggregate demand curve intersects the (vertical/ horizontal) _____ axis.

E. When disposable income equals $400 billion, the induced aggregate demand equals $_____ billion.

2. Numerical Determination of Short-run Equilibrium Output

The focus of this problem is the determination of the short-run equilibrium output within the framework of a numerical table.

(1) Output (Y)	(2) Aggregate Demand	(3) Y– AD	(4) Y = AD?
$3,000			
3,500			
4,000			
4,500			
5,000			
5,500			
6,000			

A. Assume that aggregate demand is determined by the equation AD = $500 + .9 Y. Complete column 2 of the table by calculating the amount of aggregate demand when output equals $3,000 to $6,000.

B. Complete column 3 of the table by calculating the difference between output and aggregate demand when output equals $3,000 to $6,000.

C. Complete column 4 by determining whether or not Y = AD. The equilibrium level of output equals $_____ .

D. If output equals $ 3,500, firms will (increase/decrease) _____ the level of output.

E. If output equals $ 6,000, firms will (increase/decrease) _____ the level of output.

3. The Basic Keynesian Model

This problem is designed to help you understand the fundamentals of the basic Keynesian model. You will determine the equilibrium level of income (or output) and analyze the effects of changes in investment spending on the equilibrium level of income (or output).

A. Assume the consumption function is C = $200 billion + .8Y, investment equals $ 150 billion, government purchases equal $200 billion, taxes equal $100 billion, and net exports equals minus $70 billion. Using this information, derive the aggregate expenditure function. AD = $_____ billion + _____ Y.

B. On the graph below, plot the aggregate demand curve for level of output ranging from $0 billion to $5,000 billion (label the curve AD).

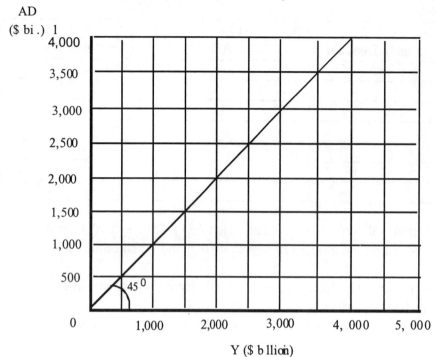

AD
($ bi .)

C. The equilibrium level of output equals $ _____ billion.

D. If firms produce $3,000 billion of output, aggregate demand would equal $_____ billion. As a result, firms would have $_____ billion of goods they intended to sell but didn't. This would cause firms (increase / decrease) _____ their level of output.

E. The MPC equals _____ . and the multiplier equals _____ .

F. If investment spending decreases by $100 billion, the aggregate demand curve will shift (upward / downward) _____ and the equilibrium output will (increase / decrease) _____ by an amount equal to the change in aggregate demand times the multiplier.

G. On the graph above, draw the aggregate demand curve after a $100-billion decrease in investment spending (label it AD$_1$). The new equilibrium output would equal $_____ billion.

H. If the potential output (Y*) equals $2,000, there would now be a (recessionary/ expansionary) _____ gap in the economy.

4. Solving the Basic Keynesian Model Numerically

This problem uses algebraic equations to determine the short-run equilibrium output. You will derive the aggregate expenditure equation and, employing the equation for the short-run equilibrium condition, calculate the short-run equilibrium real GDP, and determine the effect of changes in government purchases, taxes, and transfer payments of the short-run equilibrium output.

Use the following set of equations to answer the questions below:

$C = \$400$ billion $+ .75(Y - T)$

$T = \$200$ billion

$I^P = \$250$ billion

$G = \$300$ billion

$NX = \$50$ billion

A. Using the information above, substitute into the equation the numerical values for each component of aggregate demand. Y= \$_____ billion + _____(Y – \$_____ billion) + \$_____ billion + \$_____ billion + \$_____ billion.

B. After simplifying that equation yields the equation AD = \$ _____ billion + _____Y.

C. The definition of short-run equilibrium output implies that Y = AD. Replacing AD with the equation found in Question 4B yields Y = \$ _____ billion + _____Y.

D. Now solve for Y in Y – ____ Y = \$_____ billion, or Y = \$ _____ billion.

E. Thus, the equilibrium output equals \$ _____ billion.

F. If government purchases decrease by \$100 billion the new short-run equilibrium output will equal \$ _____ billion.

G. Starting from the level of the short-run equilibrium output in Question 4E, an increase in taxation of \$100 will result in a new short-run equilibrium output of \$ _____ billion.

H. If, instead of decreasing government purchases by \$100 billion in Question 4F, the government decreased transfer payments by \$100 billion, the new short-run equilibrium output would equal \$ _____ billion.

I. In comparing the answers to Questions 4F-H, it is apparent that a change in government purchases has a (greater/lesser/equal) _____ effect on the short-run equilibrium output than does an equal change in transfer payments or taxation.

Solutions
Self-Test: Key Terms

1. consumption function
2. aggregate demand
3. marginal propensity to consume (MPC)
4. stabilization policies
5. income-expenditure multiplier
6. menu costs
7. autonomous aggregate demand
8. short-run equilibrium output
9. automatic stabiliizers
10. induced aggregate demand

Self-Test: Multiple-Choice Questions

1. B
2. D
3. C
4. A
5. B
6. E
7. E $250 billion + [.6(Y - $200 billion)] + $180 billion + $75 billion + (-$40 billion) = $345 billion + .6Y
8. C
9. D
10. A
11. B
12. C
13. E
14. C
15. A
16. D
17. D
18. E
19. A
20. B

Self Test: Short Answer Problems

1. A.

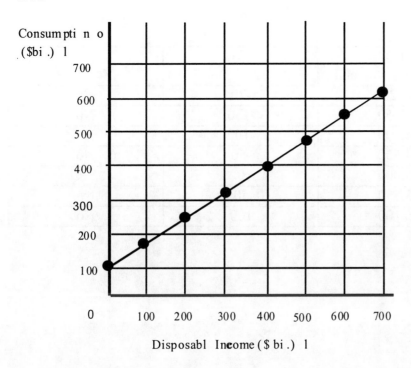

B. $175 billion + .75(Y - $100 billion) + $50 billion + $75 billion + (-$75) billion; $150 billion + .75Y

C.

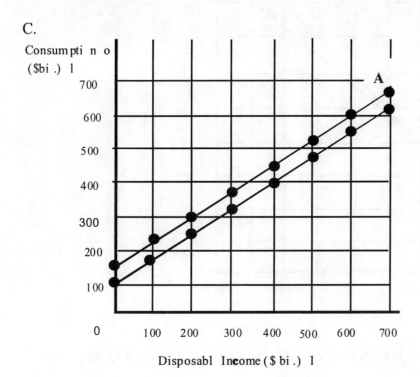

D. $150 billion (= $175 billion - $75 billion + $50 billion + 75 billion - $75 billion); vertical
E. $300 billion (= .75 x $400 billion)

2. A. B. C.

(1) Output (Y)	(2) Aggregate Demand	(3) Y– AD	(4) Y = AD?
$3,000	$3,200	$-200	No
3,500	3,650	-150	No
4,000	4,100	-100	No
4,500	4,550	-50	No
5,000	5,000	0	Yes
5,500	5,550	50	No
6,000	6,100	100	No

C. $5,000
D. increase
E. decrease

3.
A. AD = $400 billion + .8Y

B.

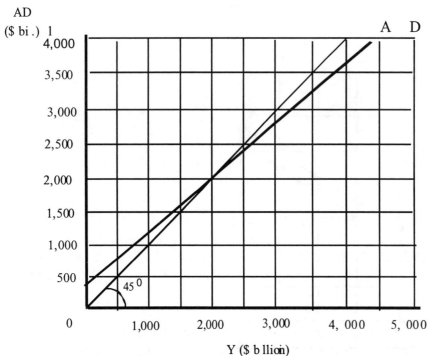

C. $2,000 billion
D. $2,800 billion (= $400 billion + .8($3,000 billion); $200 billion (Y – AD, or $3,000 billion –
$2,800 billion); decrease

E. .8 ; 5 $(=\dfrac{1}{1-.8}=\dfrac{1}{.2})$

F. downward; decrease

G.

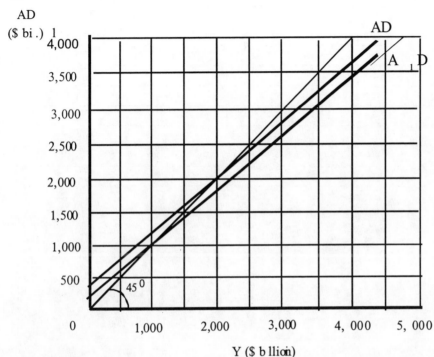

AD
($ bi .)

Y ($ b llion)

; $1,500 billion (The change in equilibrium output is − $100 billion x 5 = − $500 billion. Subtracting the change in equilibrium output from the initial equilibrium output, $2,000 billion - $500 billion, gives us the new equilibrium output)

H. recessionary

4.

A. $400 billion + .75 (Y - $200 billion) + $250 billion + $300 billion + $50 billion

B. AD = $850 billion + .75Y

C. Y = $850 billion + .75Y;

D. Y= $3,400 billion (The solution is found by first moving the .75 Y to the left side of the equation and subtracting it from Y. In equation form it is written, Y − .75 Y = $850 billion. Reducing the left-hand side yields the equation, .25Y = $850 billion. Next, divide both sides of the equation by .25. This gives us Y = $850 billion / .25, and dividing $850 billion by .25 equals $3,400 billion. Thus Y= $3,400 billion)

E. $3,400 billion

F. $3,000 billion (Y − .75Y =$750 billion, or .25Y = $750 billion, thus Y= $3,000 billion)

G. $3,100 billion (Y − .75 Y = $675, or .25Y = $775 billion, thus Y = $3,100 billion)

H. $3,100 billion (the effect a decrease in transfer payments is the same as an increase in taxation, and thus the numerical derivation is identical to the answer to 4G).

I. greater

Chapter 14
Stabilizing Aggregate Demand:
The Role of the Fed

Key Point Review

This chapter examines the workings of monetary policy, one of the two major types of stabilization policy. The chapter begins with a discussion of how the Fed uses its ability to control the money supply to influence nominal and real interest rates. The chapter concludes by building on the analysis of the basic Keynesian model to explain the effects of monetary policy and interest rates on aggregate demand and the short-run equilibrium output.

As explained in Chapter 23, the Fed uses three tools to control the money supply. This chapter shows that the Fed's control of the money supply is tantamount to controlling nominal interest rates. The nominal interest rate is the price of money and is determined by the supply and demand for money. The demand for money is the result of choices made by households and businesses. The **demand for money** is the amount of wealth an individual chooses to hold in the form of money. Households and businesses demand money to carry out transactions (i.e., use it as a medium of exchange) and as a way of holding wealth (i.e., the store of value function of money). There are, however, almost an infinite number of forms in which wealth can be held. The decision about the forms in which to hold one's wealth is called the **portfolio allocation decision**. How much money one chooses to hold is based on the costs and benefits of holding money. The opportunity cost of holding money is the interest that could have been earned if the person had chosen to hold interest-bearing assets instead of money. The higher the prevailing interest rate, the greater the opportunity cost of holding money, and hence the less money individuals and businesses will demand. The principle benefit of holding money is its usefulness in carrying out transactions. The amount of money demanded to carry out transactions is affected at the macroeconomic level by real output and the price level. An increase in aggregate real output or income raises the quantity of goods and services that people and businesses want to buy and, thus, raises the demand for money. The higher the price of goods and services, the more dollars needed to make a given set of transactions and, therefore, a higher demand for money.

Macroeconomists are primarily interested in the aggregate, or economy-wide demand for money, represented by the money demand curve. The **money demand curve** relates the aggregate quantity of money demand, M, to the nominal interest rate, i. Because an increase in the nominal interest rate increases the opportunity cost of holding money, which reduces the quantity of money demanded, the money demand curve slopes down. An increase in real output or the price level will cause the money demand curve to increase (shift to the right), while a decrease in either will cause it to decrease (shift to the left). Other factors, such as technological and financial advances, also cause the money demand curve to shift.

The supply of money is controlled by the Federal Reserve (the central bank of the United States). Its primary tool for controlling the money supply is open-market operations. Because the Fed fixes the supply of money, the money supply curve is a vertical line that intercepts the horizontal axis at the quantity of money chosen by the Fed. The equilibrium in the market for money occurs at the intersection of the supply and demand for money curves. The equilibrium amount of money in circulation is the amount of money the Fed chooses to supply. The equilibrium nominal interest rate is the interest rate at which the quantity of money demanded by the public equals the fixed supply of money made available by the Fed. When the Fed increases the money supply by purchasing government bonds from the public, it drives up the price of bonds and, thus, lowers the equilibrium nominal interest rate. When the Fed decreases the money supply through open-market sales of government bonds to the public, the price of bonds is driven down and, therefore, the equilibrium nominal interest rate must rise.

Although there are thousands of different interest rates determined in the financial markets, the textbook authors use the phrase *the nominal interest rate* to refer to an average measure of these interest rates because they tend to rise and fall together. Of all the market interest rates, the one that is most closely watched by the public, politicians, and the media, however, is the federal funds rate. The **federal funds rate** is the interest rate commercial banks charge each other for very short-term (usually overnight) loans. It is closely watched because for the past 35 years, the Fed has expressed its policies in terms of a target value for the federal funds rate. Because interest rates tend to move together, an action by the Fed to change the federal funds rate generally causes other interest rates to change in the same direction. The tendency of interest rates to move together, however, is not an exact relationship. This means that the Fed's control over other interest rates is somewhat less precise than its control over the federal funds rate.

Similarly, the Fed's control over real interest rates is less complete than its control over nominal interest rates. The real interest rate equals the nominal interest rate minus the rate of inflation. Because inflation tends to change relatively slowly in response to changes in policy or economic conditions, actions by the Fed to change nominal interest rates allows it to control real interest rates in the short run. In the long run, however, the inflation rate and other variables will adjust, and the balance of saving and investment will determine the real interest.

Because the Fed can control the money supply and interest rates (at least, in the short run), monetary policy can be used to eliminate output gaps and stabilize the economy. Consumption and planned investment spending are inversely related to real interest rates, that is, a decrease in real interest rates will cause consumption and planned investment spending to increase. Because consumption and planned investment spending are components of aggregate demand, changes in real interest rates cause changes in aggregate demand. By adjusting real interest rates, the Fed can move aggregate demand in the desired direction. For example, an **expansionary monetary policy**, or monetary easing, is a reduction in interest rates by the Fed, made with the intention of reducing a recessionary gap. If the economy faces a recessionary gap, the Fed could reduce real interest rates to stimulate consumption and investment spending. This will increase aggregate demand and, as a result, output will rise and the recessionary gap will be reduce or eliminated. When the economy experiences inflationary pressures, the Fed may implement a **contractionary monetary policy**, or monetary tightening, by increasing interest rates with the intention of reducing an expansionary gap.

Economists often try to summarize the behavior of the Fed in terms of a **policy reaction function,** describing how the action a policymaker takes depends on the state of the economy. An example of a monetary policy reaction function is the Taylor rule, first proposed by John Taylor in 1993. The Taylor rule can be written as $r = 0.01 - 0.5 \ (Y^* - Y)/Y^* + 0.5\pi$, where r is the real interest rate, $(Y^* - Y)/Y^*$ is the output gap measured as a percentage of potential output, and π is and the rate of inflation. Thus, according to the Taylor rule, the Fed responds to both output gaps and the rate of inflation. It is important to understand, however, that the Taylor rule is not a legal restraint on the Fed. The Fed is perfectly free to deviate from it and does so when circumstances warrant. It is up to the Fed to determine its policy reaction function. Doing so is a complex process, involving a combination of statistical analysis of the economy and human judgment. In practice, monetary policymaking is as much an art as a science.

Knowledge and Skills

The student must master the knowledge and skills listed below each number topic.	Key Terms	Multiple-Choice Questions	Short Answer/ Problems
1. The Federal Reserve and Interest Rates			
A. Define portfolio allocation decision and explain how it relates to the demand for money	1	1	
B. Define demand for money and money demand curve	7		
C. Apply cost-benefit analysis to the money demand decision		2, 13	1
D. Discuss macroeconomic factors that affect the demand for money and the effects of changes on the money demand curve	4	3, 14	1
E. Identify the money market equilibrium			2
2. The Federal Reserve's Control of Interest Rates			
A. Explain how monetary policy is used to control nominal interest rates		4, 15	2

The student must master the knowledge and skills listed below each number topic.	Key Terms	Multiple-Choice Questions	Short Answer/ Problems
B. Define the federal funds rate and explain why the Fed has focused on it.	3	5	
C. Discuss the Fed's ability to control the real rate of interest		6, 16	
3. Effects of Federal Reserve Actions on the Economy			
A. Explain how interest rates affect consumption and investment spending, aggregate demand, and short-run equilibrium output		7, 8, 17	3
B. Define expansionary and contractionary monetary policy and explain when and how the Fed would implement each	2, 6	9, 10, 18, 19	3
C. Define and discuss the Fed's policy reaction function	5	11	
D. Apply Taylor's rule			3
E. Discuss the art and science of monetary policymaking		12, 20	

Self-Test: Key Terms
Use the terms below to complete the following sentences. (Answers are given at the end of the chapter.)

contractionary monetary policy
demand for money
expansionary monetary policy
federal funds rate
money demand curve
policy reaction function
portfolio allocation decision

1. The choice about which forms to hold one's wealth is called the _____ .

2. A reduction in interest rates by the Fed, made with the intention of reducing a recessionary gap, is achieved through _____ .

3. For the past 35 years, the Fed has expressed its policies in terms of a target value for the _____ .

4. An increase in real output or the price level will cause the _____ to shift to the right.

5. The Taylor rule is an example of a(n) _____ .

6. If the economy faces an expansionary gap, the Fed could increase real interest rates by implementing a(n) _____ .

7. The amount of wealth an individual chooses to hold in the form of money is that person's _____ .

Self-Test: Multiple-Choice Questions

Circle the letter that corresponds to the best answer. (Answers are given at the end of the chapter.)

1. The portfolio allocation decision is related to the demand for money because
   A. money can be used to buy a portfolio.
   B. money is one of the many forms in which wealth can be held and is a part of most asset portfolios.
   C. the portfolio allocation decision determines how much of an individual's money is going to be held in the form of currency and how much in the form of balances in a checking account.
   D. money is the main form of wealth for most people.
   E. portfolio allocation explains why the amount of money people hold is directly related to interest rates.

2. E-Buy, a web-based auction firm receives an average of $25,000 in payments for its services each day that it deposits in its bank account at the end of each day. E-Commerce Management Systems, Inc. proposed a computerized cash management system to track E-Buys' inflows and outflows of payments and electronically transfer the funds to an interest-bearing bank account. The cost of the system is $500 per year and E-Buys estimates that it would reduce its cash holding by approximately $10,000 per day. E-Buy should
   A. accept the proposal.
   B. reject the proposal.
   C. accept the proposal if the average interest rate they can earn on the funds is at least 10 percent.
   D. reject the proposal if the average interest rate they can earn on the funds is less than 10 percent.
   E. accept the proposal if the average interest rate they can earn on the funds is greater than 5 percent.

3. As the number of ATM machines increases in a country
   A. the supply of money will increase.
   B. the supply of money will decrease.
   C. people will hold more of their wealth in the form of money. (i.e., the demand for money will increase).
   D. people will hold less of their wealth in the form of money (i.e., the demand for money will decrease).
   E. interest rates will increase.

4. When the Fed buys government bonds, bond prices
   A. increase and interest rates fall.
   B. decrease and interest rates fall.
   C. increase and interest rates rise.
   D. decrease and interest rates rise.
   E. and interest rates fall.

5. The Fed communicates its monetary policy to the public in terms of targets for the federal funds rate because it is
   A. the only interest rate that they can control.
   B. the interest rate that most individuals pay when they borrow money to buy a car, a household appliance, or a house.
   C. the interest rate that the Fed has the greatest control over.
   D. one of the tools of monetary policy.
   E. the most important of all the interest rates that are determined in the various financial markets.

6. The real interest rate
   A. cannot be controlled by the Fed because monetary policy only affects nominal interest rates.
   B. can be controlled by the Fed in the short run, but not in the long run.
   C. can be controlled by the Fed in the long run, but not in the short run.
   D. equals the nominal interest rate plus the inflation rate.
   E. equals the inflation rate minus the nominal interest rate.

7. If the Fed implements an open-market sale of government bonds, the
   A. money market equilibrium interest rate will rise.
   B. money market equilibrium interest rate will fall.
   C. price of bonds will rise.
   D. supply of money will increase.
   E. demand for bonds will decrease

8. If the Fed implements an open-market purchase of government bonds, this will cause a(n)
   A. decrease in consumption spending, an increase in investment spending, and an increase in aggregate demand.
   B. increase in consumption and investment spending, and an increase in aggregate demand.
   C. decrease in consumption and investment spending, and an increase in aggregate demand.
   D. decrease in consumption spending, a decrease in investment spending, and an increase in aggregate demand.
   E. increase in consumption spending, a decrease in investment spending, and a decrease in aggregate demand.

9. To close a recessionary gap the Fed should
   A. sell government bonds to increase bond prices and lower interest rates, causing consumption, investment spending, and aggregate demand to increase.
   B. sell government bonds to decrease bond prices and lower interest rates, causing consumption, investment spending, and aggregate demand to increase.
   C. buy government bonds to increase bond prices and lower interest rates, causing consumption, investment spending, and aggregate demand to increase.
   D. buy government bonds to decreases bond prices and increase interest rates, causing consumption, investment spending, and aggregate demand to decrease.
   E. buy government bonds to decreases bond prices and lower interest rates, causing consumption, investment spending, and aggregate demand to increase.

10. An expansionary monetary policy will cause a(n)
    A. decrease in interest rates, an increase in aggregate demand, and is designed to reduce an expansionary gap.
    B. increase in interest rates, a decrease in aggregate demand, and is designed to reduce an expansionary gap.
    C. decrease in interest rates, a decrease in aggregate demand, and is designed to reduce a recessionary gap.
    D. decrease in interest rates, an increase in aggregate demand, and is designed to reduce a recessionary gap.
    E. increase in interest rates, increase in aggregate demand, and is designed to reduce a recessionary gap.

11. The Fed's policy reaction function
    A. is mandated by the Taylor rule.
    B. is approximated by the Taylor rule.
    C. can be determined by statistical analysis of the economy.
    D. is determined by its short-run target rate of inflation.
    E. only provides information about the central bank's inflation target.

12. Monetary policymaking is based on
    A. scientific analyses, to apply detailed statistical modeling of the economy.
    B. the judgment of the members of the Federal Open Market Committee based on their experience as policymakers.
    C. a mathematical model of Taylor's rule.
    D. scientific analyses and art, (i.e., the judgement of the members of the Federal Open Market Committee).
    E. a mathematical model of Taylor's rule and art, (i.e., the judgement of the members of the Federal Open Market Committee).

13. The higher the price of bonds, with no change in the cost of transferring funds between bonds and checkable deposits, the
    A. more likely people are to hold their wealth in the form of bonds than money.
    B. more likely people are to hold their wealth in the form of money than bonds.
    C. the greater the differential between nominal and real interest rates.
    D. the smaller the quantity of money demanded.
    E. the greater the demand for money.

14. A decrease in aggregate real output or income will
    A. decrease the quantity of goods and services that people and businesses want to buy and sell and, thus, decrease the demand for money.
    B. decrease the quantity of goods and services that people and businesses want to buy and sell and, thus, increase the demand for money.
    C. increase the quantity of goods and services that people and businesses want to buy and sell and, thus, decrease the demand for money.
    D. increase the quantity of goods and services that people and businesses want to buy and sell and, thus, increase the demand for money.
    E. decrease the quantity of goods and services that people and businesses want to buy and sell, but have no effect on the demand for money.

15. A contractionary monetary policy
    A. is achieved if the Fed implements an open-market purchase of government bonds.
    B. will decrease the money market equilibrium interest rate.
    C. will increase the money market equilibrium interest rate.
    D. will raise the price of bonds.
    E. will shift the money supply curve to the right.

16. The Fed can control real interest rates only in the short run because
    A. the U.S. Congress has not given it the legal authority to control interest rates in the long run.
    B. nominal interest rates only adjust slowly to changing economic conditions and policy.
    C. saving and investment are not relevant to short-run real interest rates.
    D. saving and investment are not relevant to long-run real interest rates.
    E. the inflation rate only adjusts slowly to changing economic conditions and policy.

17. If the Fed wants to lower the money market equilibrium interest rate, it should
    A. decrease the supply of money.
    B. shift the supply of money to the left.
    C. sell government bonds.
    D. purchase government bonds.
    E. decrease the price of bonds.

18. A contractionary monetary policy is designed to produce a(n)
    A. increase in aggregate demand, and reduce an expansionary gap.
    B. decrease in aggregate demand, and reduce an expansionary gap.
    C. increase in aggregate demand, and reduce a recessionary gap.
    D. decrease in aggregate demand, and reduce a recessionary gap.
    E. increase in aggregate demand, and increase an expansionary gap.

19. If the Fed purchases government bonds, this will cause a(n)
    A. increase in aggregate demand and output and reduce a recessionary gap.
    B. increase in aggregate demand and output and reduce an expansionary gap.
    C. decrease in aggregate demand and output and reduce a recessionary gap.
    D. decrease in aggregate demand and output and reduce an expansionary gap.
    E. increase in aggregate demand, decrease output, and reduce an expansionary gap.

20. The "art" of monetary policymaking is necessary because
    A. of Taylor's rule.
    B. the Fed does not have precise information about the size of the money supply and the level of interest rates.
    C. the Fed does not have precise information about the level of potential output and the size and speed of the effects of its actions.
    D. the Fed does not have precise information about the level of actual output and the size and speed of the effects of its actions.
    E. the Fed does not have precise information about the level of aggregate demand, and the size and speed of the effects of its actions.

Self Test: Short Answer Problems
(Answers and solutions are given at the end of the chapter.)

1. Cost and Benefit of Holding Money
The following table shows the estimated annual benefits to Siam of holding different amounts of money.

Average Money Holdings	Total Annual Benefit	Marginal Annual Benefit
$1,000	$60	XXXXXXXX
1,100	72	
1,200	82	
1,300	90	
1,400	96	
1,500	100	
1,600	102	
1,700	102	

A. Complete column 3 by calculating the extra benefit of each additional $100 in money holdings greater than $100.

B. How much money will Siam hold if the nominal interest rates is 10 percent? $_____; if the nominal interest rates is 8 percent? $_____; if the nominal interest rates is 6 percent? $_____; if the nominal interest rate is 4 percent $_____; if the nominal interest rate is 2 percent $_____?

C. On the graph below plot Siam's money demand curve for nominal interest rates between 2 and 12 percent.

Interest Rate
(%)

12

10

8

6

4

2

0   1100   1200   1300   1400   1500   1600   1700

Quantity of Money Demanded

D. If Siam won a million-dollar lottery, his money demand curve shift to the (right/left) _____ representing a(n) (increase/decrease) _____ in the demand for money.

2. Money Market and Equilibrium Interest Rate

This problem focuses on the Fed's control of the money supply to achieve targeted nominal interest rates. Assume the aggregate demand for money (in millions of dollars) is given by the equation $M = P(0.33Y - 15,000i)$, the price level (P) equals 1.5, and real output (Y) equals $9,000.

A. If the Fed wants to set the nominal equilibrium interest rate at 4 percent, it should set the nominal money supply at $ _____.

B. If real GDP increases to $10,000, and the Fed wants to keep the nominal equilibrium interest rate at 4 percent, it should (increase/decrease) _____ the nominal money supply to $ _____.

C. If the Fed now wants to raise the nominal equilibrium interest rate to 5 percent, it should (increase/decrease) _____ the nominal money supply to $ _____.

D. If the price level rises to 2.0 and the Fed wants to keep the nominal equilibrium interest rate at 5 percent, it should (increase/decrease) _____ the nominal money supply to $_____.

3. Monetary Policy and Short-Run Equilibrium Output

This problem will help you to better understand the relationship between interest rates, aggregate demand, output, and monetary policy. The aggregate demand for the economy of Hinderland is given by the following equations:

$C = \$750 + 0.75(Y - T) - 300r$

$IP = \$400 - 600r$

$G = \$500$

$T = \$400$

$NX = -\$55$

A. If the Fed sets the nominal interest rate (r) at 0.05 (5 %), the aggregate demand for the Hinderland economy would be represented by the equation $AD = \$$_____ $+ .75Y$.

B. Given the Hinderland aggregate demand, the short-run equilibrium output would equal $\$$_____ .

C. If potential output (Y^*) in the Hinderland economy equals $5,050, there would be a(n) _____ gap of $\$$_____ .

D. If the Fed wanted to close the output gap, it should implement a(n) (expansionary/ contractionary) _____ monetary policy.

E. To close the gap, the Fed would need to (decrease/ increase) _____ nominal interest rates to _____ percent.

F. Following the expansionary monetary policy, assume the recessionary gap is closed at $Y = \$5,050$, and the Fed determines that the inflation rate is 1.5%. Applying the Taylor rule, this would suggest that the real interest rate in the economy would equal_____ %.

Solutions
Self-Test: Key Terms

1. portfolio allocation decision
2. expansionary monetary policy
3. federal funds rate
4. money demand curve
5. policy reaction function
6. contractionary monetary policy
7. demand for money

Self-Test: Multiple-Choice Questions

1. B
2. E $10,000 x 0.05 = $500. Therefore, an interest rate of greater than 5% would imply that the benefit would be greater than the cost.
3. D
4. A
5. C
6. B
7. A
8. B
9. C
10. D
11. B
12. C
13. B
14. A
15. B
16. E
17. D
18. B
19. A
20. C

Self-Test: Short Answer/Problems

1.

A.

Average Money Holdings	Total Annual Benefit	Marginal Annual Benefit
$1,000	$60	XXXXXXXX
1,100	72	12
1,200	82	10
1,300	90	8
1,400	97	7
1,500	103	6
1,600	107	4
1,700	109	2

B. $1,200; $1,300; $1,500; $1,600; $1,700

C.

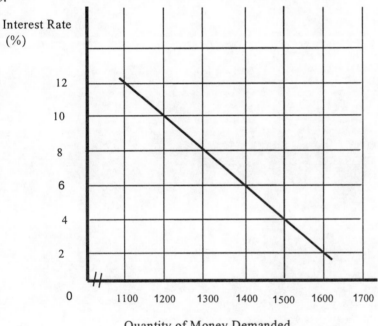

Quantity of Money Demanded

D. right; increase

2.

A. $3,600 {M= 1.5[(.33 x 9,000) – (15,000 x .04)], or M = $4,500 – 900}

B. $,4050 {M= 1.5[.33 x 10,000) – (15,000 x .04)], or M = $4,950 – 900}

C. $3,825 { M= 1.5[.33 x 10,000) – (15,000 x .05)], or M = $4,950 – 1,125}

D. increase; $5,100 { M= 2.0[.33 x 10,000) – (15,000 x .05)], or M = $6,600 – 1,500}

3.

A. $1,250 ($750 + .75(Y − $300) − $300(.05) + $400 − $600(.05) + $500 + (−$55)

B. $5,000 (Y = $1,250 + .75 Y, or .25Y = $1,250, thus Y = $1,250/.25)

C. recessionary gap; $50 (Y* − Y = output gap)

D. expansionary

E. decrease; 3.6 ($5,050 = $1,295 + .75($5,050) − 900i, or $5,050 = $1,295 + $3,787.5 − 900$i$.
Combining the constant values gives us −$32.5 = − 900$i$., or 3.6 = i)

F. 1.75 [r = 0.01 − 0.5 $(\dfrac{\$5,050 - \$5,050}{\$5,050})$ + 0.5(.015)]

Chapter 15
Inflation, Aggregate Demand, and Aggregate Supply

Key Point Review

This chapter introduces a framework for understanding inflation and the policies used to control it. The basic Keynesian model introduced in the previous chapters assumes preset prices and, thus, cannot explain inflation. The basic Keynesian model must be extended to allow for inflation. The extended Keynesian model is represented in a new diagram called the aggregate demand/aggregate supply diagram. The extended model shows the causes of ongoing inflation, how macroeconomic policies affect inflation and output, and illustrates the difficult tradeoffs policymakers sometimes face.

To incorporate inflation into the model, a new relationship is introduced between aggregate demand (AD) and the rate of inflation (π). Graphically, this relationship is called the aggregate demand curve. Because short-run equilibrium output equals aggregate demand, the **aggregate demand curve** not only shows the relationship between AD and inflation, but also shows the relationship between short-run equilibrium output and inflation. When the Fed raises real interest rates in response to higher inflation rates, aggregate demand and the short-run equilibrium output decrease. The aggregate demand curve is, therefore, downward sloping. In addition to the effect of inflation on monetary policy, there are three other reasons why inflation reduces aggregate demand. First, higher inflation reduces the real value of money held by households and businesses causing them to restrain spending and, thus, reduces aggregate demand. Second, higher inflation affects income distribution as it redistributes resources from relatively high-spending, less-affluent households to relatively high-saving, more-affluent households, causing overall spending to decline. Third, as domestic goods become relatively more expensive to prospective foreign purchasers, export sales decline, reducing aggregate demand. To summarize, changes in the Fed's response to higher inflation, and the effects of inflation on the real value of money, income distribution, and net exports, cause a movement along the aggregate demand curve.

The downward slope of the aggregate demand curve reflects the fact that, all other factors held constant, a higher level of inflation will lead to a lower aggregate demand and short-run equilibrium output. In addition to the above factors that cause movements along the aggregate demand curve, there are also factors that cause the aggregate demand curve to shift. For a given level of inflation, any change in the economy that affects the aggregate demand and short-run equilibrium will cause the AD curve to shift. This chapter focuses on two sorts of changes in the economy that shift the aggregate demand curve: changes in autonomous aggregate demand and changes in the Fed's reaction function. The components of autonomous aggregate demand include autonomous consumption, taxes, autonomous investment spending, government purchases, and net exports. An increase in any of the components of autonomous aggregate demand will cause the AD curve to shift to the right, while a decrease in any of these components will cause the AD curve to shift to the left. If the Fed's reaction function shifts upward, (i.e., the Fed chooses a "tighter" monetary policy by setting the real interest rate higher than normal for a given rate of inflation), the aggregate demand curve will shift to the left. An easing of monetary policy (the Fed's reaction function shifts downward) causes the AD curve to shift to the right.

The aggregate supply component of the extended Keynesian model (the AD/AS diagram) is represented by two curves, the long-run aggregate supply line and the short-run aggregate supply line. The **long-run aggregate supply line**, or LRAS line, is a vertical line at the economy's potential output (Y*). The **short-run aggregate supply line**, or SRAS line, is a horizontal line showing the current rate of inflation, as determined by past expectations and pricing decisions. In the model, the current rate of inflation is determined by past expectations and pricing decisions to reflect the fact that, in low-inflation industrial economies, inflation tends to change relatively slowly from year to year (inflation inertia). Inflation inertia is due to (1) the public's inflation expectations for the next few years, which are highly influenced by the recent inflation experience, and (2) long-term wage and price contracts, which tend to build the effects of people's inflation expectations into current price level. Although the rate of inflation is inertial, it does change over time. An important factor influencing the rate of inflation is the output gap. If the output gap is zero, the rate of inflation will tend to remain the same. When an expansionary gap exists, the rate of inflation will tend to increase; and a recessionary gap tends to cause the rate of inflation to decrease.

The adjustment of inflation in response to output gaps can be shown using the AD/AS diagram. The AD/AS diagram can be used to determine the level of output prevailing at any particular time, called the short-run equilibrium output. The **short-run equilibrium** occurs when inflation equals the value determined by past expectations and pricing decisions and output equals the level of short-run equilibrium output that is consistent with that inflation rate. Graphically, the short-run equilibrium occurs at the intersection of the AD curve and the SRAS line. If the short-run equilibrium output indicates an output gap exists, the economy will not remain at that level of output. For example, if a recessionary gap exists at the short-run equilibrium output, it will cause the inflation rate to fall. As the inflation rate gradually declines, the SRAS line shifts downward. Also, as the inflation rate declines, the Fed lowers real interest rates and, as a result, the short-run equilibrium output point moves down the AD curve. The recessionary gap is eventually closed and cyclical unemployment declines. At this point there is no further downward pressure on inflation. This point is referred to as the long-run equilibrium of the economy. The **long-run equilibrium** occurs where actual output equals potential output and the inflation rate is stable. Graphically, long-run equilibrium occurs when the AD curve, the SRAS line and the LRAS line all intersect at a single point. An expansionary gap at the short-run equilibrium output would set in motion a similar adjustment process, but in the opposite direction (e.g., inflation rate would rise, SRAS line shifts upward).

The AD/AS diagram makes the important general point that the economy tends to be self-correcting. That is, given enough time, output gaps tend to disappear without changes in monetary or fiscal policy. This view contrast with the basic Keynesian model, which does not include a self-correcting mechanism. This difference derives from the fact that the basic Keynesian model concentrates on the short-run period, during which prices do not adjust, while the extended AD/AS model focuses on the changes in prices and inflation over the long-run period. Whether monetary and fiscal policies are needed to stabilize output then depends crucially on the speed with which the self-correction process takes place. If self-correction takes place slowly, active use of monetary and fiscal policy can help to stabilize output. If it takes place rapidly, however, an active stabilization policy is not only unnecessary, but is probably harmful. The speed with which a particular economy corrects itself depends upon the prevalence of long-term contracts and the efficiency and flexibility of product and labor markets. In addition, the larger the size of the output gap, the longer the self-correction will take. The self-correcting tendency of the economy also explains why the income-expenditure multiplier is smaller in practice than the basic Keynesian model suggests.

The analysis of the AD/AS diagram indicates that inflation rises and falls in response to output gaps. An expansionary output gap may result from excessive aggregate demand that puts upward pressure on prices. Wars and military buildups have historically been one reason for excessive aggregate demand. Monetary or fiscal policy, however, can be used to offset excessive aggregate demand and prevent higher inflation from emerging. Inflation may also arise from an **aggregate supply shock**, either an inflation shock or a shock to potential output. An **inflation shock** is a sudden change in the normal behavior of inflation, unrelated to the nation's output gap. For example, a large runup in energy or food prices shifts the SRAS line upward. An inflation shock creates stagflation, a combination of recession and higher inflation, creating a difficult dilemna for policymakers. If they take no action, eventually inflation will subside and output will recover, but in the interim the economy may suffer a protracted period of recession. Monetary or fiscal policy can be used to shorten the recession, but will also lock in higher inflation. A **shock to potential output** is a sharp change in potential output, shifting the LRAS line. Like an inflation shock, an adverse shock to potential output results in stagflation. The adverse shock to potential output, however, implies that productive capacity has fallen and, therefore, output does not recover as it does following an inflation shock.

In order to achieve a low and stable inflationary environment that is conducive to sustained economic growth, policymakers can reduce inflation through tight monetary policies that reduce aggregate demand. In the short run, the main effect of monetary tightening is reduced output and higher unemployment as the economy experiences a recessionary gap. The recessionary gap eventually will cause **disinflation**, a substantial reduction in the rate of inflation. As the inflation rate falls output and employment will return to normal levels. A tight monetary policy, thus, inflicts short-term pain (lower output, and higher unemployment and real interest rates) to achieve a long-term gain (a permanent reduction in inflation).

Knowledge and Skills

The student must master the knowledge and skills listed below each number topic.	Key Terms	Multiple-Choice Questions	Short Answer/ Problems
1. Aggregate Demand and Inflation			
A. Define aggregate demand curve	3		
B. Explain why the AD curve slopes downward		1, 9, 17	
C. Discuss the factors that cause the AD curve to shift		2, 10, 18	
D. Draw an AD curve and show appropriate shifts			1
2. Inflation and Aggregate Supply			
A. Identify the causes of inflation inertia		3, 11	
B. Explain the causal relationship between output gaps and inflation		4, 12	
3. The Aggregate Demand/Aggregate Supply Diagram			
A. Define long-run and short-run aggregate supply lines, and short-run and long-run equilibrium	2, 4, 7, 8		
B. Explain the adjustment of inflation to output gaps		5, 13	
C. Use the AD/AS diagram to analyze output and inflation			2
D. Discuss the self-correcting tendency of the economy		6, 14	
4. Sources of Inflation			
A. Define aggregate supply shocks, inflation shock and shock to potential output	1, 6		
B. Discuss the sources of inflation		7, 15	
C. Show the effects of excessive aggregate demand and supply shocks on the economy			3, 4
5. Controlling Inflation			
A. Define disinflation	5		
B. Explain the effects of monetary tightening in the short run and long run		8, 16	

Self-Test: Key Terms
Use the terms below to complete the following sentences. (Answers are given at the end of the chapter.)

aggregate demand (AD) curve
aggregate supply shock
disinflation
inflation shock
long-run aggregate supply (LRAS) line
long-run equilibrium
short-run aggregate supply (SRAS) line
short-run equilibrium

1. Inflation may arise from excessive aggregate demand or from a(n) _____ .

2. In the AD/AS diagram, a horizontal line showing the current rate of inflation, as determined by past expectations and pricing decisions, is called the _____ .

3. In the AD/AS diagram, the relationship between AD and inflation, as well as the relationship between short-run equilibrium output and inflation, is shown by the _____ .

4. When the AD curve, the SRAS line, and the LRAS line all intersect at a single point the economy is at the _____ .

5. A substantial reduction in the rate of inflation is called _____ .

6. A sudden change in the normal behavior of inflation that is unrelated to the nation's output gap is caused by a(n) _____ .

7. In the AD/AS diagram, a vertical line is drawn at the economy's potential output (Y*) to represent the _____ .

8. When inflation equals the value determined by past expectations and pricing decisions and output equals the level of short-run equilibrium output that is consistent with that inflation rate, the economy is at its _____ .

Self-Test: Multiple-Choice Questions
Circle the letter that corresponds to the best answer. (Answers are given at the end of the chapter.)

1. When the Fed responds to higher inflation by raising real interest rates
    A. consumption and investment spending rise and, thus, aggregate demand increases.
    B. consumption and investment spending fall and, thus, aggregate demand increases.
    C. consumption and investment spending rise and, thus, aggregate demand decreases.
    D. consumption and investment spending fall and, thus, aggregate demand decreases.
    E. the Fed changes its policy reaction function.

2. A decrease in taxes will cause a
   A. movement downward along the AD curve.
   B. movement upward along the AD curve.
   C. rightward shift in the AD curve.
   D. leftward shift in the AD curve.
   E. decrease in AD.

3. Inflation inertia is attributable to
   A. inflation shocks and shocks to potential output.
   B. output gaps and inflation shock.
   C. disinflation and inflation shock.
   D. output gaps and disinflation.
   E. inflation expectations and long-term wage and price contracts.

4. When an expansionary gap exists, the rate of inflation will
   A. tend to rise.
   B. tend to fall.
   C. remain unchanged.
   D. become disinflation.
   E. shift the SRAS line downward.

5. If, at the short-run equilibrium output, a recessionary gap exists, the
   A. SRAS line will move upward until actual output equals potential output.
   B. SRAS line will move downward until actual output equals potential output.
   C. LRAS line will move upward until actual output equals potential output.
   D. LRAS line will move downward until actual output equals potential output.
   E. LRAS line and SRAS line will move upward until actual output equals potential output.

6. The tendency for the economy to be self-correcting
   A. is highlighted by the AD/AS diagram.
   B. is highlighted by the basic Keynesian model.
   C. is an underlying assumption of all macroeconomic models.
   D. implies that fiscal and monetary policies are not needed to stabilize output.
   E. has been called into question by the analysis of the AD/AS diagram.

7. Excessive aggregate demand can result in
   A. a recessionary gap and a rising inflation rate.
   B. too many goods chasing too little spending.
   C. an expansionary gap and an increasing inflation rate.
   D. an expansionary gap and an increasing unemployment rate.
   E. a recessionary gap and a rising unemployment rate.

8. If the Fed decides to tighten monetary policy because the inflation rate has risen to a level inconsistent with economic efficiency and long-term growth,
    A. in the short run the SRAS curve will shift downward and a recessionary gap will be created.
    B. in the long run the AD curve will shift to the left and the long-run equilibrium will be restored.
    C. in the short run the AD curve will shift to the right and an expansionary gap will be created.
    D. in the short run the AD curve shifts to the left and a recessionary gap will be created.
    E. in the short run the AD curve shifts to the right and a recessionary gap will be created.

9. The distributional effects of inflation contribute to a downward-sloping AD curve because inflation redistributes income from
    A. less affluent, lower-spending families to more affluent families who spend more, causing overall spending to decline.
    B. relatively higher-spending, less-affluent families to relatively higher-saving, more-affluent families, causing overall spending to decline.
    C. relatively lower-spending, more-affluent families to relatively higher spending, less-affluent families, causing overall spending to decline.
    D. relatively lower-spending, less-affluent families to relatively higher spending, more-affluent families, causing overall spending to decline.
    E. relatively higher-spending, more-affluent families to relatively lower saving, less-affluent families, causing overall spending to decline.

10. If the Fed were to shift its policy reaction function downward (i.e., an easing of monetary policy), the
    A. SRAS line would shift upward causing an increase in the inflation rate.
    B. LRAS line would shift upward causing an increase in the inflation rate.
    C. SRAS line would shift downward causing a decrease in the inflation rate.
    D. AD curve would shift to the left.
    E. AD curve would shift to the right.

11. A current high rate of inflation will tend to promote a
    A. virtuous circle of high expected inflation and a high rate of actual inflation.
    B. virtuous circle of low expected inflation and a low rate of actual inflation.
    C. vicious circle of high expected inflation and a high rate of actual inflation.
    D. vicious circle of low expected inflation and a low rate of actual inflation.
    E. built-in expectation of low inflation in the future.

12. A short-run equilibrium with an output gap of zero implies
    A. zero inflation in the near future.
    B. the rate of inflation will remain the same.
    C. the rate of inflation will rise.
    D. the rate of inflation will fall.
    E. firms have no incentive to raise the prices of their goods and services.

13. If, at the short-run equilibrium output, an expansionary gap exists, the
    A. SRAS line will move upward until actual output equals potential output.
    B. SRAS line will move downward until actual output equals potential output.
    C. LRAS line will move upward until actual output equals potential output.
    D. LRAS line will move downward until actual output equals potential output.
    E. LRAS line and SRAS line will move downward until actual output equals potential output.

14. If the self-correction process of the economy takes place very slowly, so that actual output differs from potential output for protracted periods of time, then active
    A. stabilization policies are probably not justified.
    B. stabilization policies may end up doing more harm than good.
    C. use of monetary and fiscal policy can cause actual output to overshoot potential output.
    D. use of monetary and fiscal policy can help to stabilize output.
    E. stabilization policy can cause the output gap to become larger.

15. Inflation escalated to the double-digit level in the United States during the 1970s because of
    A. excessive aggregate demand due to the military buildup under President Reagan.
    B. an adverse inflation shock caused by the military buildup under President Reagan.
    C. adverse inflation shocks caused by two oil crises that significantly raised world oil prices.
    D. a positive inflation shock that resulted in high inflation and a recessionary gap.
    E. a positive inflation shock that resulted in two periods of stagflation.

16. In late 1979, under the guidance of Federal Reserve Chairman Paul Volcker, the Fed dramatically tightened monetary policy. The result of the policy was
    A. strong economic growth and disinflation during 1980-82, and a recessionary gap during 1983-85.
    B. a recessionary gap during 1980-82, and strong economic growth and disinflation during 1983-85.
    C. lower nominal and real interest rates during 1980-82, and strong economic growth and disinflation during 1983-85.
    D. an expansionary gap during 1980-82, and strong economic growth and disinflation during 1983-85.
    E. an expansionary gap during 1980-82, and weak economic growth and disinflation during 1983-85.

17. At high rates of inflation, the purchasing power of money
    A. declines and households restrain their spending, causing aggregate demand to decline.
    B. rises and household increase their spending, causing aggregate demand to rise.
    C. rises and households restrain their spending, causing aggregate demand to decline.
    D. declines and households restrain their spending, causing aggregate demand to increase.
    E. declines and households increase their spending, causing aggregate demand to decline.

18. The development of new cost-saving technology would
    A. increase autonomous consumption spending and, thus, shift the AD curve to the right.
    B. increase autonomous consumption spending and, thus, shift the AD curve to the left.
    C. increase autonomous investment spending and, thus, shift the AD curve to the right.
    D. increase autonomous investment spending and, thus, shift the AD curve to the left.
    E. increase net exports and government purchases and, thus, shifts the AD curve to the right.

19. A short-run equilibrium with an recessionary gap implies that
    A. firms will raise the prices of their goods and services more than needed to fully cover their increases in costs.
    B. firms will raise the prices of their goods and services as much as needed to fully cover their increases in costs.
    C. negative inflation.
    D. firms have incentives to lower the relative prices of their goods and services..
    E. firms have incentives to raise the relative prices of their goods and services.

20. Unlike an adverse inflation shock, a shock to potential output causes
    A. lower output and higher inflation.
    B. higher output and lower inflation.
    C. no output losses.
    D. only temporary output losses.
    E. permanent output losses.

Self-Test: Short Answer/Problems
(Answers and solutions are given at the end of the chapter.)

1. Aggregate Demand Curve
This problem is designed to help you better understand why the AD curve is downward sloping and the factors that can cause the AD curve to shift. Assume the aggregate demand is given by the equation, $AD = \$950 + .75Y - 900r$

A. Complete the table below by calculating the level of aggregate demand, AD, for rates of inflation from 0 to 4 percent.

Inflation rate, π	Interest rate, r	aggregate demand, AD
0.00	0.03	
0.01	0.04	
0.02	0.05	
0.03	0.06	
0.04	0.07	
0.05	0.08	
0.06	0.09	

B. On the graph below, draw the AD curve that is shown in the above table, label it AD.

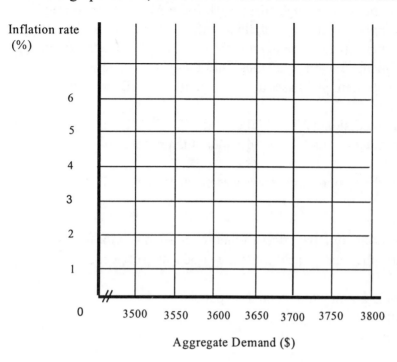

Aggregate Demand ($)

C. Assume that the Fed shifts its policy reaction function downward by reducing the nominal interest rates 1% at each rate of inflation. Complete column 2 of the following table, by indicating the new interest rates for rates of inflation from 0 to 6 percent.

Inflation Rate, π	Interest Rate, r	Aggregate Demand, AD
0.00		
0.01		
0.02		
0.03		
0.04		
0.05		
0.06		

D. Complete column 3 of the above table, by calculating the new levels of aggregate demand for rates of inflation from 0 to 6 percent.

E. On the graph above, draw the new AD curve shown in the above table and label it AD_1.

F. If new technological innovations caused the autonomous investment spending to increase by $20, in the table below calculate the new levels of aggregate aggregate demand for rates of inflation from 0 to 6 percent.

Inflation Rate, π	Interest Rate, r	Aggregate Demand, AD
0.00	0.02	
0.01	0.03	
0.02	0.04	
0.03	0.05	
0.04	0.06	
0.05	0.07	
0.06	0.08	

G. On the graph above, plot the new AD curve shown in the last table and label it AD_2.

2. AD/AS Diagram

This problem will give you practice drawing the SRAS and LRAS lines, determining the short-run and long-run equilibria, analyzing output gaps, and analyzing the economic adjustments to output gaps.

A. Assume the current inflation rate in the economy is 3 percent, and draw the short-run aggregate supply (SRAS) line on the graph below.

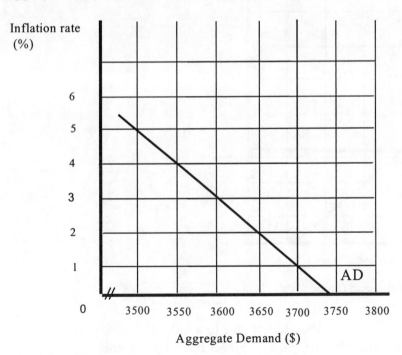

B. Given the AD curve and SRAS line on the graph above, the short-run equilibrium output is $_____ .

C. Assuming the potential output in the economy is $3,650 billion, draw the long-run aggregate supply (LRAS) line on the graph above.

D. Given the short-run equilibrium output and the potential output, the graph indicates that a(n) _____ gap exists.

E. The output gap will cause the inflation rate to (increase/decrease/ remain unchanged) _____ .

F. As the inflation rate adjusts to the output gap, the (SRAS/LRAS) _____ line will shift (upward/downward) _____ until the actual output equals the potential output.

G. When the actual output equals potential output, the economy will settle into its _____ equilibrium at $_____ .

3. Sources of Inflation
This problem focuses on the effects of excessive aggregate demand on the economy in the short run and long run. Assume the economy is initially in long-run equilibrium at the point where the AD curve, and the SRAS and LRAS lines intersect on the graph below.

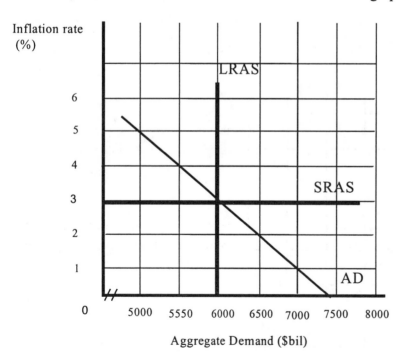

A. Suppose government purchases increase by $500 billion due to a military buildup in anticipation of a potential war. As a result, the (AD curve / SRAS line / LRAS line) _____ will shift _____. Draw the new curve on the graph above.

B. The new short-run equilibrium output will equal $ _____ billion.

C. In the short run, the military buildup has caused the actual output to become (greater than / less than / equal to) _____ the potential output, creating a(n)

_____.

D. The output gap eventually will cause the inflation rate to (rise / fall) _____ and the (AD curve / SRAS line / LRAS line) _____ will shift

_____.

E. Draw the new curve on the above graph showing its location when the self-correcting process is complete.

F. The economy will achieve its long-run equilibrium output at $ _____ billion and the inflation rate will equal _____ percent.

G. The long-run equilibrium output after the military buildup is (greater than / less than / equal to) _____ the initial long-run equilibrium output, and the inflation rate is (greater than / less than / equal to) _____ the initial long-run equilibrium inflation rate.

H. If the policymakers decided that the inflation rate had risen to a level incompatible with long run economic growth, the Fed might implement a(n) (tight / easy) _____ monetary policy that would shift the (AD curve / SRAS line / LRAS line) _____ to the

_____.

I. In comparison to a "do nothing policy," in the short run such a monetary policy would cause a(n) _____, with output (increasing/decreasing / remaining unchanged) _____, and the rate of inflation (increased/decreased/ unchanged)

_____.

J. In the long run, such a monetary policy would leave output (greater than / less than / equal to) _____ a "do nothing policy," and the rate of inflation would be (greater than / less than / equal to) _____ a "do nothing policy."

4. Aggregate Supply Shocks

This problem focuses on the effects of aggregate supply shocks on the economy in the short run and long run. Assume the economy is initially in long-run equilibrium at the point where the AD curve and that the SRAS and LRAS lines intersect on the graph below.

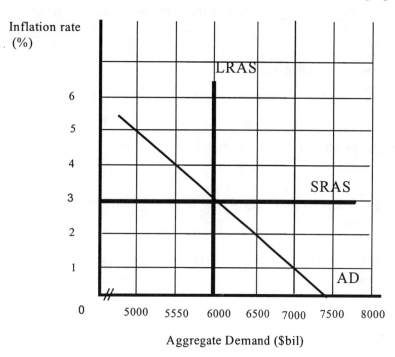

A. Because of a disruption in the worldwide supply of crude oil, the price of energy rises and drives the inflation rate to 4%. As a result, the (AD curve / SRAS line / LRAS line) _____ will shift _____. Draw the new curve on the graph above.

B. The new short-run equilibrium output will equal $ _____ billion.

C. The adverse supply shock has created a(n) _____, combined with a (higher / lower) _____ rate of inflation. This combination is referred to as _____.

D. The output gap eventually will cause the inflation rate to (rise / fall) _____ and the (AD curve / SRAS line / LRAS line) _____ will shift _____.

E. When the self-correcting process is complete, the economy will achieve its long-run equilibrium output at $ _____ billion, and the inflation rate will equal _____ percent.

F. The long-run equilibrium output after the adverse supply shock is (greater than / less than / equal to) _____ the initial long-run equilibrium, and the inflation rate is (greater / less / equal) _____ the initial long-run equilibrium.

G. If the policy makers chose to eliminate the output gap more quickly than the self-correcting process, the Fed might implement a(n) (tight / easy) _____ monetary policy that would shift the (AD curve / SRAS line / LRAS line) _____ to the

_____.

H. If the policymakers chose to eliminate the output gap more quickly, the long-run equilibrium output would be (greater than / less than / equal to) _____ a "do nothing policy," and the inflation rate would be (greater than / less than / equal to) _____ a "do nothing policy".

Solutions
Self-Test: Key Terms

1. aggregate supply shock
2. short-run aggregate supply (SRAS) line
3. aggregate demand (AD) curve
4. long-run equilibrium
5. disinflation
6. inflation shock
7. long-run aggregate supply (LRAS) line
8. short-run equilibrium

Self-Test: Multiple-Choice Questions

1. D
2. C Taxes are a component of autonomous aggregate demand and a decrease in taxation, therefore, cause the AD curve to shift to the right.
3. E
4. A
5. B
6. A
7. C
8. D
9. B
10. E
11. C
12. B
13. A
14. D
15. C
16. B
17. A
18. C
19. D
20. E

Self-Test: Short Answer/Problems

1.

A.

Inflation Rate, π	Interest Rate, r	Aggregate Demand, AD
0.00	0.03	$3,692
0.01	0.04	3,656
0.02	0.05	3,620
0.03	0.06	3,584
0.04	0.07	3,548
0.05	0.08	3,512
0.06	0.09	3,476

B.

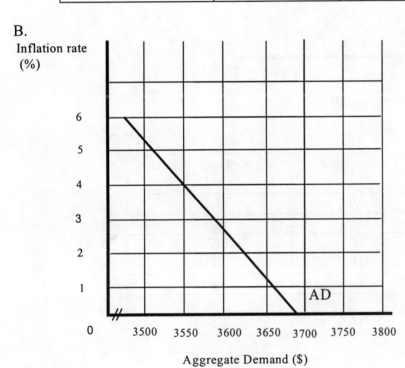

Aggregate Demand ($)

C. , D.

Inflation Rate, π	Interest Rate, r	Aggregate Demand, AD
0.00	0.02	$3,728
0.01	0.03	3,692
0.02	0.04	3,656
0.03	0.05	3,620
0.04	0.06	3,584
0.05	0.07	3,548
0.06	0.08	3,512

E.

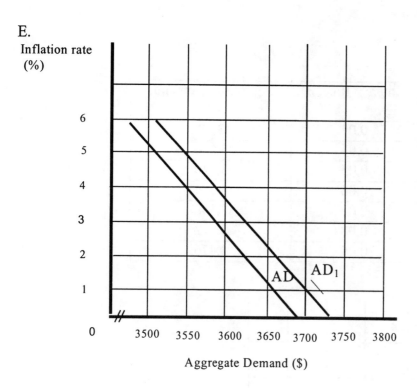

Aggregate Demand ($)

F.

Inflation Rate, π	Interest Rate, r	Aggregate Demand, AD
0.00	0.02	$3,808
0.01	0.03	3,772
0.02	0.04	3,736
0.03	0.05	3,700
0.04	0.06	3,664
0.05	0.07	3,628
0.06	0.08	3,592

G.

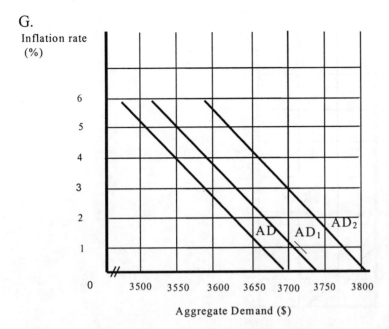

Aggregate Demand ($)

2.

A.

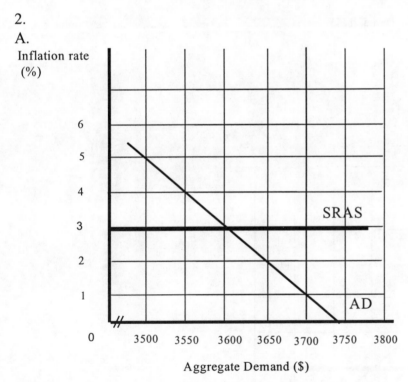

Aggregate Demand ($)

B. $3,600

C.

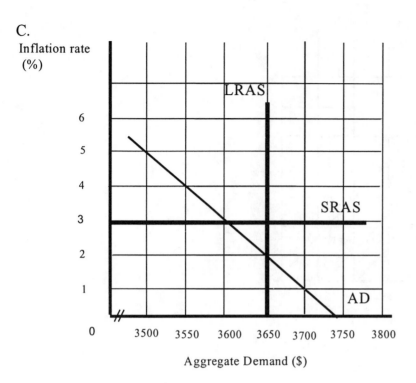

Aggregate Demand ($)

D. recessionary
E. decrease
F. SRAS; downward
G. long-run; $3,650

3.
A. AD curve; rightward;

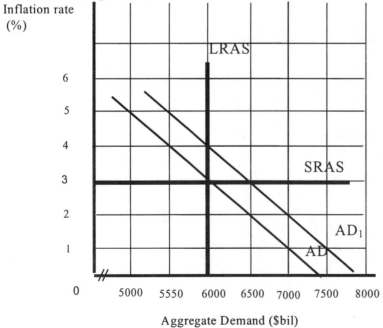

Aggregate Demand ($bil)

B. $6,500 billion

C. expansionary gap; greater than

D. rise; SRAS line; upward

E.

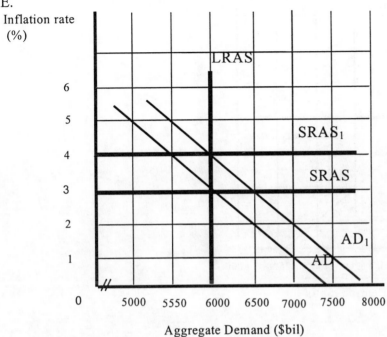

Aggregate Demand ($bil)

F. $6,000 billion; 4 percent

G. equal; greater

H. tight; AD curve; left

I. recessionary gap; decreasing; unchanged;

J. equal; less

4.

A. SRAS line; upward;

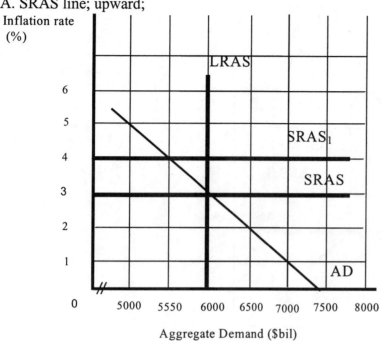

Aggregate Demand ($bil)

B. $5,500 billion
C. recessionary gap; higher; stagflation
D. fall; SRAS line; downward
E. $6,000 billion; 3
F. equal; equal
G. easy; AD curve; right
H. equal; greater

Chapter 16
International Trade and Capital Flows

Key Point Review

This chapter addresses the topic of international trade and its effects on the broader economy. It begins with a review of comparative advantage and the benefits of trade, and is followed by a discussion of the reasons for opposition to trade and an analysis of the effects of trade restrictions. The chapter concludes by examining the crucial role of international capital flows in modern economies.

As we learned in Chapter 3, factors such as climate, natural resources, technology, workers' skills and education, and culture provide countries with comparative advantages in the production of various goods and services. The principal of comparative advantage tells us that we can all enjoy more goods and services when each country produces according to its comparative advantage and then trades with other countries. In demonstrating how international trade benefits an individual country, production and consumption opportunities in a closed economy are contrasted with the opportunities in an open economy. A **closed economy** is one that does not trade with the rest of the world, while an **open economy** is one that does trade with the rest of the world. In a closed economy, a society's production possibilities are identical to its **consumption possibilities**, (i.e., the combinations of goods and services a country's citizens might feasibly consume). A closed economy is an example of **autarky**, a situation in which a country is self-sufficient. This contrasts with an open economy where a society's consumption possibilities are typically greater than (and will never be less than) its production possibilities.

Despite the fact that a country can improve its overall consumption possibilities by trading with other countries, not everyone gains from an open economy. Opening an economy to trade with other countries may create groups of winners and losers among producers, even as it helps consumers. The gains and losses are demonstrated using supply and demand analyses to compare domestic and world prices for imported and exported goods and services. The **world price** is the price at which a good or service is traded on international markets. The analysis shows that in a closed economy if the price of a good or service is greater than the world price, and that economy opens itself to trade, the economy will tend to become a net importer of that good or service. Alternatively, if the price of a good or service in a closed economy is lower than the world price, and that economy opens itself to trade, the economy will tend to become a net exporter of that good or service. When a country becomes a net importer of a good or service, the domestic consumers benefit from free trade, but domestic producers are hurt by free trade. When, on the other hand, a country is a net exporter of a good or service, the domestic producers benefit from free trade, while the domestic consumers are hurt by free trade.

Despite the overall efficiency of free trade, when some groups lose from trade, political pressures may be created to block or restrict trade. The view that free trade is injurious and should be restricted is known as **protectionism**. Supporters of this view believe the government should attempt to protect domestic markets through the imposition of tariffs or quotas. A **tariff** is a tax imposed on an imported good. A **quota** is a legal limit on the quantity of a good that may be imported. Supply and demand analysis indicate that a tariff raises the price of the imported good or service, harming the domestic consumer, but helping the domestic producers and government. Similarly, a quota on a good or service raises the price of the imported good or service by an identical amount as a tariff does, harming the domestic consumer and helping the domestic producer. The government, however, is not helped through quotas because it does not collect additional tax revenues, as it does when a tariff is imposed.

Such protectionist policies are inefficient because they reduce the total economic pie. Because those who benefit from these restrictions are often politically better organized than the losers are, lawmakers are sometimes persuaded to enact the restrictions. The fact that free trade increases the overall economic pie, however, suggests an alternative to trade restrictions. In general, winners from free trade should be able to compensate losers in such a way that everyone become better off. Government programs that assist and retrain workers displaced by import competition are an example of such compensation. Nonetheless, economic interests do not motivate all protectionism. Environmental concerns have also been a cited by supporters of protectionism. While protecting the environment is an important and laudable goal, the efficiency principle again suggests that restricting trade is not the most effective means of achieving that goal. Furthermore, much of the income loss from trade restrictions is absorbed by poor nations trying to develop their economies.

When an economy is open to trade, its **trade balance**, the value of a country's exports minus the value of its imports in a particular period, may be positive or negative. A country is said to have a **trade surplus** for a period when the value of its exports exceeds the value of its imports. Alternatively, a country is said to have a **trade deficit** for a period, when the value of its imports exceeds the value of its exports. In addition to the trade of goods and services that is captured in the trade balance, trade among countries occurs in real and financial assets. Purchases or sales of real and financial assets across international borders are known as **international capital flows**. From the perspective of a particular country, purchases of domestic assets by foreigners are called **capital inflows**, and purchases of foreign assets by domestic households and firms are called **capital outflows**. Capital inflows are related to real interest rates and investment risk in a country. The higher the real interest rate in a country, and the lower the risk of investing there, the higher its capital inflows. Capital inflows expand a country's pool of saving, allowing for more domestic investment and economic growth. A drawback, however, to using capital inflows to finance domestic investment is that the interest and dividends on the borrowed funds must be paid to foreign savers rather than domestic residents.

There is a precise link between the trade balance and international capital flows. In any given period, the trade balance and net capital inflows add up to zero, or NX (net exports) + KI (net capital inflows) = 0. This link suggests the primary cause of a trade deficit is a country's low rate of national saving. A low-saving, high-spending country is likely to import more and export less than a high-saving, low-spending country. It is also likely to have higher real interest rates, attracting capital inflows. Because the sum of the trade balance and capital inflows is zero, a high level of net capital inflows is consistent with a large trade deficit.

Knowledge and Skills

The student must master the knowledge and skills listed below each number topic.	Key Terms	Multiple-Choice Questions	Short Answer/ Problems
1. Production and Consumption Possibilities and the Benefits of Trade			
A. Review the principle of comparative advantage			1
B. Define closed economy, open economy, consumption possibilities, and autarky	2, 5, 6, 8	17	
C. Analyze the production possibilities and consumption possibilities curves for a closed and an open economy			1, 2
D. Explain the benefits of trade		1, 9	
2. Supply-and-Demand Perspective on Trade			
A. Define world price	3		
B. Identify trade winners and losers		2, 10	3
3. Protectionist Policies: Tariffs and Quotas			
A. Define protectionism, tariff, and quota	1, 7, 11		
B. Analyze the economic effects of tariffs and quotas		3, 11, 18	3, 4
C. Explain why governments may impose protectionist policies		4, 12	
4. Capital Flows and the Balance of Trade			
A. Define trade balance, trade surplus, and trade deficit	9, 12, 14		
B. Define international capital flows, capital inflows, and capital outflows	4, 10, 13		
C. Explain the link between the trade balance and capital flows		5, 13, 19	
D. Identify the determinants of capital inflows		6, 14	
E. Discuss the relationships among capital inflows, saving, and investment		7, 15, 20	
F. Explain the cause of trade deficits		8, 16	

Self-Test: Key Terms

Use the terms below to complete the following sentences. (Answers are given at the end of the chapter.)

autarky
capital inflows
capital outflows
closed economy
consumption possibilities
international capital flows
open economy
protectionism
quota
tariff
trade balance
trade deficit
trade surplus
world price

1. The view that free trade is injurious and should be restricted is known as

    _____ .

2. A society that does not trade with the rest of the world has a(n)

    _____ .

3. The price at which a good or service is traded on international markets is the

    _____ .

4. From the perspective of a particular country, purchases of domestic assets by foreigners are
    called _____ .

5. The combinations of goods and services a country's citizens might feasibly consume are its

    _____ .

6. A situation in which a country is self-sufficient is referred to as _____ .

7. Legal limits are placed on the quantity of a good that may be imported when a government
    imposes a(n) _____ .

8. A society that trades with the rest of the world has a(n) _____ .

9. Another term for a country's net exports is its _____ .

10. Purchases or sales of real and financial assets across international borders are known as

    _____ .

11. A tax imposed on an imported good is called a(n) _____ .

12. When the value of a country's exports exceeds the value of its imports for a period, it has a(n)

    _____ .

13. From the perspective of a particular country, purchases of foreign assets by domestic
    households and firms are called _____ .

14. If the value of a country's imports exceeds the value of its exports for a period, it has a(n)

    _____ .

Self-Test: Multiple-Choice Questions
Circle the letter that corresponds to the best answer. (Answers are given at the end of the chapter.)

1. To maximize its gains from trade, a nation should
   A. maximize net exports (or its trade surplus).
   B. export products in which it has a comparative advantage.
   C. export as many products as possible by subsidizing domestic producers that could not otherwise compete with foreign producers.
   D. create jobs by subsidizing industries that employ the large numbers of workers.
   E. subsidize the purchase of imports in order to achieve the highest level of total consumption.

2. If Sierra Leone has a comparative advantage in the production of coffee, and its previously closed economy is opened to trade coffee for imported steel, Sierra Leone's
   A. steel industry will benefit at the expense of its steel consumers.
   B. steel industry will benefit at the expense of its coffee industry.
   C. steel consumers will benefit, as will its steel producers.
   D. coffee producers will benefit and as will its coffee drinkers.
   E. steel consumers and coffee producers will benefit.

3. If quotas are imposed on French clothing imported into the United States
   A. both French and American consumers are penalized when they buy clothing.
   B. both French and American producers of clothing are penalized.
   C. American producers and consumers of clothing are penalized.
   D. American clothing producers benefit but American consumers of clothing are penalized.
   E. French producers and consumers of clothing benefit.

4. Protectionist policies are implemented by governments because
   A. they benefit the domestic consumers
   B. they benefit politically powerful groups.
   C. they are efficient and, therefore, increase the total economic pie.
   D. its unfair for domestic workers and producers to have to compete with the low wages and costs in poor countries.
   E. it is the most effective way to protect the global environment.

5. When American investors pay cash for stock in a French corporation, from the perspective of
   A. the United States, it is a capital inflow.
   B. France, it is a capital outflow.
   C. the United States, it is a capital outflow.
   D. France, it is a trade deficit.
   E. the United States, it is a trade deficit.

6. If interest rates in Japan increase relative to international interest rate levels, all else being equal, Japan's net capital
   A. inflows will tend to increase, and the pool of funds for domestic investment will tend to decrease.
   B. inflows will tend to increase, and the pool of funds for domestic investment will tend to increase.
   C. outflows will tend to increase, and the pool of funds for domestic investment will tend to decrease.
   D. outflows will tend to increase, and the pool of funds for domestic investment will tend to increase.
   E. inflows will tend to decrease, and the pool of funds for domestic investment will tend to decrease.

7. The sum of national saving and capital inflows from abroad must equal
   A. domestic investment in new capital goods.
   B. capital outflows.
   C. aggregate demand.
   D. the trade deficit.
   E. the trade surplus.

8. The U.S. trade deficit is mainly caused by
   A. production of inferior goods in the country.
   B. unfair trade restrictions imposed by other countries on imports.
   C. a low rate of national saving.
   D. cheap labor in other countries.
   E. inadequate safety and environmental protections in other countries.

9. A country will benefit the most from trade if it
   A. has a closed economy to protect its producers from low-cost, inferior goods produced in low-income countries.
   B. exports to the rest of the world while maintaining protectionist policies on imports into its economy.
   C. has an open economy and subsidizes its less-competitive producers.
   D. has an open economy and produces those goods in which it has the lowest opportunity cost and exchanges them for other goods.
   E. has an open economy and produces those goods in which it has the highest opportunity cost and exchanges them for other goods.

10. The voluntary export restraints (VERs) on the importation of Japanese automobiles into the United States benefited
    A. Japanese and American automotive producers.
    B. Japanese and American automotive consumers.
    C. American automotive producers and consumers.
    D. Japanese automotive producers and consumers.
    E. Japanese automotive producers and American automotive consumers.

11. Compared to a quota, a tariff on shoe imports
    A. avoids an increase in the price of domestic shoes.
    B. does not harm foreign shoe producers, whereas a quota does.
    C. does not harm domestic shoe producers, whereas a quota does.
    D. does not harm foreign shoe consumers, whereas a quota does.
    E. generates revenue for the government, whereas a quota does not.

12. In all likelihood, the U.S. government chose to negotiate quotas (VERs) on the importation of Japanese automobiles during the early 1980s rather than imposing tariffs because
    A. quotas generated tax revenues for the government that tariffs would not have created.
    B. quotas are less harmful to domestic consumers than are tariffs.
    C. they reduced the probability of retaliation by the Japanese government.
    D. the Japanese auto producers wanted to raise the price of their cars.
    E. the VERs had less adverse effects on capital outflows from the United States to Japan.

13. Which of the following transactions would cause a capital inflow to a country?
    A. exports of goods or services
    B. import of goods or services
    C. purchasing financial assets (e.g., a corporate bond) from abroad
    D. purchasing real assets (e.g., a factory) abroad
    E. lending money abroad

14. The illegal drug trade has increased the political instability in Colombia and has
    A. reduced net capital outflows from Colombia.
    B. reduced net capital inflows to Colombia.
    C. increased net capital inflows to Colombia.
    D. increased Colombia's trade deficit.
    E. decreased Colombia's trade surplus.

15. An increase in net capital inflows to a country will
    A. increase its real interest rates.
    B. increase its imports.
    C. decrease its exports.
    D. decrease its real interest rates.
    E. decrease its investment in new capital.

16. During the 1960s and 1970s, the U.S. trade balance was close to zero, but during the 1980s the trade deficit ballooned to unprecedented levels due to
    A. an inability of U.S. companies to compete in the international market.
    B. a decline in private saving that resulted from an upsurge in consumption.
    C. a decline in national saving caused largely by rapidly rising government budget deficits.
    D. a worldwide recession that made it difficult for U. S. companies to sell their products abroad.
    E. unfair protectionist policies imposed by U. S.s' major trade partners.

17. Autarky is a situation created by
    A. a trade deficit.
    B. a trade surplus.
    C. protectionist policies.
    D. an open economy.
    E. a closed economy.

18. Quotas and tariffs are similar in that both
    A. generate revenues for the government that imposes them.
    B. increase the prices of goods and services in the domestic markets.
    C. increase the revenues of the firms importing the goods and services.
    D. harm domestic and foreign producers.
    E. harm domestic and foreign consumers.

19. A country's trade balance and its net capital inflows
    A. Add up to zero.
    B. determine the size of the pool of saving available for capital investment.
    C. must always equal the sum of the four components of aggregate demand.
    D. must equal domestic investment in new capital goods.
    E. are identical in open and closed economies.

20. Capital inflows used to finance capital investment in some developing countries have
    A. decreased domestic saving.
    B. benefited domestic savers because of higher interest rates paid on saving accounts.
    C. caused debt crises because the returns on the investments were less than the interest cost of the capital.
    D. caused debt crises because the returns on the investments were greater than the interest cost of the capital.
    E. had economic benefits without costs.

Self-Test: Short Answer/Problems
(Answers and solutions are given at the end of the chapter.)

1. Production Possibilities in a Three-Person Economy
In this problem you will draw a production possibilities curve for a three-person economy, reviewing the implications of the principal of comparative advantage for production.

Assume the country of Islandia has only 3 workers, Maria, Tom and Patty, each of whom works 50 weeks per year. Maria can produce 100 shirts or she can catch 10 pounds of fish per week. Tom can produce 50 shirts or catch 20 pounds of fish per week. Patty can produce 200 shirts or catch 40 pounds of fish per week.

A. Maria's opportunity cost of producing 1 pound of fish per week is _____ shirts, Tom's opportunity cost of producing 1 pound of fish per week is _____ shirts, and Patty's opportunity cost of producing 1 pound of fish per week is _____ shirts.

B. Maria's opportunity cost of producing 1 shirt per week is _____ pounds of fish, Tom's opportunity cost of producing 1 shirt per week is _____ pounds of fish, and Patty's opportunity cost of producing 1 shirt per week is _____ pounds of fish.

C. Based on their respective opportunity costs, if Islandia were to allocate resources to the production of shirts, _____ would be the first worker to begin producing shirts, _____ would be the second worker to begin producing shirts, and _____ would be the third worker to begin producing shirts.

D. On the graph below construct the annual production possibilities curve for Islandia, identify the location of the "kinks" in the curve (label them A and B), and label each section of the curve to indicate who is producing the shirts.

Fish
(pounds)

3500
3000
2500
2000
1500
1000
500

0   2,500   5,000   7,500   10,000   12,500   15,000   17,500

Shirts

E. To produce 1 to 5,000 shirts, the opportunity cost of producing shirts in Islandia is _____ pounds of fish. To produce 5,001 to 15,000 shirts the opportunity cost of producing shirts in Islandia is _____ pounds of fish. To produce 15,001 to 17,500 shirts the opportunity cost of producing shirts in Islandia is _____ pounds of fish.

F. Thus, as Islandia allocates more resources to the production of shirts, the opportunity cost of producing shirts (increases / decreases / remaines constant) _____ . This reflects the core principle of _____ .

G. As a result of the above core principle, the shape of Islandia's production possibilities curve is

_____ .

2. Consumption Possibilities With and Without International Trade

This problem will help you better understand the gains that a country can achieve by opening its economy to international trade. You will determine the opportunity cost of producing goods, draw a consumption possibilities curve, and calculate the gains from trade.

Assume the country of Nordica has two workers, Ian and Michelle. Ian can produce 1,500 bicycles per year or 1,500 articles of clothing. Michelle can produce 1,500 bicycles or 750 articles of clothing per year.

A. Ian's opportunity cost of producing 1 bicycle is _____ articles of clothing, and Michelle's opportunity cost of producing 1 bicycle is _____ articles of clothing.

B. Michelle's opportunity cost of producing 1 article of clothing is _____ bicycles, and Ian's opportunity cost of producing 1 article of clothing is _____ bicycles.

C. If Nordica has a closed economy and Ian only produces articles of clothing and Michelle only produces bicycles, identify the point of Nordica's production (label it A) on the graph below.

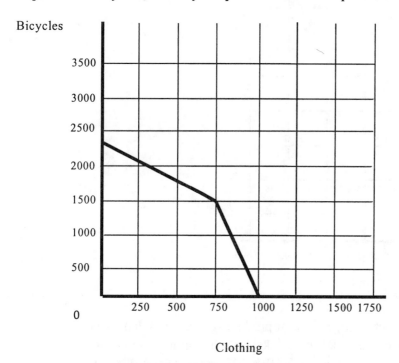

D. Assume the world prices are such that 2 bicycles can be traded for 1 article of clothing. If Nordica opens its economy to world trade, on the above graph draw its consumption possibilities curve such that it just touches (i.e., is tangent to) Nordica's production possibilities curve at point A.

E. If Nordica chose to trade 250 of the 750 articles of clothing it is producing on the world markets, it could obtain _____ bicycles.

F. On the graph above, locate the point on Nordica's consumption possibilities curve (label it B) that would represent the amount of bicycles and articles of clothing it could consume after it traded 250 articles of its clothing. After the trade, the consumption possibilities curve indicates that Nordica can consume _____ articles of clothing and_____ bicycles.

G. Had Nordica remained a closed economy, it could produce 500 articles of clothing and _____ bicycles.

H. By comparison to a closed economy, opening its economy to world trade resulted in Nordica gaining _____ bicycles.

3. Closed versus Open Economy

In this problem you will analyze the economic impact of a closed and an open economy using the supply and demand model. The following graph shows the domestic supply and demand for wool in Upperlandia.

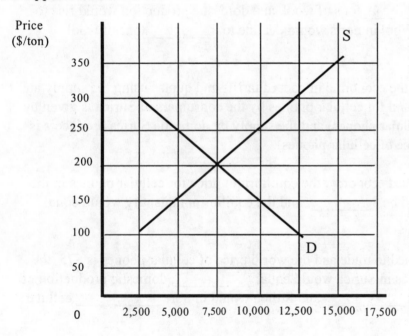

A. If Upperlandia has a closed economy, the equilibrium price of wool would equal $_____ per ton and Upperlandia would produce _____ tons of wool.

B. Assume the world price of wool is $150 per ton. On the graph above, draw a curve representing the world price of wool (label it P_w).

C. Given the domestic supply and demand for wool and the world price of wool, if Upperlandia opened its economy to trade it would produce _____ tons of wool, consume _____ tons of wool, import _____ tons of wool, and the domestic price of wool would fall to $ _____ per ton.

D. As a result of opening the Upperlandian economy to trade, the trade winners would be the (domestic wool producers / foreign wool producers / domestic consumers / foreign consumers) _____ and (domestic wool producers / foreign wool producers / domestic consumers / foreign consumers) _____ , while the trade losers would be the (domestic wool producers / foreign wool producers / domestic consumers / foreign consumers) _____ and (domestic wool producers / foreign wool producers / domestic consumers / foreign consumers) _____ .

E. Assume the domestic wool producers convinced the Upperlandia government to impose a quota of 1,000 tons of imported wool. On the graph above, draw the curve that would reflect the effect of the quota on the Upperlandia wool market (label it $P_w + Q$).

F. As a result of the quota, the price of wool in Upperlandia would rise to $_____, domestic consumption would equal _____ tons of wool, and domestic production would rise to _____ tons of wool. Wool imports would decline to _____ tons of wool.

4. Trade Protectionism

In this problem you will analyze the economic impact of tariffs and quotas using the supply and demand model. Assume the demand for cellular phones by the consumers of Surica is given by Demand = 320 – 0.6 (price of cellular phones) and the supply by domestic Surica producers is given by Supply = 200 + 0.6 (price of cellular phones).

A. Assuming that Surica is a closed economy, the equilibrium price for cellular phones in the domestic Surica market would be $_____, and the equilibrium quantity would equal _____ .

B. If the Surica economy is opened to trade and the world price of cellular phones is $75, the consumption of cellular phones in Surica would equal _____, domestic production of cellular phones would equal _____, and Surica would import _____ cellular phones.

C. Assume that, at the request of Surica cellular phone producers, the Surica government imposes a tariff of $20 per cellular phone. After the imposition of the tariff, Surica consumption of cellular phones would equal _____, domestic production would equal _____ cellular phones, and Surica would import _____ cellular phones.

D. The tariff raised the price of cellular phones by $_____ and reduced imports by _____ .

E. The Surica government would receive $_____ from the tariff.

Solutions
Self-Test: Key Term

1. protectionism
2. closed economy
3. world price
4. capital inflows
5. consumption possibilities
6. autarky
7. quota
8. open economy
9. trade balance
10. international capital flows
11. tariff
12. trade surplus
13. capital outflows
14. trade deficit

Self-Test: Multiple-Choice Questions

1. B
2. E
3. D
4. B
5. C
6. B
7. A
8. C
9. D
10. A
11. E
12. C
13. A
14. B
15. D
16. C
17. E
18. B
19. A
20. C

Self-Test: Short Answer/Problems

1.
A. 10 (=100/10); 25; 5
B. .1 (=10/100); .4; . 2
C. Maria, Patty, Tom
D.

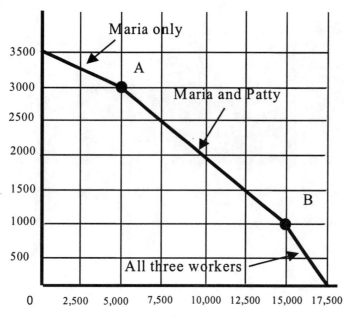

E. 1 (Maria has a comparative advantage in producing shirts and she can produce a maximum of 5,000 per year. Because she would be the first worker to produce shirts, Islandia's opportunity cost would equal her opportunity cost); 2; 4
F. increases; increasing opportunity cost
G. bowed outward

2.
A. 1 (=1500/1500); 1/2
B. 2 (1500/750); 1

C.

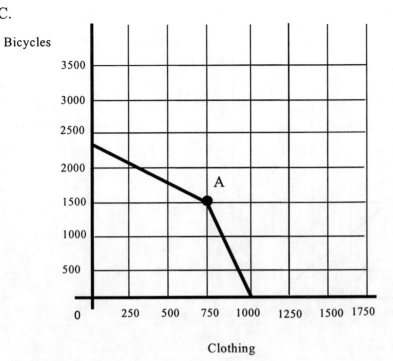

Clothing

D.

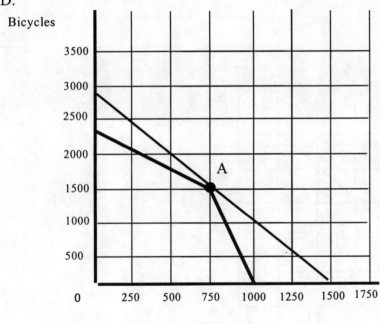

Clothing

E. 500 (The world price is 2 bicycles = 1 article of clothing. Thus, 250 x 2 = 500)

F.

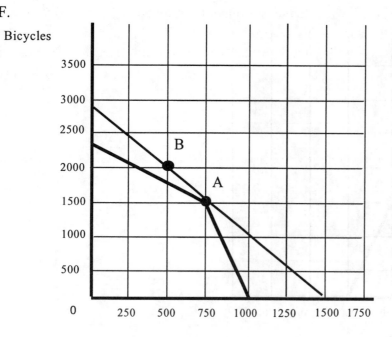

Clothing

; 500; 2000

G. 1,750

H. 250 (= 2,000 − 1,750)

3.

A. $200; 7,500

B.

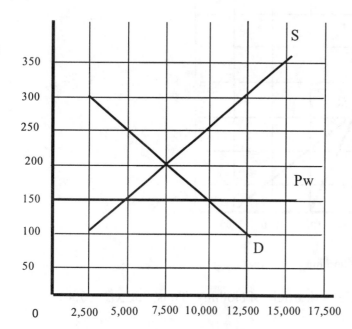

Tons of wool

C. 5,000 (at the world price of $150 per ton of wool, the quantity supplied is 5,000); 10,000 (at the world price of $150, the quantity supplied is 10,000); 5,000 (10,000 – 5,000)

D. domestic consumers; foreign wool producers; domestic wool producers; foreign consumers

E.

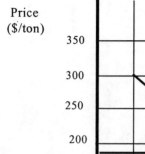
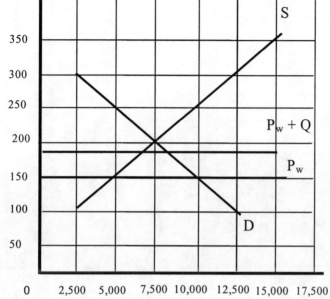

Tons of wool

F. $190; 7,000; 8,000; 1,000

4.

A. $100 (320 – 0.6p = 200 + 0.6p, or 120 = 1.2p. Thus, 120/1.2 = p); 260 (320 –0.6 x 100, or 320 – 100)

B. 275 (D= 320 –0.6 x 75, or 320 – 45); 245 (S= 200 + 0.6 x 74, or 200 + 45); 30 (275 – 245)

C. 266 (D= 320 – 0.6 x 95, or 320 – 54); 254 (S= 200 + 0.6 x 95, or 200 + 54); 12 (266 – 254)

D. $20; 18 (30 – 12)

E. $240 (20 x 12)

Chapter 17
Exchange Rates and the Open Economy

Key Point Review

This chapter explains the role of exchange rates in open economies. The discussion begins by distinguishing between the nominal exchange rate and the real exchange rate. This is followed by an analysis of how flexible and fixed exchange rates exchange rates are determined. The chapter concludes with a discussion of the relative merits of fixed and flexible exchange rates.

The economic benefits of trade between nations in goods, services, and assets are similar to the benefits of trade within a nation. There is, however, a difference between the two cases. Trade within a nation normally involves only a single currency, while trade between nations involves different currencies. Because international transactions generally require that one currency be traded for another currency, the relative values of different currencies are an important factor in international economic relations. The rate at which two currencies can be traded for each other is called the **nominal exchange rate**, or simply the exchange rate. Exchange rates can be expressed as the amount of foreign currency needed to purchase one unit of domestic currency, or as the number of units of the domestic currency needed to purchase one unit of the foreign currency. These two ways of expressing the exchange rate are equivalent; each is the reciprocal of the other. Although the exchange rate can be expressed either way, to simply the discussion, the textbook authors have chosen to define the nominal exchange rate (e) as the number of units of foreign currency that domestic currency will buy.

Exchange rates can be of two broad types: flexible or fixed exchange rates. A **flexible exchange rate** is not officially fixed, but varies according to the supply and demand for the currency in the **foreign exchange market**–the market in which currencies of various nations are traded for one another. Flexible exchange rates change over time. An increase in the value of one currency relative to other currencies is called **appreciation,** and a decrease in the value of that currency relative to other currencies is called **depreciation. A fixed exchange rate** is an exchange rate whose value is set by official government policy.

It is important to distinguish the nominal exchange rate from the real exchange rate. As indicated above, the nominal exchange rate tells us the price of the domestic currency in terms of a foreign currency. The **real exchange rate** tells us the price of the average domestic good or service in terms of the average foreign good or service, when prices are expressed in terms of a common currency. The real exchange rate is equal to the nominal exchange rate times the price of the average domestic good divided by the price of the average foreign good. Consequently, the nominal and real exchange rates tend to move in the same direction. The real exchange rate has important implications for a nation's trade. A high real exchange rate implies that domestic producers will have a hard time exporting to other countries, while foreign goods will sell well in the home country. Thus, when the real exchange rate is high, net exports will tend to be low. Conversely, if the real exchange rate is low, domestic producers will find it easier to export and foreign producers will have difficulty selling in the domestic market. Net exports, therefore, will be high when the real exchange rate is low. This cause-and-effect relationship suggests that a strong currency does not necessarily reflect a strong economy.

What determines the value of flexible exchanges rates? The most basic theory of how nominal exchange rates are determined is called **purchasing power parity**, or PPP. To understand the PPP theory, one first has to understand the law of one price. The **law of one price** states that if transportation costs are relatively small, the price of an internationally traded commodity must be the same in all locations. If the law of one price were to hold for all goods and services, then the value of the exchange rate between two currencies would be determined by dividing the price of the average good in one country by the price of the average good in the other country. An implication of the PPP theory is that, in the long run, the currencies of countries that experience significant inflation will tend to depreciate. The rationale is sound because inflation implies that a nation's currency is losing purchasing power in the domestic market, while exchange-rate deprecation implies that the nation's currency is losing purchasing power in international markets.

Empirical studies have found that the PPP theory is useful for predicting changes in nominal exchange rates over the long run. The theory is less successful, however, in predicting short-run movements in exchange rates. One reason that the PPP works less well in the short run is that the law of one price works best for standardized commodities that are widely traded. Not all goods, however, are standardized commodities and not all goods are traded internationally. In general, the greater the share of traded and standardized goods and services in a nation's output, the more precisely the PPP theory will apply to the country's exchange rate.

Supply and demand analysis is more useful for understanding the short-run movements of exchange rates. Anyone who holds a currency is a potential supplier of that currency, but, in practice, the principal suppliers of a currency to the foreign exchange market are that nation's households and firms. The demanders of a currency are, in practice, households and firms that want to purchase foreign assets or goods and services. The supply curve of a currency is upward sloping and the demand curve is downward sloping. The equilibrium value of a currency, also called the **fundamental value of the exchange rate**, is the exchange rate at which the quantity supplied equals the quantity demanded. Factors that cause shifts in the supply and demand for a currency will cause the equilibrium value of the currency to change. Some factors that cause an increase in the supply of the domestic currency are an increased preference for foreign goods, an increase in the domestic real GDP, and an increase in the real interest rate on foreign assets.

Factors that will cause an increased demand for the domestic currency are an increased preference for domestic goods, an increase in real GDP abroad, and an increase in the real interest rate on domestic assets. Of the many factors affecting a country's exchange rate, among the most important is the monetary policy of a country's central bank. A tightening of a country's monetary policy increases domestic real interest rates, raising the demand for its currency and causing the currency to appreciate. Easing of monetary policy has the opposite effects. In an open economy with a flexible exchange rate, the exchange rate serves as another channel for monetary policy that reinforces the effects of real interest rates. Higher interest rates, for example, reduce domestic consumption and investment. They also cause appreciation of the currency and, as a result, imports rise and exports fall, reducing net exports. The decline in net exports, thus, reinforces the domestic effects of the tightened monetary policy. Monetary policy, therefore, is more effective in an open economy with flexible exchange rates.

Fixed exchange rates are a historically important alternative to flexible exchange rates. Fixed exchange rates also are still used in many countries, especially small and developing nations. The value of a fixed exchange rate is determined by the government (in practice, usually the by the finance ministry or treasury department, in cooperation with the country's central bank). Fixed exchange rates today are usually set in terms of a major currency (e.g., the dollar or yen), or relative to a "basket" of currencies, typically those of the country's trading partners. Historically, currency values were fixed in terms of gold or other precious metals. Once an exchange rate has been fixed, the government usually attempts to keep it unchanged for some time. Economic circumstances, however, can force the government to change the value of the exchange rate. A reduction in the official value of a currency is called **devaluation**; and increase in the official value is called a **revaluation**.

Fixed exchange rates are not always consistent with the fundamental value of a currency (as determined by supply and demand). When the officially fixed value of an exchange rate is greater than its fundamental value, the exchange rate is **overvalued,** and when it is less that its fundamental value, it is **undervalued**. When the officially set value of an exchange rate is overvalued, the government has several alternatives for dealing with the inconsistency. It could devalue its currency, restrict international transactions, or become a demander of its currency. The most common approach is for the government to become a demander of its currency. To be able to purchase its own currency and maintain an overvalued exchange rate, a government (usually the central bank) must hold foreign-currency assets called **international reserves**, or simply reserves. Because a government must use part of its reserves to maintain an overvalued currency, over time its reserves will decline. The net decline in a country's stock of international reserves over a year is called its **balance-of-payments deficit**. Conversely, if a country experiences a net increase in its international reserves over a year, it has a **balance-of-payments surplus**. Although a government can maintain an overvalued exchange rate for some time by purchasing its own currency, there is a limit to this strategy because no government's reserves are unlimited. Eventually a government will run out of reserves, and the fixed exchange rate will collapse. A **speculative attack**, involving massive selling of domestic-currency assets by financial investors, can quickly end a government's attempt to maintain an overvalued currency.

Such an attack is most likely to occur when financial investors fear that an overvalued currency will be devalued. A speculative attack, therefore, can be self-fulfilling.

As an alternative to trying to maintain an overvalued currency, a government can take actions to try to increase the fundamental value of its currency and eliminate the overvaluation problem. The most effective way to increase the fundamental value of a currency is through monetary policy. A tightening of monetary policy that raises real interest rates will increase the demand for a currency and, in turn, will raise its fundamental value. Although monetary policy can be used in this manner, it has some drawbacks. In particular, if monetary policy is used to set the fundamental value of the exchange rate equal to the official value, it is no longer available for stabilizing the domestic economy. The conflict between using monetary policy to set the fundamental value of a currency or using it to stabilize the domestic economy is most severe when the exchange rate is under a speculative attack.

There are two important issues in comparing flexible and fixed exchange rates – the effects on monetary policy and the effects on trade and economic integration. A flexible exchange rate strengthens the impact of monetary policy on aggregate demand, when a fixed exchange rate prevents policymakers from using monetary policy to stabilize the domestic economy. Large economies should almost always employ flexible exchange rates because it seldom makes sense for them to give up the power to stabilize the domestic economy via monetary policy. For small economies, however, giving up this power may make sense when their history suggests an inability to use monetary policy to control domestic inflation. On the issue of trade and economic integration, supporters of fixed exchange rates have argued that an officially fixed exchange rate reduces or eliminates uncertainty about future exchange rates and, thus, provides incentives for firms to expand export business. The problem with this argument is that a fixed exchange rate is not guaranteed to remain fixed forever, especially if the currency comes under a speculative attack. Some countries, such as eleven western European nations, have tried to solve the problem of uncertain exchange rates by adopting a common currency.

Knowledge and Skills

The student must master the knowledge and skills listed below each number topic.	Key Terms	Multiple Choice Questions	Short Answer/ Problems
1. Exchange Rates			
A. Define nominal exchange rate, appreciation, and depreciation	8, 13, 18		
B. Calculate the nominal exchange between two currencies		1	1
C. Define flexible and fixed exchange rates, foreign exchange market, and real exchange rate	3, 7, 10, 14		
D. Calculate the real exchange rate between two currencies		2	1
E. Discuss the effects of real exchange rates on net exports		3, 11	

The student must master the knowledge and skills listed below each number topic.	Key Terms	Multiple Choice Questions	Short Answer/ Problems
2. The Determination of the Exchange Rate			
A. Define the law of one price and purchasing power parity (PPP)	6, 16		
B. Explain the PPP theory and its implications		4, 12	
C. Discuss the shortcomings of the PPP theory		5, 13	
D. Use supply-and-demand analysis to determine the equilibrium exchange rate			2, 3
E. Define fundamental value of the exchange rate	1	14	
F. Identify the factors that cause changes in the equilibrium exchange rate		6, 15, 19	2
G. Explain the links between monetary policy and the exchange rate		7, 16	2
3. Fixed Exchange Rates			
A. Explain how a fixed exchange rate is set		8	
B. Define devaluation, revaluation, and overvalued and undervalued exchange rates	2, 5, 12, 15		
C. Discuss the alternatives actions a government can take when its currency is overvalued		9, 17	
D. Define international reserves and balance-of-payments deficit and surplus	9, 11, 17	18	
E. Calculate the balance-of-payments deficit			3
F. Define speculative attack	4		
G. Compare flexible and fixed exchange rate systems		10, 20	

Self-Test: Key Terms
Use the terms below to complete the following sentences. (Answers are given at the end of the chapter.)

appreciation
balance-of-payments deficit
balance-of-payments surplus
depreciation
devaluation
fixed exchange rate
flexible exchange rate
foreign-exchange market
fundamental value of the exchange rate
international reserves
law of one price
nominal exchange rate

overvalued exchange rate
purchasing power parity (PPP)
real exchange rate
revaluation
speculative attack
undervalued exchange rate

1. The exchange rate at which the quantity supplied equals the quantity demanded is the

    _____ .

2. When the officially set value becomes a(n)_____ , the government
    must either devalue its currency, restrict international transactions, or become a demander of
    its currency.

3. The nominal exchange rate times the price of the average domestic good divided by the price
    of the average foreign good equals the _____ .

4. A government's attempt to maintain an overvalued currency can quickly end when it
    encounters a(n) _____ of massive selling of domestic-
    currency assets by financial investors .

5. A reduction in the official value of a currency is called a _____ .

6. If transportation costs are relatively small, the price of an internationally traded commodity
    must be the same in all locations, according to the _____ .

7. An exchange rate that varies according to the supply and demand for the currency is a(n)

    _____ .

8. The rate at which two currencies can be traded for each other is called the

    _____ .

9. To be able to purchase its own currency and maintain an overvalued exchange rate, a
    government (usually the central bank) must hold _____ .

10. An exchange rate whose value is set by official government policy is a(n)

    _____ .

11. If a country experiences a net increase in its international reserves over a year, it has a(n)

    _____ .

12. When the officially fixed value of an exchange rate is less than its fundamental value, the
    country has a(n) _____ .

13. An increase in the value of a currency relative to other currencies is called

    _____ .

14. Flexible exchange rates are determined in the _____ , where
    currencies from various nations are traded for one another.

15. An increase in the official value of an exchange rate is called _____ .

16. If the law of one price were to hold for all goods and services, then the value of the exchange
    rate between two currencies would be determined in accordance with the theory of

    _____ .

17. The net decline in a country's stock of international reserves over a year is equal to its

    _____ .

18. A decrease in the value of a currency relative to other currencies is called

    _____ .

Self-Test: Multiple-Choice Questions
Circle the letter that corresponds to the best answer. (Answers are given at the end of the chapter.)

1. During summer 2000, the nominal exchange rate was one U.S. dollar to 9.5 Mexican pesos. The dollar per peso equivalent exchange rate equaled
    A. 9.5 dollars per peso.
    B. .095 dollars per peso.
    C. 10.5 dollars per peso.
    D. .105 dollars per peso.
    E. 105 dollars per peso.

2. A disposable camera cost $8 in the United States and 110 peso in Mexico during the summer of 2000. The exchange rate at that time was 9.5 pesos per dollar. The real exchange rate of the dollar (for disposable cameras) equaled
    A. 9.5.
    B. .69.
    C. .84.
    D. 92.6.
    E. .105.

3. During the 1980s, the United States had a balance-of-payments deficit with South Korea and Taiwan. The U.S. government complained that the governments of those two nations were manipulating their exchange rates to promote exports to the United States. Apparently, the White House believed that the
    A. currencies of South Korea and Taiwan were overvalued relative to the dollar.
    B. currencies of South Korea and Taiwan were undervalued relative to the dollar.
    C. South Korean currency was overvalued relative to the currency of Taiwan.
    D. South Korean currency was undervalued relative to the currency of Taiwan.
    E. dollar should be allowed to appreciate against the currencies of South Korea and Taiwan.

4. Between 1973 and 1999, annual inflation in developing nations that export mainly manufactured goods averaged 23 percent, while inflation averaged 59 percent in countries that mainly export raw materials. Other things equal, the PPP theory would predict that, in the long run, the currencies of the raw materials exporting countries should have
    A. been approximately stable relative to the currencies of countries exporting manufactured goods.
    B. appreciated relative to the currencies of countries exporting manufactured goods.
    C. depreciated relative to the currencies of countries exporting manufactured goods.
    D. had no predictable relationship to the currencies of countries exporting manufactured goods.
    E. been perfectly stable relative to the currencies of countries exporting manufactured goods because they maintained fixed exchange rates.

5. The PPP theory works less well in the short run than it does in the long run because
    A. the law of one price only pertains to the long run.
    B. not all goods and services are traded internationally, and not all goods are heterogeneous commodities.
    C. all goods and services are traded internationally, and not all goods are heterogeneous commodities.
    D. not all goods and services are traded internationally, and not all goods are standardized commodities.
    E. all goods and services are traded internationally, and all goods are standardized commodities.

6. In the early 1980s, high interest rates in the United States attracted enormous amounts of capital into the United States to buy stocks, bonds, real estate, and other assets. All other things equal, supply-and-demand analysis of exchange rates would predict that the U.S. dollar would experience _____ relative to other currencies.
    A. depreciation
    B. appreciation
    C. devaluation
    D. revaluation
    E. purchasing price parity

7. During 1999 and 2000, the U.S. Federal Reserve Bank tightened its monetary policy and interest rates in the United States increased in order to reduce domestic consumption and investment spending. In the short-run, one would predicate a(n)
    A. depreciation of the dollar and an increase in net exports.
    B. depreciation of the dollar and a decrease in net exports.
    C. devaluation of the dollar and a decrease in net exports.
    D. appreciation of the dollar and an increase in net exports.
    E. appreciation of the dollar and a decrease in net exports.

8. The value of a fixed exchange rate in contemporary economies is
    A. determined by the supply and demand for a currency in the foreign exchange market.
    B. set by the government, usually in terms of gold or some other precious metal.
    C. set by the government, usually in terms of the currency (or basket of currencies) of the country's major trading partner(s).
    D. set by agreement of the central banks of the major trading countries of the world.
    E. determined by economic forces.

9. During the 1990s, the government of Malaysia fixed the exchange rate of the Baht to the dollar. During the spring of 1998, investors perceived that the Baht was overvalued and a speculative attack ensued. What alternatives did the Malaysian government have to deal with this problem?
   A. It could have revalued the Baht, limited international transactions, purchased Baht on the foreign exchange market, or tightened domestic monetary policy.
   B. It could have devalued the Baht, limited international transactions, purchased Baht on the foreign exchange market, or tightened domestic monetary policy.
   C. It could have devalued the Baht, limited international transactions, sold Baht on the foreign exchange market, or tightened domestic monetary policy.
   D. It could have revalued the Baht, limited international transactions, sold Baht on the foreign exchange market, or eased domestic monetary policy.
   E. It could have revalued the Baht, limited international transactions, sold Baht on the foreign exchange market, or tightened domestic monetary policy.

10. During the 1930s, the United States was on the gold standard, creating a system of fixed exchange rates between the dollar and other currencies whose values were also set in terms of gold. As a result, monetary policy
   A. could not be used to stabilize the U.S. economy during the Great Depression.
   B. could be used to stabilize the U.S. economy during the Great Depression.
   C. was immune to a speculative attack because devaluation was not possible.
   D. was eased to counteract the banking panic and the bank failures during the Great Depression.
   E. was used to decrease interest rates to counteract the economic decline brought on by the bank failures during the Great Depression.

11. When the real exchange rate of a country's currency is low, the home country will;
   A. find it easier to import, while domestic producers will have difficulty exporting.
   B. find it easier to export, while domestic residents will buy more imports.
   C. find it harder to export, while domestic residents will buy fewer imports.
   D. find it easier to export, while domestic residents will buy fewer imports.
   E. find it harder to export, while domestic residents will buy more imports.

12. Between 1990 and 1999, inflation in the United States averaged 2-3% per year, while Mexico experienced double-digit average annual inflation rates. Since the Mexican government did not try to maintain a fixed exchange rate, the PPP theory would suggest that, in the long run, the Mexican peso would
   A. appreciate against the dollar and Mexico's net exports to the United States decreased.
   B. appreciate against the dollar and Mexico's net exports to the United States increased.
   C. depreciate against the dollar and Mexico's net exports to the United States increased.
   D. depreciate against the dollar and Mexico's net exports to the United States decreased.
   E. remain stable relative to the dollar, with no change in Mexico's net exports to the United States.

13. The PPP theory would be most useful in predicting
    A. short-run changes in the exchange rate for a country that mainly produces heavily traded, standardized goods.
    B. long-run changes in the exchange rate for a country that mainly produces heavily traded, standardized goods.
    C. short-run changes in the exchange rate for a country that mainly produces lightly traded, standardized goods.
    D. long-run changes in the exchange rate for a country that mainly produces lightly traded, non-standardized goods.
    E. short-run changes in the exchange rate for a country that mainly produces lightly traded, standardized goods.

14. The fundamental value of a country's exchange rate is
    A. constant over a prolonged period of time.
    B. determined by the supply of the country's currency in the foreign exchange market.
    C. determined by the demand for the country's currency in the foreign exchange market.
    D. determined by the supply of and demand for the country's currency in the domestic financial market.
    E. determined by the supply of and demand for the country's currency in the foreign exchange market.

15. During the latter half of the 1990s, real GDP in the United States grew faster than in most other industrial countries. All other things equal, supply-and-demand analysis of exchange rates would predict that, in the short run, the U.S. dollar would _____ relative to the currencies of the other industrialized countries.
    A. appreciate
    B. depreciate
    C. devaluate
    D. revaluate
    E. remain constant

16. If the central bank of England were to respond to a slowdown in the domestic economy by easing monetary policy, all other things equal, one would predict in the short run a(n)
    A. increase in the real interest rate, an increase in demand for the pound, and an appreciation in the pound.
    B. decrease in the real interest rate, an increase in demand for the pound, and an appreciation in the pound.
    C. decrease in the real interest rate, a decrease in demand for the pound, and a depreciation in the pound.
    D. increase in the real interest rate, a decrease in demand for the pound, and a depreciation in the pound.
    E. increase in the real interest rate, an increase in demand for the pound, and a depeciation in the pound.

2. Supply and Demand Analysis of the Exchange Rate

Supply and demand analysis is applied to the determination of the exchange rate in this problem. You will determine the equilibrium exchange rate and analyze the effects of changes in various factors on the supply of or demand for dollars to determine the impact on the equilibrium exchange rate. Answer the questions below based on the following graph illustrating the supply and demand for dollars in the euro-dollar market.

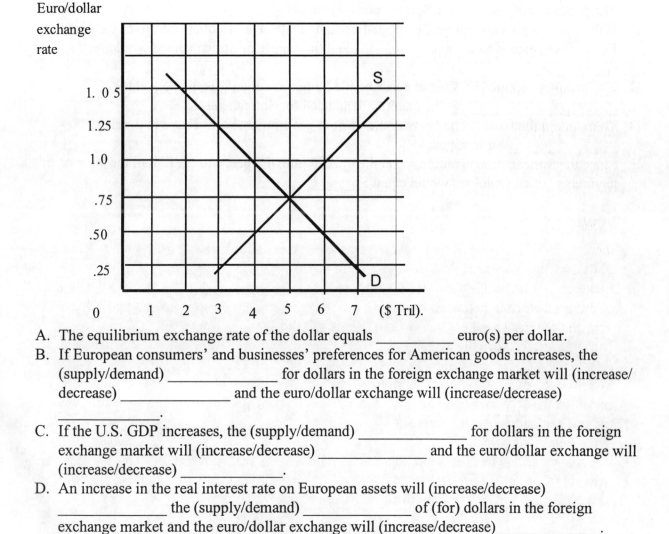

Euro/dollar
exchange
rate

A. The equilibrium exchange rate of the dollar equals _____ euro(s) per dollar.

B. If European consumers' and businesses' preferences for American goods increases, the (supply/demand) _____ for dollars in the foreign exchange market will (increase/decrease) _____ and the euro/dollar exchange will (increase/decrease) _____.

C. If the U.S. GDP increases, the (supply/demand) _____ for dollars in the foreign exchange market will (increase/decrease) _____ and the euro/dollar exchange will (increase/decrease) _____.

D. An increase in the real interest rate on European assets will (increase/decrease) _____ the (supply/demand) _____ of (for) dollars in the foreign exchange market and the euro/dollar exchange will (increase/decrease) _____.

E. If the Fed tightens U.S. monetary policy, the (supply/demand) _____ for dollars in the foreign exchange market will (increase/decrease) _____ and the euro/dollar exchange will (increase/decrease) _____.

3. Fundamental Value of a Currency and the Balance of Payments Deficit

The demand and supply for Surican pesos in the foreign exchange market are given by the following equations (e is the Surican exchange rate measured in dollars per Surican peso).
Demand = 55,000 − 88,000 e
Supply = 25,000 + 32,000 e

A. The fundamental value of the Surican peso (e) equals _____ .

B. If the Surican government set the official exchange rate at .333 dollars per peso, the demand for Surican pesos would equal _____, and the supply of Surican pesos would be

   _____ .

C. The quantity supplied of Surican pesos would be (greater than/less than/equal to)

   _____ the quantity demanded for Surican pesos.

D. To maintain the fixed exchange rate, the Surican government would have to purchase

   _____ Surican pesos.

E. Since the Surican peso is purchased at the official rate of 3 pesos to the dollar, the balance of payments deficit in dollars would equal $_____ .

Solutions
Self-Test: Key Terms

1. fundamental value of the exchange rate
2. overvalued exchange rate
3. real exchange rate
4. speculative attack
5. devaluation
6. law of one price
7. flexible exchange rate
8. nominal exchange rate
9. international reserves
10. fixed exchange rate
11. balance-of-payments surplus
12. undervalued exchange rate
13. appreciation
14. foreign-exchange market
15. revaluation
16. purchasing power parity (PPP)
17. balance-of-payments deficit
18. depreciation

Self-Test: Multiple-Choice Questions

1. D (=1/9.5)
2. B (=[9.5*8] / 110)
3. A
4. C
5. D
6. B
7. E
8. C
9. B
10. A
11. D
12. C
13. B
14. E
15. A
16. C
17. B
18. D
19. A
20. B

Self-Test: Short Answer/Problems

1.
A., B.

Country	Foreign currency / dollar	Dollar / foreign currency
Britain (Pound)	.6582 (=1/1.5193)	1.5193
Canada (Dollar	1.4833	.6742
Europe (Euro)	1.0499	.95250
Germany (Mark)	2.054	.4869 (=1/2.054)
Japan (Yen)	105.06	.009518
Mexico (Peso)	9.91	.100908

C. 1.23 (= [9.91 x 18,995]/ 152,100)
D. more; U.S.

2.
A. .75
B. demand; increase; increase
C. supply; increase; decrease
D. increase; supply; decrease
E. demand; increase; increase

3.
A. .25 ($55,000 - 88,000e = 25,000 + 32,000e$ or $30,000 = 120,000e$)
B. 25,636 (=55,000 - 88,000 x .333); 35,656 (=25,000 + 32,000 x .333)
C. greater than
D. 10,020 (=35,656 - 25,636)
E. $3,340 (=10,020 / 3)

Study Schedule: Chapters 8-14 (9-14)

no chptr 11 (12

Monday

7 - 9
- Chapter 9 (Workers, Wages and Unemployment)
- Chapter 10 (Saving and Wealth)

Night
- Chapter 11 (Money, Prices & the Fed. Reserve)
- Chapter 12 (Short-term Economic Fluctuations)

Tuesday

Day
- Chapter 13 (A.D. & Output in Short Run)
- Chapter 14 (A.D.: Role of Fed)